SCHOOL LEADERSHIP
IN TIMES OF URBAN REFORM

TOPICS IN EDUCATIONAL LEADERSHIP

Larry W. Hughes, Series Editor

SCHOOL LEADERSHIP
IN TIMES OF URBAN REFORM

～～～～～

Edited by

Marilyn Bizar
Rebecca Barr
National-Louis University

LAWRENCE ERLBAUM ASSOCIATES, PUBLISHERS
2001   Mahwah, New Jersey   London

Lawrence Erlbaum Associates, Inc., Publishers
10 Industrial Avenue
Mahwah, New Jersey 07430-2262

Cover design by Shawn Calvert

Library of Congress Cataloging-in-Publication Data

School leadership in times of urban reform / editors, Marilyn Bizar and Rebecca Barr ; authors Rebecca Barr ... [et al.].
    p.   cm. — (Topics in educational leadership)
Includes bibliographical references (p.) and index.
ISBN 0-8058-2451-0 (pbk. : alk. paper)
    1. Educational leadership—Illinois—Chicago—Case studies. 2. School improvement programs leadership—Illinois—Chicago—Case studies. 3. Education, Urban leadership—Illinois—Chicago—Case studies. I. Bizar, Marilyn. II. Barr, Rebecca. III. Series.

LB2806 .S3418 2000
371.2'009773—dc21

                                                                00-039381

Books published by Lawrence Erlbaum Associates are printed on acid-free paper, and their bindings are chosen for strength and durability.

Printed in the United States of America
10 9 8 7 6 5 4 3 2 1

Contents

Foreword

This book demonstrates the strengths of case studies when they are put together with care and imagination; in this instance, the cases are done in ways that make them particularly compelling. They incorporate a variety of perspectives, make us aware of the human, emotional side of change, and are well constructed; combined with the thoughtful observations made by Rebecca Barr and Marilyn Bizar, they stimulate thought and generate ideas, ideas that can lead to productive research and more effective practice.

Reading these cases underscores the complexity of large-scale reform and makes it clear that understanding the events involved in such major change requires subtle and sustained analysis. We empathize with principals and teachers and the concerns of a committed parent; we are reminded, if that be needed, that no one of the groups engaged in schooling our children is composed primarily (or even markedly) of villains nor, for that matter, entirely of heroes. The authors and editors bring alive one of the most significant meanings of complexity; they help us to appreciate that tough problems are built right into efforts to improve schools, that such change is inherently difficult. Recognizing such complexity inoculates us against the oversimplifications we often encounter in public discourse on educational change, oversimplifications that can come from monolithic belief systems—ideologies that locate all knowledge "in the people" or idealize business management or assume that all will be well if we simply "leave the teachers alone."

The strong feelings that people develop around their work shine through in these pages as we glimpse emotions that accompany change, emotions arising from new opportunities or from new sources of distress. We see the excitement teachers feel as they exert major influence for the first time and we sense the quiet pride of principals whose actions produce the outcomes for which they hoped. One case reveals less happy feelings, the frustration and despair that persuades a principal to surrender a position in which she has invested much of herself. All too frequently, discussions of change ignore this human side, an omission that reduces our chances of understanding what really happens when we try to alter work arrangements.

It is important that these stories about real people and real events are well prepared, either as written documents or as the product of interviewers whose knowledge permits them to ask acute questions. This is more than the important issue of literary quality—it is necessary to draw in the reader to the point where it produces reflection.

I can support the claim that this book produces such reflection by discussing some of the ideas that it stimulated for me as I read the book.

One of the issues that emerges in the pages that follow revolves around the concept of time. There are two senses in which I mean this—one is that change requires "enough" time to succeed, whereas the other recognizes the serial nature of change, that change occurs over time in ways which can reveal distinct phases with particular leadership requirements.

Schools, the authors make clear, do not change rapidly, and the implementation of significant change is not something that we should expect to happen quickly. I concur, strongly. It is evident, moreover, that wider appreciation of the need for sufficient time is truly necessary. Take, for example, the projected gains in standardized scores included in the first version of the Reform Act discussed in this book, vast percentage gains, to be attained within a few years, were listed as expected results of the reform, larger gains, I'd wager, than have ever been recorded in the history of American schooling. As I recall it, there was no public questioning of those projections, no newspaper editorials expressing skepticism. (One wonders, why this happens. Are we unwilling to undertake the hard work of changing things unless we talk ourselves into expecting rapid and vast results? Do grandiose expectations, unfulfilled, doom further efforts to press for change?)

The question of "enough" time, however, is more complicated than setting reasonable schedules and voicing reasonable expectations. There is considerable irony here, for to implement significant change may require not only sufficient time, but a degree of stability, that is, the absence of change—in other parts of the system. Furthermore, there are structural features in our school districts that make it hard to ensure that such stability will prevail when it is needed. Let me illustrate the point with a short (and highly condensed) "case" based on personal familiarity.

A school district, urged on by a strong teacher association, sought to improve the evaluation of classroom teachers, seeking to make it meaningful for tenured teachers as well as useful in making retention decisions about new teachers. An overall plan was developed which included, among other features, evaluation of teachers by teachers as well as by principals; a new assistant superintendent was appointed to serve as coordinator of the project. Finding the need for more precise language to frame their classroom observations, a group composed of teachers, principals and other professional staff spent many hours over many months refining the terms and procedures to be used. Observers both inside and outside the district, some of whom had expressed a lot of skepticism, were much impressed by the enthusiasm, serious effort and high quality of the work produced by the staff. At the point where the undertaking had undergone considerable testing (successfully) and was ready for expansion to the district-at-large, the superintendent accepted a position elsewhere, and, a little later, substantial change took place in the composition of the school board. Within months, the budget that had supported the project was reduced, and before long eliminated; it became clear that the new persons in charge of the district had other priorities. The outcome may not surprise those who have watched school districts in operation; they have seen how innovative projects are vulnerable to the prevalence of high turnover among superintendents and board members. Although this is obviously only one of the factors that affects the fate of proposed changes in schools, a lack of long-range commitment resulting from instability may be one of the reasons why we seem to hear so much more talk about innovation than we see translated into action.

The serial nature of change shows up in two cases, Amundsen High School and The Best Practice High School. The first deals with matters that occur in conventionally organized districts as well as those undergoing restructuring, the second in more fluid situations. But both illustrate instances where there are phases in the process of school development, phases that call for different kinds of leadership.

The principal in the Amundsen case brought order to a disorganized school, a level of order that was needed before instruction could proceed in normal ways. I have encountered similar instances in my own research where a principal "turned the school around," taking it from the brink of chaos to a going concern where the normal activities of teaching and learning could take place. The Amundsen case suggests, however, that this principal was neither inclined nor, perhaps, well equipped, to move the school much beyond the point it had reached. It seems likely that the school would have benefitted from a new principal who could establish fresh goals and move people toward their realization. But for this to occur, the current principal would have to be removed by the school council, retire or be promoted to a central or district office position. None of these alternatives makes much sense to me. The first two remove from the educational scene a person with proven capacities to bring order to a school, whereas the third does not capitalize on the particular skills he has demonstrated and may, in fact, require abilities he does not possess.

The point I wish to make is this: We have not developed the practice in public schools of recognizing and acknowledging that the skills of administrators can be specialized. Nor have we learned to make the most of such capacities when they do appear. There seems little doubt that a large school district like Chicago (or, for that matter, another district entirely) could use this principal's abilities in a problem school if mechanisms existed to arrange for it. Our habits of thought seem so tied to hierarchical definitions of success and recognition that we lack the flexibility to use scarce talent when it is displayed, we seem unaware of the possibilities that lie in less rigid and more lateral conceptions of managerial careers in public education. Perhaps it is time for those engaged in governing school districts (and other influentials) to consider alternatives that would be less wasteful and to develop new kinds of career systems that better match the ways in which change occurs over time.

The Best Practice High School is placed in a novel context that may prove to be significant in the years ahead. It is a context that consists of small schools, highly innovative in program and governed by norms that differ markedly from those we find in the traditional structures of American school districts, structures organized around vertical authority encased in a bureaucratic framework. A famous precursor is, of course, Deborah Meier's school in District 4, New York City, and one presumes that many of the charter schools being created across the country will be similar in important respects. These developments suggest that we are beginning (at least in some places) to decouple school leadership from its traditional loci in the offices of principals and central officials, to create conditions where those who work directly with the students have enormous influence on the day-to-day decisions made in the school. In addition, student participation is often a matter of family choice, itself a departure from the historic authority of school officials to decide which children go to which schools. Does choice within the public sector imply changes in "accountability?" Do families who choose their schools signal a larger degree of responsibility than they express under more coercive arrangements? If so, does this encourage new kinds of relationships between families and school personnel that are less likely in traditional arrangements? Those are possibilities we should perhaps watch for as more people send their children to charter and other public schools where choice prevails.

Concentrating for the moment on one aspect of Best Practice High changes in leadership as it moved from design to operation, we see that the planners, based in universities, had to accept declines in the influence they initially possessed. Leadership, as a matter of course, moved to those charged with doing the day-in, day-out work of the school. This case strongly suggests that when people from organizations outside schools (e.g., universities, consulting agencies, state offices) become heavily engaged in schools, those involved should be prepared to cope with the irony of losing influence as their efforts prove successful!

The rich material in this book tempts one to go on and on, to react at greater and greater length. Come to think of it, I can think of no stronger recommendation for a set of cases and commentaries. So now it's your turn—read, ponder and react.

—*Dan C. Lortie*
Professor Emeritus
University of Chicago

Preface

PURPOSE

Many urban schools are in dire circumstances that cannot be addressed in traditional ways. Major restructuring efforts are being undertaken by inner-city districts due to the nature of the problems they face and their resistance to traditional solutions. Serious attempts to restructure schools seek to alter the fundamental ways in which schools operate in areas of either curriculum or governance with the hope of improving student learning. Those involved in reform efforts are aware of the complexity of school problems and the resistance of schools to change efforts.

This volume deals with the various ways in which the schools in Chicago implemented strategies that called for whole school change and system reform. The many challenges that were faced by the individual schools in Chicago exemplify similar efforts for reforming schools all over the country, and can be used by the reader as templates against which to examine their own schools.

The reform movement places emphasis on the value and importance of leadership in our schools. Although the literature on effective schools stresses the importance of top administrative leadership, educators have come to understand how more diverse, school-based leadership can help make school improvement a reality. We have long recognized the importance of the school principal, but lately there is an emerging concern with other school leaders including parents, teachers, and students. This volume focuses attention on these important participants in their various school communities and in their evolving leadership roles.

In our roles as university professors, we have been participant-observers in the process of reform, and although reform in Chicago was implemented districtwide, what we have found most interesting is the process that plays out in each individual school. The call to restructure the schools in Chicago was resounding, and the chosen course of action was designed to empower parents and community members in a decentralized form of administration. The reform legislation passed in 1988 has been called the largest experiment in site-based management ever undertaken. Although we were aware that site-based management was far from a panacea, we observed that leadership opportunities were created for persons who were willing to accept the challenge. What was needed were creative, committed individuals willing to redefine leadership roles.

This volume gives voice to persons who accepted the challenge to lead, not at the district level, but in their individual schools. Each of the cases, written by school leaders, lays bare the complexities of the change process in eight different schools. These eight cases ask the reader to rethink the concept of school leadership and to conceive of it more broadly to include teachers, parents, and community members as active participants in the process of urban school change.

AUDIENCE

This volume will be helpful to teachers, principals, and particularly to students who seek to understand the complexities of schools and the process of school change. The cases, followed by reflective questions and activities, uncover the differences in schools and their cultures, and will help the reader understand the nature of schools, how they are alike, and how they are different. All schools are alike in having a very specific mission to support the learning and development of children. But the cultures of schools are unique in ways that influence the balance of power and the forms of leadership exercised. What works in one school may not work in another. These cases provide a window into eight different school cultures that provide an opportunity to examine the context of each and the ways in which alternative forms of leadership are supported or resisted. Our hope is that these cases will be used as catalysts for dialogue, problem solving, and self-examination.

THE CONTENT

This volume is divided into six sections. In Section 1, we discuss school leadership and how it is influenced by reform. The following four sections are made up of two cases that we placed together because of similarities. Section 2, The Response of Schools to the Initial Years of Reform, examines two schools with very different cultures and their readiness for taking on the new leadership roles that site-based management called for. Section 3, Tensions Between the Local School Council and the Principal, deals with issues of power and responsibility. Section 4, Reform as an Opportunity for Creating Responsive Instruction, examines two schools in their struggles to use reform as a lever to improve teaching and learning. Section 5, New Beginnings: Making Changes in High School Instruction and Learning, looks at two very different high schools; a large high school that has been in existence for many years, and a newly created small school. In Section 6, we consider similarities and differences among the cases and suggest some conclusions.

ANONYMITY

The authors of the eight cases have made different choices about anonymity. In five of the cases, the schools are identified, and in three of the cases, pseudonyms are used. The authors of Case 1, Case 4, and Case 6 have chosen to keep their schools anonymous. The other five cases identify both the schools and the participants by name.

VOICE

The stories are told in the individual voices of various school leaders and have the biases that come from authors being imbedded in their cases. We supported the authors in telling their stories with the full realization that they represent individual perspectives. At the same time, their richness derives from the passion with which these stories are told. We offer these cases as textured, complex, powerful stories that will provide the reader with much to think and talk about.

ACKNOWLEDGMENT

We thank the teachers, administrators, students, and parents from the schools represented in the case studies. Making schools better places to learn and work is a challenge that requires deep commitment day by day. The case studies give readers an inside look at the realities of school life as those who work in schools attempt to find their way through the maze of changes and demands that reform requires.

The editorial staff of Lawrence Erlbaum Associates, Publishers provided support at every stage in the writing and production of this book. We are particularly grateful to Naomi Silverman, our editor at Erlbaum, for her patience and faith: patience in allowing us more time, and the faith to know that we would get the job done. We are pleased to be part of the series edited by Larry W. Hughes on "Topics in Educational Leadership." His careful reading and thoughtful comments helped us to examine more closely the larger issues that the cases address.

Our cover was designed by Shawn Calvert. The more we reflect on it, the process of people finding their way through a maze is an apt metaphor for the forward and sometimes backward motion in navigating the complexities of school reform. We benefited from the insights and comments of our colleagues at National-Louis University, and thank Linda Tafel in particular for her interest in our work in Chicago schools. Finally, we thank our families for their unfailing encouragement and support.

—*Marilyn Bizar*
—*Rebecca Barr*

SECTION 1

Conceptualizing Leadership in the Context of School Reform

Rebecca Barr
Marilyn Bizar
National-Louis University

Urban schools, faced with problems of poverty, gangs, violence, underachievement, bloated bureaucracies, and limited resources, are attempting to make changes in governance, instruction, and learning. The schools in Chicago are no exception. In this book, we examine schools in Chicago where the largest experiment in site-based management and accountability is being enacted. Chicago schools are representative of other urban schools in the problems they face and in the solutions they are attempting. Thus, a detailed analysis of Chicago school cases permits us to pursue an agenda concerned with educational reform and school leadership.

The decentralization of authority (legislated in 1988) and accountability standards (implemented in 1995) created, in quite different ways, new sets of contingencies that school leaders had to address. Our focus in this book is on school leaderhsip. We explore how principals working in quite different settings responded to the new opportunities and pressures of reform. We are particularly interested in the different ways they defined their administrative roles. We are intrigued by the concept of shared leadership. We examine the role of teachers: the settings and ways in which some became empowered to assume new leadership roles. The legislation passed in 1988 gave community members and teachers an important role in school decision making. We explore how elected community members took up this authority and how their relation with the principal evolved. Finally, the framers of the reform legislation believed that changes in school leadership and culture would have the consequence of improving school achievement. We explore whether and how this occurred. In sum, the focus of the book is on the nature of school leadership and its consequences for teacher roles, school culture, community involvement, and student achievement.

1

This chapter is organized into four sections. First, we focus on the nature of school leadership, explore the nature of administrative management and leadership, and consider the leadership contributions that may be made by teachers and community members as well as by school administrators. Second, we examine various forms of school reform, including those involving decentralization. We delve into the nature of decentralized forms of school governance and consider the history of their implementation in other large cities. Third, we describe reform as it is occurring in Chicago, both in terms of the history of its legislative mandate and the way it has materialized. We consider the impact of the Chicago reform on various forms of school leadership and consider areas in which tensions might be expected to arise. Fourth, we describe the eight case studies included in this book and discuss how they enable us to think clearly about the unique ways in which leadership opportunities were shaped by the history and special circumstances of each school. We also consider the questions framing our case analyses.

School Leadership

The term *leadership* conjures up different images. We may think of historically important leaders such as Napoleon and Alexander the Great or current-day business or political leaders who are particularly successful. Leadership is defined as "a person or thing that leads," who goes "before or with to show the way." However, the limited usefulness of a generic definition in clarifying the nature of school leadership highlights the extent to which the meaning of any term is specified by its situational context. Being a leader in a school entails a somewhat different set of skills and activities from being a civic, military, political, or business leader.

As we examine leadership and the ways different people exert leadership in schools, we ponder what sort of organizations school are and what forms of leadership are needed. According to Sergiovanni (1996), how schools and other organizations differ has not been pursued sufficiently; we import our theories of leadership from "corporations, baseball teams, armies, transportation systems, and other organizations" (p. xiii). Moreover, he argued that the assumptions and practices that come with these imported theories provide models for the organization of schools that do not take into consideration the specific and unique characteristics of schools.

Schools differ from other organizations such as businesses and industries in important ways. Schools are characterized by elusive, complex, and controversial goals, inconsistent standards for determining effectiveness, unpredictable problems and solutions, and a technology that is unclear at best (Norris, 1999; Weick, 1982). Take, for example, complications in the area of goals. An important shift has occurred in the consensus of what constitutes useful learning. As we enter the "information age," students who learn skills and information by rote memory are no longer prepared for the future. The sort of "knowledge workers" that are needed in the 21st century are those who can define and solve problems thoughtfully. Students will need to have a role in thinking about the nature of tasks in which they engage (Brooks & Brooks, 1993).

Concurrent changes have also occurred in conceptions of knowledge and its construction and the nature of learning. Whereas behaviorist formulations dominated instruction in the past, these have given way to constructivist theories of learning in which learners play an active role in making sense of their experiences, whether through reading, listening, observation, or actually doing (Paris, Wasik, & Turner, 1991). The value of students sharing diverse interpretations based on shared experiences is well documented (Pearson & Fielding, 1991). A consequence of these trends is the need for teachers to begin involving students in decisions about their learning to a greater extent. Moreover, one way that teachers learn to share aspects of decision making with their students is by participating in such collaborative activities with school colleagues. Thus, a variety of forces converge to encourage the rethinking of traditional forms of instruction.

These views of learning and teaching have implications for the roles of principals. They would seem to demand a form of administration that not only preserves what is best of traditional practice, but is also willing to take risks in exploring new forms of leadership. When thinking of administration, it may be useful to distinguish "leadership" from "management" (Hughes, 1999). Management functions are undertaken to get the school's work done. They consist of doing business in ways that are known within the school community—making requests, communicating, disciplining, filing complaints, making plans, and the like. Management preserves the status quo, the often unwritten set of roles and expectations for getting business done, "the way it is usually done." In contrast, leadership activities may be defined as those creative activities focused in revitalizing and reforming certain aspects of school practice.

There has been a tendency to think about these terms in dichotomous ways and to assign value to them, with leadership viewed in positive terms and management in negative (Cuban, 1990). Within these formulations, leadership connotes progress, change, and innovation and is thus positively valued. In contrast, management is viewed negatively as a reactive force maintaining the status quo. Achilles, Keedy, and High (1999) cautioned that this dichotomous thinking oversimplifies the complexities inherent in school leadership. They argued instead for viewing school administration as composed of leadership as well as management dimensions, both of which may be pursued in positive or negative ways.

The importance of management in establishing and maintaining school culture is revealed by Keedy's (1991) study of four principals in out-of-control schools. The case involving Principal Burke is particularly instructive. Burke entered the chaotic school with two goals in mind: to make it safe for all students and to provide an appropriate curriculum for them. His first task was to deal with personnel problems—clarifying teaching and administrative roles, equalizing class and teaching loads, and establishing a new departmental leadership structure. He also had to get students under control, which led to a number of physical confrontations and time spent in court hearings. As summarized, "Burke and the other three principals in the study gained control over their schools by assessing situations quickly, by laying down the law, and by enforcing the law" (Achilles et al., 1999, p. 31).

The case illustrates how the power of an administrator may be used unilaterally to establish the procedures and structures that permit the work of the school to occur. Negotiations are at the level of saying, "Here's what I expect of you. Here's what you can expect from me" (Achilles et al., 1999, p. 33). As shown by the case, establishing the norms of the culture, as well as the values and beliefs that support compliance to them can be a lengthy and complicated process. Although the power was used unilaterally, interactions were characterized by consideration, mutual respect, and trust, in keeping with the norms being established. The principal modeled the conduct he was trying to establish. Once standard operating procedures and roles were in place, the managerial role of the principal became one of conserving roles, policies, and procedures that work well.

Most individual schools are characterized by established ways of doing business. The culture is, however, so familiar that it becomes invisible to participants: the water unknown to the fish that swim in it. It is when a school is in disarray, as it was for the principals that Keedy (1991) studied, that the importance of management functions become apparent. Once rules, responsibilities, and agreed-upon ways of doing business were in place, *then* these principals were free to engage in leadership activities to establish a more shared form of governance. Though the management responsibilities continued, once cultural norms were established, principals were able to pursue them in more flexible and less unilateral ways.

The principal of a school is responsible for maintaining the critical balance between management tasks to conserve the existing culture and leadership initiatives to create new or revised goals, policies, and procedures. Particularly in an era when the goals of education are contested and new forms of student involvement in their own learning are being advocated, different teacher roles and community involvement in school decision making will also emerge and be supported by some administrators.

Shared leadership depends to a greater extent than management on the personal traits of the principal because the leadership role, by definition, is less bound by traditional ways of doing things, is less institutionalized. Some administrators possess the personal traits, such as degrees of imagination, planning skills, and singleness of purpose (Hughes, 1999), the absence of a preconceived vision and ability to respond to situational opportunities (Keedy, 1991), as well as the ability to cope with "turbulence" (Duane, Bridgeland, & Stern, 1986), that enable them to experiment with new forms of governance. Such creative forms of leadership depend on the ability of the principal to make decisions collectively, nurture leadership in others, and give voice to teachers and community members (Moore, 1992). Reform creates the opportunity for various forms of shared leadership. It demands a realignment in the balance between management and leadership in which the leadership tasks, as well as the power entailed, are shared with others such as teachers and community members.

Hughes and Ubben (1994) described five administrative functions in schools. These include curriculum development, instructional improvement, pupil services, community relations, and financial and facility management. It is easy to see how teacher leadership might make significant contributions, particularly in the areas of curriculum development and instructional improvement. Indeed, Norris (1999) noted in her chapter on cultivating creative cultures the importance of leadership "as the pivotal force necessary for shaping the creative attitude of an organization—not only through the personal creativeness displayed by leaders, but through the inspiration provided to others to encourage them to contribute as well" (p. 60). Yet, the empowerment of teachers and others to take leadership roles is a complicated process. Research involving site-based management suggests that even when teachers are given responsibility to assume new leadership roles, often little change occurs (Malen, Ogawa, & Kranz, 1990). Instead, teachers were often responsive to what they thought their principal might want; hence, only limited creative thinking occurred. The lesson is that an open climate encouraging the questioning of existing practice must be modeled by principals to promote the culture in which teachers become entitled and trusting. New ways of interacting must be learned before teachers will trust their own creative thinking (Darling-Hammond, Bullmaster, & Cobb, 1995; Hess, 1994). It must become the cultural norm to question existing norms and practices as new situations emerge and to develop forms of work that are more suited to the changing needs of schools (Argyris, 1982; Argyris & Schon, 1974; Deal & K. D. Peterson, 1999).

Whereas teachers might be expected to assume leadership roles in the areas of curriculum development and instructional innovation, what leadership roles might draw on the unique expertise of parents and community members? Though parents and community members may have useful insights concerning the curriculum and instruction, they may be particularly valuable participants in forming policies and procedures concerning pupil services and community relations. Yet, a long history exists in which parents perceive themselves to be unwelcome in schools. Their contributions are typically limited to collecting report cards, serving on parent–teacher association meetings, and dealing with problems concerning their children. Thus, how to expand the traditionally circumscribed set of roles of parents and community members constitutes a puzzle for school personnel. What is the appropriate set of activities in which the insights of parents and community members should be encouraged and how should this be done?

These forms of shared leadership do not relieve the principal of the responsibility for managing an organization to meet its goals. Ultimately, it is the principal who is responsible for tasks such as those delineated by Hughes and Ubben (1994): curriculum development, instructional improvement, pupil services, community relations, and financial and facility management. Principals are seeking ways to involve teachers and community members leadership roles to promote creative decision making, while they must, at the same time, enforce agreed-upon standards and procedures so that the organization will work well (Bryk & Rollow, 1992; Cordeiro, 1999).

In this book, we plan to explore the different roles that principals and other leaders play in schools that are being reformed. We test these emerging roles against existing theories of school leadership. We explore, for example, the leadership role of the principals and how they engage in management and leadership activities. We consider the extent to which leadership in schools becomes shared with teachers and the activities around which this shared leadership is organized. Finally, we examine how principals interact with community members as they attempt to forge new roles.

As we pursue issues of leadership, we explore how the culture of the school changes as the opportunities created by the reform are pursued or not. Do principals, teachers, parents, and students accept responsibility for developing a school community that values constructivist views of teaching and learning? Do principals and other school leaders facilitate the development of a school learning community where all are engaged in the act of nurturing an educational and moral environment for children? These cases also lay out the complexities involved in changing the culture of authority (i.e., beliefs, fears, traditions, and the larger policy environment) in a school site and system.

Reform of Urban Schools

Overview.   When problems of public education are discussed, schools in suburban areas and small towns are usually not the focus. Rather, people are concerned about urban schools—those serving large numbers of poor children. Achievement differences between urban and nonurban schools are dramatic, with urban students achieving an average of 20 percentile points below those in nonurban schools in reading, and even lower in mathematics and science (Olson & Jerald, 1998). When high-poverty urban and nonurban schools are compared, the gap is even wider.

Only 24% of all students are enrolled in urban districts, but 43% of minority students are in such schools. W. J. Wilson (1987) discussed the plight of the poor living in inner-city neighborhoods characterized by lack of employment opportunities, poverty, and isolation. Education, which might serve as an escape from this underclass existence, adds to the set of problems confronted. Reforming schools to serve poor inner-city students better has been a priority in many states, but one that has met with limited success.

A constellation of factors facing urban schools militate against easy solutions: apathy or hostility from state lawmakers, huge bureaucracies that are unresponsive to the needs of local schools, inadequate resources, high rates of teacher and student mobility, high rates of teacher and student absenteeism, and high rates of students dropping out of school. These features translate into classrooms that are composed of a heavy concentration of low-achieving children, where a quarter to a third may be absent on any given day, and where resources and teaching are inadequate. In addition, barriers to school reform exist at the district level in the form of bloated bureaucracies and entrenched power structures.

School reforms come in many guises. Some aim to affect the incentive structure of school, by focusing on goals and accountability. In the past decade, an increasing number of states has sought to influence student learning through the development and use of state assessment systems. Some assume that accountability procedures will lead directly to changes in student learning; others believe that decisions about how learning can be improved should be made locally and that assessment will provide the impetus for doing so. Another variant, standards-based reform, asserts the importance of specifying worthy goals and then holding schools accountable for achieving them (O'Day & Smith, 1993). The means are to be locally determined. Some districts, such as District 2 in New York City and the San Diego schools, meet this challenge by developing comprehensive systems of professional development so that teachers can envision how they may change their instruction to meet the agreed-upon standards.

An alternative method of reform focuses on the curriculum. Most noteworthy in recent years has been the specification of the curriculum to be used for reading instruction. In states such as Texas and California, for example, the use of curricular materials focusing on phonics instruction in the primary grades has been mandated. Similarly, districts often select new instructional materials in mathematics and other areas as a way to define the curriculum as a means of changing instruction and learning.

Some reform initiatives focus on the structural organizations of schools. Some reformers advocate the formation of small schools. Sergiovanni (1996), for example, emphasized the important role of small schools as a vehicle for building community. Large schools with their chains of command, departmentalization, and fragmentation have not worked. "Two conditions help to develop the bonding and binding necessary for community building—continuity of place and manageability of scale. It is easier for a small school to provide both" (p. 100). Sergiovanni viewed schools as learning communities, emphasizing their moral and humanistic role.

Another form of restructuring may involve a shift away from the traditional pattern of about 25 children working with a teacher for about a 9-month period and then moving onto another teacher during the next year. Greer and Short (1999) described several alternatives to schools that involve students of various ages working with one or several teachers over a multiple-year period. The purpose for restructuring is to enable teachers and students to engage in their work in new ways that are responsive to student needs.

Decentralization of School Governance.
Some approaches to reform focus directly on the decision-making power structure of schools. Decentralization is a reform that seeks to distribute the governance of schools away from the district office so that local schools have authority in decision making. Advocates range from those who see central bureaucracies as unresponsive and entrenched and thus desire community control of schools (e.g., Rogers, 1968) to parents who want a voice in their children's education. They make the assumption that decentralized school governance or site-based management will lead to improved performance. Through responsive decision making based on knowledge of the needs of children and their parents' goals, advocates believe that appropriate instruction will be developed, leading to high achievement.

Not always is the promise of decentralization realized. Schlechty (1991), for example, took a dim view of site-based decision making and called it "a good idea gone awry." He believed that in implementing site-based decision making, the emphasis is too often on what to do rather than on what is to be accomplished. "In such a context, discussions of who has the right to make a given decision become more important than which decisions are the right ones to make" (p. 115). He asserted that site-based decision making as it is currently being carried out in too many school districts may only aggravate further some of the problems that exist in schools. Moreover, Malen et-al., (1990) and P. Peterson (1976) found that the partnerships between parents and professional educators have tended to be superficial.

A common assumption of those advocating decentralization is that through the involvement of local stakeholders the instruction and learning of students will be improved. A number of studies focus on this issue. Site-based management was implemented in New Zealand's 2,666 schools in 1989. Based on surveys of trustees, principals, teachers, and parents, Wylie (1995-1996) reported that "there are no definitive answers" (p. 56) about whether decentralizing governance has had an impact on student learning. Positive outcomes include better methods of assessing the learning of students and improved communication with parents. Administrators report an increase in work load from about 48 to 60 hours per week following reform.

In the state of Washington, Jenkins, Ronk, Schrag, Rude, and Stowitschek (1994) examined the impact of school-based decision making on the performance of low-achieving students in 23 schools. Principals worked with teachers to design special interventions to improve the instruction for their lowest achieving students, and most teachers reported that they supported the program (87%) and had input into the new program (75%). Nevertheless, the test results comparing students in the program with a control sample indicated no significant differences in reading, spelling, or mathematics, nor in the behavior of students. These results suggest a cautionary note: It is not necessarily true that when decision-makers have intimate knowledge of students, programs will lead to higher achievement. Site-based management may open opportunities for more responsive programming, but this in itself may not be sufficient to realize increased learning on the part of students (Latham, 1998).

School System Studies.   District studies also provide insight into the workings of decentralized forms of school governance. The problems of low achievement that plague urban schools have not just recently emerged; they are of long-standing duration. Ravitch (1974), speaking of the New York City schools, noted that "the education of lower-class children has been from 1805 until the present the most vexing dilemma" (p. 401). In the late 1960s, a series of teacher strikes and militant action on the part of community representatives from the Ocean Hill–Brownsville area and Intermediate School 201 left the New York City schools in disarray. Ravitch described the opposing forces of the conflict. Those supporting the United Federation of Teachers included most of organized labor, conservative Jews who saw "an impartial merit system as a protection against discrimination," and White ethnic groups who saw their jobs and neighborhoods threatened by a growing minority population. On the side of community control were militant spokespersons for poor Blacks and Puerto Ricans, radical intellectuals from universities and foundations, political activists, wealthy patricians associated with social-welfare organizations, and representatives from the corporate elite. Because such a small proportion of teachers and administrators were from minority groups, community forces argued that unresponsive administrators and teachers were contributing to the genocide of poor Black and Puerto Rican children by withholding a proper education. Hence, the solution they proposed was a school governance plan that would involve community members and parents directly in the education of their children.

On April 30, 1969, both houses of the New York State Legislature enacted legislation enabling community control of the New York City schools. As described by Ravitch (1974) the new law established an interim board of education, empowered the interim board to divide the New York City district into about 30 school districts, and provided for the election of community school boards with substantial operating powers. The law also directed that a chancellor with wide-ranging powers, including suspension or removal of community school boards, be appointed by the board and that the board of examiners be retained to examine prospective supervisors and teachers.

Community activists anticipated that African Americans and Puerto Ricans would take control of many of the community school boards because more than 60% of schoolchildren were from these minority groups. Because all the voters of the city, not just parents, could vote in the elections, because low-income persons vote less regularly than those from middle- and high-income groups, and because there was a low voter turn out (15%), fewer African Americans and Puerto Ricans than had been anticipated were elected. The next few years were plagued by distrust and ethnic conflict between African Americans and Puerto Ricans. C. Wilson (1971) noted, in relation to the "interminable debates" that occurred: "Reason took a back seat to flamboyant rhetoric and to, of all things, old school traditions!" (pp. 235–237). The schools of New York City later reverted to a more centralized form of governance.

As the same time as the Ocean Hill–Brownsville controversy, the Detroit Public Schools became embroiled in a similar issues. Mirel (1993) described this period of history. During the 1960s, Detroit was beset by overwhelming social and economic changes including student walkouts to protest inadequate education, the riots in 1967, relocation of major industries to the suburbs coupled with White flight, a teacher strike for higher wages, increasing violence and decay in the inner city, and Black militant rejection of liberal reforms. Leadership of the schools was exercised by a fragile coalition among liberals, African Americans, and labor, including the Detroit Federation of Teachers (DFT). Similar to New York, the gulf between a predominantly White middle-class teaching force and ghetto schools with a majority of African-American students precipitated the charge by African-American activists that the schools were part of a White racist conspiracy committed to miseducating African-American youth.

As described by Mirel (1993), African-American leaders advocated the solution of community control of schools, and in 1969, the Michigan legislature passed a bill developed by Coleman Young that transferred powers from the central school board to regional boards. Two provisions demanded by the DFT were part of the bill: Regional boards had to operate under guidelines developed by the central board and the rights of tenure, seniority, and other benefits were protected. Desegregation issues, culminating in the 1971 Supreme Court decision (*Milliken v. Bradley I*) establishing that desegregation remedies could not go beyond city limits, complicated the decentralization process.

Eight decentralized regions were created, four with a majority of African Americans and four with a majority of Whites. Regional elections in 1970 resulted, however, in Whites controlling six of the eight regions and a large majority of the central board (10 of 13 members). During the next decade, as it became apparent that the quality of education had failed to improve, opposition to decentralization increased. By 1980 when African Americans controlled both the schools and city government, Detroit voters voted overwhelmingly to recentralize the schools.

School Reform in Chicago

Historical Perspective. Chicago experienced many of the same problems that beset New York and Detroit in the 1960s: riots, inadequate education, tensions between a predominantly White teaching force and a large number of minority students, and strikes by teachers. Although minor reform initiatives were put in place, the Chicago Public Schools (CPS) did not become the focus of a major decentralization effort until much later. Some tensions were eased over time as the numbers of African-American teachers and administrator in schools and the central office began to match more closely the compositional characteristics of Chicago students.

What had become clear in Chicago was that various reforms, such as continuous progress and mastery learning, had not led to higher student achievement. In 1984, only one out of three high school seniors could read at or above the national average. Between 43% and 53% of high school students never graduated (Walberg, Bakalis, Bast, & Baer, 1988). The CPS bureaucracy was enormous. Approximately 3,300 employees were assigned to the central and district offices to perform administrative tasks (Banas, 1987). In addition to being bloated at the top, the administrative bureaucracy was generally unresponsive to the teachers and students it was designed to serve.

A 19-day teacher strike in the fall of 1987 outraged voters and hardened the resolve of community organizations, politicians, business people, and organized lobbies to reform Chicago schools. The process of rethinking Chicago schools was initiated under the leadership of Mayor Harold Washington through summits with business leaders, politicians, parents, educators, and community members (Shipps, 1997). Similar to New York City, a coalition of political activists, intellectuals from foundations and universities, and community leaders argued for a decentralized form of administration designed to empower parents (Katz, Fine, & Simon, 1997). Professional educators and their organizations did not play a major role in the design of the legislation.

The supporters of reform believed that the restructuring had the potential to transform disadvantaged schools and their communities. They argued that prior efforts involving decentralization in large urban areas, such as New York and Detroit, had not gone far enough beyond the subdistrict level (Hess, 1991). That is, decentralization had not reached the local school level so that parents in the neighborhood would be directly involved in the decision making involving their children. Site-based management was selected as a more locally responsive form of decentralization that might avoid earlier problems. Some opponents of reform, nevertheless, feared that the legislation would bring machine-style politics of patronage down to the school level. Others feared that the reforms would only be structural and that classroom practice would not be affected.

The Chicago school reform legislation (SB 1840), which was passed by the Illinois legislature in 1988, challenged parents, teachers, and community representatives to come forward and assume leadership in the schools to help deal with problems about which they had firsthand knowledge.

Although the reform legislation was generally described as a governance reform, its ultimate goal was to improve the educational opportunities provided to the children of Chicago. A key intent of the legislation was to build a bridge between each local school and its neighborhood. Establishing ties with local communities had previously not been viewed as a priority of schools, especially in areas of urban poverty.

The legislation addressed the issue of bridge building by providing for local school councils, one in each Chicago elementary and high school. The Local School Council (LSC) was composed of six parents, two community residents, two teachers, and the school principal. According to the legislation, the LSC was responsible for hiring the principal of the school and had broad approval powers over a school improvement plan and the discretionary funds that the principal now managed.

Later legislation mandated that the LSCs would receive training in three areas: budget, personnel, and educational theory. Training was offered by a variety of community organizations. Following the training during the first year of reform, the LSC in each school was to participate in developing a school improvement plan that reflected its school's particular needs, had the support of the school community, and could be implemented in the following 3 years. Some of the issues that the plan had to address were spelled out in the law: curriculum, attendance and dropout rates, parent involvement, and student transition into mainstream society. These tasks and decisions became an opportunity to involve both parents and school professionals in decision making and problem solving that would affect school and classroom activities. Embedded in these decisions was the explicit understanding that the LSC was responsible for stimulating quality education; they were given 5 years to improve learning substantially.

Critical responsibilities also accrued to the school principals under the legislation. The principals' key activities included hiring of faculty, conducting the school needs assessment, developing a school improvement plan, and developing a budget plan for using the school's discretionary funds. All of this was to be done with the approval of the LSC.

In addition, the legislation created a Professional Personnel Advisory Committee (PPAC), whose role was advisory to the LSC and the principal, especially in areas of curriculum and instruction. The PPAC was made up of teachers that were either elected or appointed in a way determined by the teachers. Sarason (1990) attributed the limited success of most school change efforts to the failure to see teachers as a constituency that needs to be informed and involved at all stages of the change. He argued that it is naive to ignore the power that teachers have in deciding the fate of the change effort. Reform in Chicago schools all but ignored the power of this constituency. The Principals' Association and the Chicago Teachers Union did not play a proactive role in the design of the law. In fact, the establishment of the PPAC was a last-minute effort at involving this important constituency, which had been left out in the first versions of the legislation.

The Impact of Reform.   How did these reform initiatives work in terms of local governance, classroom practice, and student achievement? One useful source, *Catalyst: Voices of Chicago School Reform,* features case-study portraits and issue-focused articles detailing both problems and success stories. In addition, several reviews of the Chicago reform have also appeared. Hess (1991, 1995) framed the Chicago reform historically in terms of the broader reform literature and considers the import of the legislation for the roles of principals and teachers, as well as parents and community residents. The Consortium on Chi-

cago School Research, composed of researchers from a variety of institutions including universities, the CPS, advocacy groups, a regional laboratory, and the
State Board of Education, surveyed teachers and principals to assess their views
on reform (Sebring & Bryk, 1993). Their report on elementary schools was encouraging, showing that about a third of the schools had developed innovative
programs. Moreover, they reported a relation between the democratic functioning of the LSCs and educational innovation (Bryk, Easton, Kebow, Rollow, &
Sebring, 1993).

In addition to reports by those living in Chicago, Katz et al., (1997) as reformers from outside the city interviewed key participants and developed case
studies of three schools. In 1994, they concluded that after a period of antago-
nism between the central office and local schools, a new alignment was emerging and that the schools were entering "a period of quiet progress" (Katz &
Simon, 1994). Yet when the 5-year trial period of reform ended in 1995, test
scores and other indicators of learning had, according to some, barely budged
(Walberg & Niemiec, 1996). Others documented substantial progress in about
a third of the elementary schools, but less in others for modest average learning
gains; no change was found in high schools. Concurrently, the system was faced
by a $300 million projected deficit. In this context, in May 1995 the Illinois
State Legislature amended the School Reform Act to place control of the
school system in the hands of the mayor, who was to appoint a five-member
board of trustees and a CEO to manage the system.

Paul Vallas, who had been Mayor Daley's budget chief, was drafted as the
new CEO of the CPS. During the 1st year, Vallas and the new trustees solved the
budgetary deficit, and negotiated a salary increase for teachers contingent on
their agreement not to strike for 4 years. The training of LSC members was required, and due to the scheduling of LSC elections on the same day report cards
were picked up, election turnout increased (but remained small overall). Although principals gained more control over budgeting and over personnel in
their buildings, including engineers, a major source of their discretionary funding, state Chapter I funds, was frozen at 1995 levels. Accountability became the
dominant theme in the system, and direct instruction of students the recommended means for enhancing achievement. Poorly performing schools were
targeted for probation, followed by "reconstitution" of the school administration and teaching force, if gains in achievement did not occur. As part of this
process, aspects of local authority have become recentralized.

Ten years have gone by since the initial legislation was passed. The 562
schools in Chicago have navigated the waters of reform in different ways. In a
recent survey of local school council members conducted by the Consortium on
Chicago School Research, it was reported that 10% to 15% of the local school

councils are not viable governing entities (Ryan, Bryk, Lopez, & Williams, 1997). The causes of variability in council effectiveness were found to be more complex than factors of race, ethnicity, income level, and poverty. Instead, key aspects in the school community such as leadership, training, and cooperative adult relations were crucial differentiating factors.

Moore and colleagues (Designs for Change, 1998), in their analysis of achievement trends in elementary schools from 1990 to 1997, found that nearly half (49%) of the schools showed significant progress or maintained above-average scores in the area of reading. Of these, 26% made impressive gains, 17% improved their scores, and 6% showed no change or slight gains. Nearly half (48%) maintained below-average test scores. Of these, 36% showed slight gains and 12% realized slight losses. The remaining 3% were "tending down" or "substantially down." Moore and colleagues noted that schools improving their scores received higher ratings on indicators of good school practice. Among these, schools with increased achievement have "principals who are instructional leaders and closely supervise the change process, and teachers who are more involved in decision making" (p. 12). In addition, teachers rated the LSC as having contributed to improving the school environment and educational programs.

Case Study Description of Chicago School Reform

School Case Studies.   As previously discussed, the Chicago reform initiative has been documented by educational researchers from a variety of perspectives. This system-wide research is valuable in describing the features of reform, characterizing groups of participants relative to one another, and tracing changes in student learning. Although school case studies appear occasionally in the context of a broader analysis, the story has not been told from the perspective of participants by the participants themselves.

In this book, we are particularly interested in the forms of leadership that the reform made possible, and how they came about. The reform, by distributing powers to the local level, particularly in the form of hiring personnel and control over discretionary funds, created the possibility for new forms of leadership. These were taken up in some schools, but not in others. We believe that the lessons offered will let us think more clearly about leadership in all schools undergoing some aspect of school reform.

These school case studies were written by participants—principals, teachers, parents, supportive professionals. We examine reform in the eight schools through the eyes of participant-observers. With the participants, we explore the paths that each school took during the years of reform. Together the stories develop a textured portrait of a school system undergoing radical change. As we examine the issue of how school restructuring affected the lives of the various participants in the case study schools, we follow an interpretive approach. Voice is given to the perspectives of participants as they engage in school activities. Thus, when reading the cases, it must also be remembered that the story of a school could have been told by any number of individuals, each with their unique "take" on what was happening. We have made the choice to feature a particular perspective.

Through this series of eight school case studies, we make visible the complex set of conditions that interact to give rise to new forms of leadership, as well as the factors that inhibit such occurrence. Six of the cases explore issues in elementary schools as they operate under the umbrella of reform; two focus on high schools. The schools were chosen purposefully to be diverse in terms of neighborhood and the students they serve, and more important, in terms of the issues related to the emergence of leadership.

The first two cases provide a broad view of decision making in schools during the early years of the reform. The first case, Jackson Elementary School, is located in one of Chicago's largest housing projects. The study describes how a traditional principal deals daily with teachers and parents, and with the many problems that characterize their situation. The second school, Maria Saucedo Scholastic Academy, which serves a Hispanic student population, began to reform itself long before the beginning of the legislated reform. Its story is one of continuation of a process well under way.

The second set of two cases permits us to focus on the workings of the LSC in relation to the principal. The case of Field School, a large elementary school that has restructured itself into five small schools within the school, lays bare the power struggle that can ensue between the LSC and the principal. "W" School is a neighborhood school with a multicultural student population and an active parent community. This case, developed from the perspective of the LSC chair, details governance issues of the school, difficulties inherent in sharing power, and the attempts made to enhance student learning.

In the third set of cases, we explore two schools in which the principals and teachers actively engaged in addressing issues of student learning. Irving School, a new school at the beginning of reform, serves a low-income population in an area that is gentrifying. Gloria Anzalúa Elementary School, nestled in the side streets of a Mexican barrio, exemplifies the important leadership role of teachers in re-forming the school.

The two high school cases differ in the populations they serve and in the leadership issues they pose. In Amundsen School, administrators and teachers are exploring how to deal with the pressures posed by accountability in a positive way to enhance student participation in meaningful activities that will lead to higher achievement. The Best Practice High School, a new, public "small school" serving a diverse set of students from across the city, was created in response to the opportunities made possible through reform.

Questions Guiding the Case Study Analyses. The purpose of our case study analyses is to reflect on the nature of school leadership. Our analysis of leadership is informed by an interpretive perspective that focuses on events occurring within schools and on how participants make sense of them and the actions of other participants. Studies of organizational leadership show that the effectiveness of leaders is related to the perceptions of other participants. How leaders contribute to an organization's primary tasks and how they support the norms of the organization influences how they are viewed by others. In essence, an interpretive approach examines the processes through which leaders, finding themselves in an unfamiliar or changing school culture, "make sense" of this new setting, and how other participants, faced with new leaders "make sense" of them.

Our approach is historical in nature, examining events that have occurred prior to and during the time of the reform. The reform legislation was passed in 1988 and implemented in the fall of 1989. At that time, the schools were given 5 years to implement sweeping reforms. School leaders were asked to come forward and rethink traditional roles of principals, teachers, and parents. These role changes required educators to examine issues of power, authority, norms, values, professional development, and student learning. In the case studies, the participants who wrote the cases look back at the path that reform took in their individual schools. This history will enable us to take a long view of the change process as it works in schools with different and unique school cultures.

A window of opportunity was created in individual schools by the nature of the site-based restructuring. But the specific ways in which leadership was to be exercised were not specified. Theoretically, the principal, teachers, and the LSC (parents and community) could share power or one of the three could dominate. Or in spite of reform, principals may continue to exercise control. The LSC, through its power to hire and fire principals, may gain an upper hand. Or perhaps, the reform may enable community members to have more of a voice in governance. Alternatively, it may be that two of the three join forces against the third, such as teachers in collaboration with the LSC working for a change in principals. Finally, all three may learn to work together in a constructive fashion. Sharing of power would entail new forms of leadership by Chicago principals, who were, for the most part, accustomed to a hierarchical form of organization. Through analysis of the case studies, we propose to examine the leadership roles of these three groups as they become redefined and describe the way in which particular leaders operate.

The legislative mandate of the Illinois state government gave new powers to the school principal. These powers included hiring of faculty and developing the school budget and the school improvement plan. In our analysis of principal roles, we consider how each of the eight principals in the case studies viewed their rights and responsibilities, and how their conceptions may have shifted over time. Thus, one of our main purposes following presentation of each case study will be to reflect on how participants carved out roles for themselves, how these roles corresponded to the conceptions of the framers of the legislation, and whether they were able to support the leadership activities of others. Thus, our first questions is: *How has the leadership of school principals been shaped by the reform initiative?*

The evolving roles of teachers are also explored. It is difficult to envision how the legislation might enable teachers to learn new strategies to enhance their leadership. The legislation does provide for the creation of a PPAC. The PPAC is composed of teachers whose role is advisory to the LSC and the principal, especially in areas of curriculum and instruction. Because of the advisory nature of their role, teachers may be expected to influence curricular and instructional preparation matters only if the principal and LSC choose to heed their advice. Indeed, teachers are highly dependent on principals for inclusion in leadership positions that have consequence (Johnson, 1990). We are particularly curious about the tasks that serve to pivot teachers into leadership roles. When this occurs, we are interested in whether and how principals give voice to teachers. Thus, our second question asks: *How have the leadership roles of teachers been shaped by the reform initiative?*

The legislation established LSCs composed of parents, community representatives, teachers, and the school principal. LSCs were granted authority to approve several key actions: the contract of the principal, the school improvement plan, and the budget. What the Chicago reform did was to put in place a form of site-based management that gave greater local authority to principals, while at the same time establishing an alternative power base in the form of the LSC. The role of principals in individual schools became similar to that of superintendent in districts insofar as they would be held accountable to a local school board. The tensions inherent between the principal and the LSC get played out daily in the microcosms of individual schools. We focus in particular on how this relation evolved, by whom it was controlled and how, and how the evolving balance affected the workings of the school. Thus, a third question we ask is: *How have community members and parents on the LSC contributed to school decision making?*

Since Sarason (1971) conceptualized the enormous social and cultural complexities of schools, others have examined these important aspects of schools.

Some advocates of school reform argue that change in the organization of schools cannot occur without fundamental changes in the culture of schools. Culture is defined as the ideas, commitments, and social order that determine the rules and standard operating procedures of schools (Hawley, 1988). We view the culture of schools as composed of the values and activities of participants: the school lives of administrators, teachers, and students, what they strive for, and the way they conceptualize the nature of schooling. We suggest that the values and actions of school leaders are particularly important in establishing the culture of schools. We expect that as the leadership roles of the principal, teachers, and community members evolve, the culture of the school will correspondingly be transformed. Thus, our fourth question focuses on: *How has the culture of the school been affected by reform?*

Finally, whether the shift in leadership leads to changes in classroom instruction and learning is of central concern. As was discussed earlier, in drafting the reform legislation, participants assumed that structural changes in the governance of Chicago schools would change the way in which decisions were made in schools. The reformers also believed that the structural changes would alter the culture of schools, their instructional environments, and ultimately the learning of students. Yet, no direct mechanisms to instruction and learning existed during the first years of the reform. As Elmore, P. Peterson, and McCarthy (1996) found in their case studies of classes in three schools, the relationship between restructuring and teaching practices is weak and indirect. More generally, the initial phase of reform initiatives has produced disappointing results (Cohen & Spillane, 1992).

This failure of restructuring to show expected gains in students achievement led to an emphasis at the national level on the specification of standards that were expected to influence curriculum and learning more directly (O'Day & Smith, 1993). In keeping with this trend, when Paul Vallas assumed leadership of the CPS in 1995, he focused on accountability as a means to influence learning. Direct instruction of students became the recommended means for enhancing achievement. Thus, two quite different phases characterize the Chicago school reform with policies and initiatives that might affect teaching and learning differently. With this in mind, our fifth question asks: *How have teaching and learning been shaped by reform?*

In sum, the eight case studies presented in the book show how restructuring changed the dynamics within schools so that a new set of relationships had the impetus to emerge. The restructuring and the implementation of standards, in quite different ways, may have created new sets of contingencies that school leaders had to address. The questions we pursue include the following:

1. How has the leadership of school principals been shaped by the reform initiative?
2. How have the leadership roles of teachers been shaped by the reform initiative?
3. How have parents and the LSC contributed to school decision making?
4. How has the culture of the school been affected by reform?
5. How have teaching and learning been shaped by reform?

The book is organized into six sections. The first includes this introductory
analysis of reform and school leadership. The next four sections are organized
around the case studies. The second section focuses on "The Response of
Schools to the Initial Years of Reform." The description of Jackson School portrays events during the first year of reform to show how difficult it is for an authoritarian principal to learn new ways of collaborative decision making.
Similarly, the report for Saucedo also shows a continuation of past modes of
shared leadership involving teachers, parents, and community members along
with the principal.

The third section, "Tensions Between the Local School Council and the
Principal," includes two cases, Field School and W School, showing how the effectiveness of concerted efforts by leaders can result in building resistance that
leads to a derailing of new initiatives. In the fourth section, "Reform as an Opportunity for Creating Responsive Instruction," the case of Irving shows how a
newly relocated school evolves its culture focused on student learning through
the collaboration of the principal and teachers. The case of Anzaldúa traces
how reform permitted teachers, working with parents, to change the culture of
the school.

In the fifth section, "New Beginnings: Making Changes in High School Instruction and Learning," the case of Amundsen shows how the external force of
academic standards was used as a wedge into new instructional practices. The
Best Practice High School case, similar to Irving, shows how a new school
evolves its unique culture focused on student learning through the collaboration of administrative leaders and teacher leaders.

The closing chapter in the final section, "Insights Into Leadership During
Times of School Reform," synthesizes and discusses what we learned through
these cases concerning the leadership roles of principals, parents and community members, and teachers during the period of reform, how the cultures of
schools changed as reform progressed, and how reform impacted the instructional practices of teachers and the learning of students.

SECTION 2

The Response of Schools to the Initial Years of Reform

We have paired the first two cases because they provide an interesting contrast in terms of their readiness for reform. The first case, Jackson Elementary, located in one of Chicago 's poorest high-rise housing communities, was clearly not ready for reform. Jackson was organized in a traditional highly hierarchical manner, with a new principal who had been brought in to "clean up" the school, following an unfortunate incident involving the former principal and male students. The nature of her task, and the distrust that was engendered, did not set the stage for teachers and parents to feel comfortable taking on leadership roles.

The second case takes us to Maria Saucedo Scholastic Academy, where the principal, the teachers, and the community had built a base that enabled them to handle the demands that reform placed on the school community. At Saucedo, many factors coalesced over time to build a learning community where leadership was shared and where trust was already in place. Because the groundwork had been laid, the school community was willing and able to address the agenda of reform.

At Jackson Elementary, the teachers and parents were unwilling to assume the new roles that were mandated by the reform legislation. They went through the motions by electing a Local School Council (LSC) and by hiring their principal, but the LSC served only as a rubber stamp, and in the process of principal selection, they chose the easiest route. The school culture at Jackson was not supportive of anyone—teachers, parents, or students. Trust was not part of the culture and this lack of trust seriously inhibited changes that called for shared leadership. In contrast, at Saucedo, a sense of trust and working relationships were already in place when the legislation was enacted. A culture already existed that focused on improving student learning, developing teacher capabilities, and enhancing the community of learning for students and teachers.

21

CASE 1

Reform at Jackson Elementary: Transition to Site-Based Management

Marilyn Bizar
National-Louis University

Background

Jackson Elementary is located in one of Chicago's largest low-income, high-rise public housing communities. Many of the families have single parents, and many of these parents are children themselves. Welfare is the predominant way of life in this community.

The current enrollment at Jackson is just over 600 students, Head Start to eighth grade, with 35 faculty. Jackson's student population is 100% Black and is listed as 100% below the poverty level. All of the students at Jackson receive both a free breakfast and a free lunch. The enrollment at Jackson has dwindled greatly due to many of the residents of the projects leaving for safety reasons, and these apartments are not being filled in an effort to control the crime. At one time during the 1970s, Jackson served about 3,000 students who attended school in shifts. Today there are about 15 empty classrooms spread throughout the building.

One of the problems that plagues Jackson today is gang membership. Jackson is in a unique situation because it is located in the center of buildings that house members of rival gangs. These gangs have formed consortiums called the "People" and the "Folks." These gang consortiums are in constant conflict, and children who attend Jackson often find themselves in the midst of it. For instance, on October 13, 1992, early in the morning, when the streets were crowded with kids going to Jackson School, a 7-year-old boy was walking to school with his mother when shots rang out. There was much confusion and it soon became clear that the boy had been shot. Teachers from Jackson came to help, an ambulance was called, and he died in the ambulance on the way to the hospital.

This gang-related murder of an innocent child was particularly disturbing to Chicago and the rest of the nation. The boy was shot down at a time of day when the streets were filled with children, he was on his way to school, and he was accompanied by his mother. Surely our children should be able to walk to school safely. The national media latched on to this tragedy and Jackson was in the spotlight for many weeks afterward. The students at

23

Jackson wrote and talked about the violence that is a fact of their young lives, and it seemed as if things would be changed forever. Since this terrible event in 1992, there has been an uneasy gang truce that has enabled people to feel a bit safer in their own neighborhood.

During the 1960s, 1970s, and much of the 1980s, Jackson had a reputation of being a tough school in which to teach. To be a "tough" school in an area where none of the schools were easy meant a great deal. Substitutes did not report to Jackson. The large building, which was built in 1932, was dirty, dark, and in disrepair. Discipline was a major problem at Jackson, and noise and students spilled out of classrooms into hallways. Jackson had a number of principals during these years, and none of them was able to "clean up" the school. One of these principals was a man whose name engenders very different responses from different people. In discussing his tenure at Jackson, the teachers who are still there use such diverse phrases as "doing our own thing," laissez-faire," "out of control," "respected his teachers," and "a sad chapter at Jackson." In 1986, this principal was asked to resign when he was convicted of molesting male students.

My role at Jackson was that of an outside partner. For 4 years, my colleague Rebecca Barr and I were involved in a partnership with the teachers at Jackson Elementary School to support them in improving their reading and writing instruction. We were invited to collaborate with teachers as facilitators of change. We worked with teachers in various ways both in and out of their classrooms, engaging in a dialogue that helped them to address instructional problems. Our presence at Jackson during the critical first year of the implementation of the reform legislation afforded me the opportunity to become a participant-observer in the transition and to carefully follow their process of change.

THE CASE

During the crucial first year of the reform process, Jackson Elementary was challenged by a variety of problems that seemed to amplify through the implementation of the reform legislation. Just prior to the reform legislation, the entire Jackson School community was shaken when the news about their principal's misconduct with children reached them. The parents clearly wanted a new principal who would literally and figuratively clean up their school. Enter, in 1989, the principal who could and would do the job. Ms. Morgan, an articulate, intelligent, and extremely professional Black woman of about 55, was formerly the principal of another school in the area for 17 years. She was known for her knowledge about instruction in general and reading education in particular. At her former school, she had built a fine reputation because of the excellent rapport she developed with her teachers. She had high expectations for teachers, and exercised her leadership by spending much of her day walking through the halls and visiting classes. The district superintendent asked Ms. Morgan to apply for the position at Jackson because the school was desperately in need of a leader who could pull the faculty together. The teachers at

Ms. Morgan's former school were angry and upset about her leaving; yet many of them visited Jackson on a regular basis to say hello and offer support.

The Jackson School community interviewed several candidates and Ms. Morgan was chosen by the parents and the teachers. Her mandate was clear, and she began the task of repairing the school. The road from chaos to respectability was not easy, and she made many enemies of both teachers and parents along the way. The former principal, according to one teacher, "although he was convicted of molesting teenage boys, had a good relationship with both teachers and the community." Many teachers left Jackson because they could not accept the new regime. One teacher complained that the new principal's "methods were not appropriate with a veteran faculty." Another teacher said that "about 80% of the teachers thought that she was too top down, not responsive to teachers needs and not open to suggestion." Ms. Morgan brought some faculty with her, and others complained that they became part of an inner circle that made the rules and implemented them. "Teachers were suspicious; we were used to openness and there was a lack of trust in both directions." Decisions were made in top-down fashion, and teachers and staff were expected to follow through.

Ms. Morgan, in discussing her first 3 years at Jackson said:

I had a very hard time. Teachers were used to total freedom. The circumstances were very unfortunate that brought me here. The former principal was completely removed from instruction, and teachers did their own things, whether they were good for kids or not. I'm sure that there were those on the faculty that had some idea about what was going on. I am not saying that they knew the specifics, but too many children were involved for people not to have some idea. There were many teachers in the building who were comfortable with the status quo.

In many important ways, Jackson School was greatly improved by Ms. Morgan's leadership. According to one teacher, "I feel very positive about Ms. Morgan; she has changed herself a great deal, and the building is running smoother." The physical building became clean, colorful, and inviting. The walls were painted, and teachers were expected to create interesting bulletin boards in the halls each month. The assistant principal took pictures of students who had achieved distinction during the month, and bulletin boards displayed these pictures of good spellers, perfect attenders, and math scholars. The school became orderly, and discipline was no longer as great a problem. This sense of order and discipline characterized the school during the early days of reform. Hallways were quiet, and teachers took pains to see that students passed through the halls in an orderly fashion.

Although the school made important changes, Jackson was not a pleasant place to work for many on the faculty and staff, according to teachers interviewed about the culture at Jackson. In the words of one teacher, "The faculty is very divided. The faculty by and large are good, but there are some teachers who don't like to share, and they stay to themselves. The principal had a hard job when she came just getting the faculty stable. For some of us, Jackson is an okay place to work, but for others it is a struggle." According to another teacher, "Many teachers don't like her [the principal]. Teachers have become closed-minded. She came in heavy-handed to clean up the staff, and although it had to be done, many don't like her."

The atmosphere in the office at Jackson was formal. There was an air of efficiency, of important jobs getting done, and visitors seem to be looked upon as intrusions. There was no phone available for teachers or parents to use in private, and teachers generally asked the assistant principal to make their calls to parents. The photocopy machine was basically off limits to teachers, and one of the clerks did all of the photocopy work. Ms. Morgan had two offices, one adjacent to the main office, and another, a first-floor classroom. Teachers did not stop in informally to talk to her.

Jackson was one of the 541 elementary schools that was not prepared for reform. Teachers had no history of participating in decisions. Ms. Morgan was brought in to clean up the school and, in so doing, had established relationships that did not lend themselves to collaboration. This section of the case focuses on four key sets of interactions that serve to reveal the leadership style of Ms. Morgan, as well as to show the attempts of others to have a role in decision making. The first concerns the role of the LSC as they interacted with the principal. The second focuses on a key decision of the LSC involving the principal's contract negotiation. The third set of interactions pertains to the development of the Professional Personnel Advisory Committee (PPAC) and the attempt of faculty to develop a role in school decision making. The final set of interactions concerns the development of the school improvement plan. The body of the case is organized into these four sections.

The Local School Council

The election and composition of the Local School Council (LSC) was spelled out by the legislation. The council was to be made up of the principal, two teachers, six parents, and two community members. This composition ensured a voice for those who have had the least voice in school governance, the parents and the community members. The rules for the election were also specified by the legislation. The candidates were asked to fill out candidate statements and to participate in a forum where each candidate had 5 minutes to campaign. At Jackson, there were 12 parents, 5 community members, and 6 teachers who ran for the council.

Elections for councils across the city's 541 schools were held on October 10, 1989. Parents were asked to come in and vote for parents, community members were asked to vote for community members, and teachers for other teachers. There was much publicity for the elections both in the media generally and also at each local school. Newspapers and local news broadcasts encouraged people to go to their local schools to vote. Businesses in Chicago gave employees time to vote. Jackson school sent out flyers from the school, and individual teachers sent student-made notes home requesting parents to vote.

Election day was a very long day. It began at 7:30 AM and ended at 6:00 PM, in order to give parents and community members time to vote. The voter turnout across the city was 10% and the turnout at Jackson was considerably smaller. Teachers and the principal came out early to open the polls. Ms. Morgan arrived at school having heard a radio broadcast that exhorted people to vote and also proclaimed the principal the villain that the newly elected councils were designed to impede. A spokesman from Acorn, a community organization, said, "We have to get out and vote in order to get power, because we can't trust the principals." Ms. Morgan said that hearing those complaints on the way to school when she was coming to implement reform was both "degrading and demeaning."

The members of the council approached their task armed with media hype about councils taking "power" and "running the schools." This particular council approached their tasks with the knowledge that they did not know much about how to "run the school." At the first meeting, officers were elected and a parent was elected chair of the council. It was decided that each meeting would be started with a prayer and a quote from scripture. The chair of the council assumed this responsibility because as she said, "we need all the help we can get."

The atmosphere at the council meetings was friendly; meetings were smooth and orderly, not at all like those reported to occur in other communities where conflict prevailed. The meetings lasted from 2:30 PM to 4:00 PM, whereas other councils reported that their meetings sometimes went way into the night. Ms. Morgan served an educative function as well as a gate-keeping function. She spent some part of each meeting explaining the procedures by which things get done. She educated about the issues that the council needed to approve such as expenditures and budgets. There was a great deal of information to be assimilated and one of the teachers on the council was given the responsibility of reading directives and explaining them to the council. When issues came up to be discussed, members turned to the principal to get her opinion on the subject. The council never addressed problems or complaints of either teachers or parents and community representatives.

The start-up kit for LSC members devoted several pages to agendas. The kit specified that it was the chair's duty to keep the meeting moving, and planning an agenda before the meeting is necessary so that all members would know what is supposed to be acted on and in what order. The kit also specified that the top officer had the responsibility of preparing the agenda. At Jackson, the principal assumed the responsibility of preparing the agenda due to the inexperience of the new council members. The preparing of the agenda became a gate-keeping function for issues and ideas.

In April 1990, the chair of the council began asking questions about agenda setting. She reported calling the clerk before council meetings to find out about the agenda. She was told that the agenda was being typed and would be ready for the council meeting. The chair reported that she knew that Ms. Morgan would know most of the issues that should be dealt with, and therefore she did not make objections to the procedure. By the end of the year, however, she expressed the wish that the chair could set the agenda for the following meeting at the end of the meeting, and the principal could add items if she wished.

The meetings of the council were open to the public, and it was left up to the council to decide how the meetings would be run. At the first meeting, the issue came up about participation from the observers. The legislation stipulates that all meetings of the council are to be open meetings and conducted in that manner. The principal suggested that the meetings be conducted in the same way that the board conducted their meetings, which meant that observers could only participate at the end of the meeting after everything was already decided. The other council members agreed to this in the name of efficiency. This ruling served to keep observers from interacting with the council. At the initial meetings, teachers and parents came to observe, but as it became clear that they could not participate, fewer and fewer came. At the last meeting of the council before the summer, when the meeting was opened up for observer participation, one parent eloquently complained to the council, "You have no idea how frustrating it is to sit here and not be able to speak." The chair, concerned about the way the meetings were structured to eliminate participation, reported having conversations with people on other councils who did not run their meetings in this way. The teachers on the council were eager to hear about these alternative plans but were unaware that meetings could be run in any other way.

The legislation stipulated that each council would receive 30 hours of training in three areas: budget, personnel, and educational theory. The councils were not initially given any money to pay for this training, although later in the year each council was allotted $1,500. Many community groups and universities offered council training and the board also offered a few sessions. Jackson was already working with the Center for School Improvement, which was a collaboration between the University of Chicago, National-Louis University, and the Department of Research and Evaluation of the Chicago Board of Education. The Center offered to provide the LSC training, and the principal agreed to this arrangement.

Ms. Morgan was given a list of possible topics that could be presented by the Center and asked to share it with the council in order to set up a schedule of meetings on

Saturdays or after school. The list of possible topics was never introduced to the LSC and dates were never set. The Center, at their initiative, delivered only 6 hours of training to the LSC members, but no more. The research-practitioner from the Center frequently tried to establish dates and select topics. Ms. Morgan said, "This year we are neglecting our classrooms. We need to prioritize. We can't work on anyone's schedule, just our own. More needs to be done than can be accomplished." At another time Ms. Morgan said, "The council is just not ready for it [training]."

The Role of the Teachers on the LSC.   The teachers on the LSC were the most vocal members of the council. The parents on the council mainly listened attentively, but rarely spoke on issues unless directly asked for an opinion. The teacher members of the council both expressed skepticism about parents in their community being equal to the task of full participation on the council. One teacher on the council confided that:

> [One of the problems with reform], especially in this community, is that the teachers on the council take over the meetings. Parents have desires to help—but that's all—they will even do some work, but they can't learn what they need to. Parents can't even go through all the information. I'm talking about this neighborhood—maybe it could work in Hyde Park.

The other teacher on the council, in speculating about reform said, "Sometimes it seems its designed to fail. There is too much for someone to master in a short period of time. In our community, it's a very heavy order, but not impossible."

One of the major problems that impacted participation on the council according to one of the teacher representatives is that the parents were not even reading what they were given. He believed that parents needed much training to be able to operate in this forum and that, with 2-year terms, parents could be trained and not reelected and "then you have trained for nothing." "Truthfully it's a bunch of bull, parents [in this community] haven't been involved, why should they get involved now?" Taking a more sympathetic stance, the other teacher representative stated that "teacher members on the council should be the experts to the others on the council and hand-hold them." He assumed this role and attempted to do it in a nondemeaning way.

These teachers on the council had little faith in the ability of parents to participate fully. This lack of faith in the parents and community members combined with the skepticism about reform being able to operate in their community served to force the council to act merely as a rubber stamp. The principal determined what issues were to be discussed and the teachers dominated the process of both discussing and deciding on the issues.

In spite of the perfunctory nature of the council, or maybe because of it, council members came regularly to meetings throughout the year. Many councils around the city complained of a loss of attendance by council members as the year progressed. At Jackson, each meeting had a quorum and participants never complained about coming. At Jackson, the tasks of reform were not monumental because many of the tasks were not placed before the council. In addition, because the training was kept from the council, council membership meant only attending monthly 1-hour meetings.

The Role of the Principal on the LSC.   The principal of Jackson School operated the school in a very top-down manner. Similar to her interactions with faculty members, her participation in the proceedings of the council were also of a top-down nature as she did the job of guiding the participants through the process. Her tight control of the proceedings exemplified her reluctance to relinquish the power that had in the past enabled her to "get the job done."

Ms. Morgan had expressed the knowledge that she had a very top-down administrative style, and that she had to work on changing it. The nature of the reform effort is such that it calls upon principals to develop skills and strategies for sharing power. Ms. Morgan was well aware of her style of leadership and knew that adjustments would have to be made if she was to implement reform. According to Ms. Morgan, "The time for me to change is now. If I don't learn to share now, I never will."

In the beginning, the teachers on the council favored a strong role for the principal with the LSC. When interviewed in February, the teachers on the council agreed that the role of the principal on the council should be one of guidance and leadership. One teacher representative on the council, in discussing this guidance role, said in February, "that our principal has been very good at doing this so far." The other teacher representative said that the "principal should take a very broad role of guiding and leading. They [principals] should not make policy by themselves, but with the input of teachers and some consideration of parents."

By June, both of the teachers expressed the view that the principal had overstepped her guidance role, prevented the council from actually dealing with important issues, and kept information from the council. One teacher representative, in reflecting on the work of the council, said:

> The council functioned smoothly. The main thing was harmony. The parents trusted the principal and teachers. One problem is that things that had to be discussed came up at the last minute. We also didn't meet enough. The meetings are too short—rush, rush. The meetings should start at 2:00. Another problem is that we don't deal with specific problems. The direction needs to come away from the principal. She basically writes the agenda. Today's meet-

ing was a good example; the council looks to the principal as though she's in charge. She should be viewed as just another member of the council.

Although the faculty at Jackson generally did not attend council meetings, one of the teachers who had attended twice said, "Ms. Morgan is lucky; maybe because they are intimidated, they have been very positive, no questions asked."

Principal's Contract Negotiations

Perhaps the most awesome responsibility that the LSC had to face the first year was the decision of whether or not to rehire the principal. The procedure was stipulated by the Board of Education, and the time frame, not unlike many of the board directives, was much too short. There was a feeling among school participants that dates just came out of the sky with little justification. The councils were notified at the end of January that they had until February 28 to decide whether or not to offer their principal a 4-year performance contract. Public hearings were to be held enabling the councils the opportunity to hear the voices of their various constituencies before they took a vote. The LSC's decision to retain the current principal had to be made by six affirmative votes. The decision to select a person other than the current principal had to be made by seven affirmative votes. The council was allowed to debate in closed session, but the vote was to be taken in open session. The community was to be given 10 days' notice of the open session in order to encourage participation.

The month of February in many of the Chicago schools was a period of unrest. All of the principals had participated in a lottery in order to determine if their contracts would be evaluated in the first or second year of reform. There are 541 local councils, and half of them had to decide on principals the first year. At some schools, councils used this event to exercise their "power" for the first time. The media in Chicago, of course, focused on these events. At some schools, the community, faculty, and students became so fractionalized that violence erupted.

However, most of the schools went through a less tumultuous process. According to then Chicago School Superintendent Ted Kimbrough, in the *Chicago Sun-Times* of February 16, 1990:

> Less than 10% of the councils plan to fire their principals. I think the tide is turning to principals. At some schools, we thought principals didn't have a chance. But all of a sudden councils are dealing with the careers and futures of principals. Unless there is something blatantly wrong, the councils are unlikely to remove principals.

With this backdrop, the process at Jackson appeared to be almost too calm. On February 22, 1990, the Jackson council voted unanimously to offer their principal a

4-year contract. Ms. Morgan had requested that her contract be reviewed this first year, rather than being part of the lottery. At the February 22, meeting the principal briefed the council on why she believed she should be offered a contract. The council went into closed session in order to debate the issue and took the vote in open session. This process took place with only the principal and the members of the council present. The date of the meeting was posted in the hallway, but no effort was made to send notes home to parents and community or to poll them about their concerns.

Although Ms. Morgan was elected unanimously, the process was not as peaceful as it seemed. The principal did not respond well to being evaluated by her council. On February 23, the day after the vote, Ms. Morgan said that entire rehiring process "had been very demeaning." She was "relieved" to have been offered a contract and said that she had been "in a frenzy" over the process. She realized that the two teachers on the council had helped to keep her at Jackson. She appreciated their help and said:

> I am just now learning how to work with a faculty with this much longevity. I had a great deal of trouble at first. I am learning about my own style. I would spend a whole weekend devising a plan of one sort or another and on Monday morning I would present it to teachers and they wouldn't buy into it. I need to learn to share.

Mr. Morris, one of the teachers on the council said that he and Mr. Griffin had convinced the council, to offer Ms. Morgan a contract. He was surprised when she came to his classroom to thank him:

> Ron and I did everything to facilitate the process with the parents, and we tried to keep things fair. We were influential in bringing in a unanimous vote. She even came to my room and thanked me. I respect her, but she was used to calling the shots. I hope she can change. We met in two closed sessions with all members present. We dealt with issues especially from community members who said that the school was very closed and the principal was unresponsive. I believe that one of the community members had someone pulling her strings. We allowed her to vent all of this. Finally we got all of the negative out first. We all agreed that there was a slight human relations problem. With the other principal, the school was much more open. Now they view the school as much too formal. Then we went through all the requirements for finding and selecting a new principal, and then we decided to renew. We weren't sure what we were going to get. The building was so filthy before Ms. Morgan came. She cleaned up the school; she spruced it up. We came up with some of the positives and thought we could do worse with someone else. We would like to see her be more direct. She doesn't meet things head on. There is a problem with communication, the lack of information being given. She communicated by memo and that is not an effective mode. We need

regular faculty meetings. Sometimes we-go a month without a meeting. I have gone to her and told her that the perception of the faculty is that you don't respect us. For example, there was an old assistant principal that she totally emasculated; she made him into a clerk. He retired. Then she brought in her own cadre of people, assistant principal, clerk, teachers. The faculty resented the cadre that she brought in. I am not against her. If I saw something that would hurt her, I would warn her. I think she respects me. In my evaluations, she has recognized my leadership ability.

Although the process seemed to proceed very smoothly and the vote was unanimous, the council had debated long and hard over this issue. The chairmen of the council expressed the hope that they had done the right thing for Jackson. In offering the contract, the council expressed strong concerns in the area of parent—community relations and recommended that Ms. Morgan make a concerted effort to work on these relations.

The main issue for the parents on the LSC was that other parents had expressed to them that they did not feel welcome at Jackson. Parents believe "that Ms. Morgan thinks she is high up and they are low down." The chair said that the decision was made to rehire Ms. Morgan based on the good work she had done in "cleaning up the school" with the hope that she could act on their recommendation. Another complaint that parents had voiced to the chair was that Ms. Morgan had not shown up at last year's graduation luncheon. Moreover, she didn't attend an awards program sponsored by a neighborhood tutoring organization, although other schools in the area attended with a full complement of students, parents, teachers, and the principal. In discussing Ms. Morgan's absence from the award program, a teacher said, "She gives the idea that she doesn't like or respect the people." This seemed to indicate a lack of interest and respect.

Although the rehiring process seemed peaceful, it was actually an example of the problems that Jackson faced in implementing site-based management. The principal seemed to have little faith in the plan and resented having to implement it. In a conversation on February 1 just prior to being offered a contract, she said:

> The law did not recognize teachers and especially principals. Uneducated parents have been given power and don't know how to use it. Many principals will either be rehired or fired for the wrong reasons. I asked to have my contract evaluated this year because I didn't want to continue to put up with this.

Although the teachers on the council were responsible for convincing the council to rehire the principal, they did so without input from the faculty, in general, and the PPAC, in particular. According to one teacher, "There was no teacher input. The teachers on the LSC should meet with the PPAC after each meeting to share information. This was not done." Teachers resented that they did not have a voice in the process. One teacher who was very angry about the process said, "I'm not going to do anything to make Ms. Morgan look good. I'm glad that they decided to offer her a contract, but the process should have been more open." According to an excellent second-grade teacher:

> Many teachers don't care for the principal. Teachers have become closed-minded with respect to her. They say that she is not responsive to teacher's needs, and that's true. She's not open to suggestion. Teachers should have had more of a role in her rehiring.

The Role of the Professional Personal Advisory Committee

The legislation was vague about both the organization and operation of the PPAC. It was to be made up of teachers who would be elected or chosen in any way that the school deemed feasible. The PPAC was to serve as an advisory board to the LSC, especially in the areas of curriculum and instruction. Because the law was so vague, it was up to teachers at each individual school to organize and operate their PPACs. In March 1990, there was a city-wide meeting of teachers to talk about PPAC issues. At this meeting, it became evident that PPACs across the city were in various states of effectiveness or lack of effectiveness. It was even determined that some schools had not yet formed PPACs. For teachers to organize and operate a functional PPAC, several basic things had to be in place. First, teachers needed to believe that, in the context of their particular setting, they could actually have a voice. Second, there had to be teachers who believed in the legislation and therefore thought a PPAC would be worth the effort. Third, there had to be a core group of teachers who were willing to commit their own time because the legislation did not provide time for meeting. Fourth, there had to be a principal who would support this work or, at the very least, not stand in its way. Last, there had to be an LSC who was willing to be advised by teachers.

At Jackson, the PPAC was formed easily and quickly. The PPAC formed immediately in October. The principal suggested that there be a teacher from each grade level on the PPAC. In response to this suggestion, many teachers said that more than one from each grade wished to serve. Therefore it was decided that everyone who wished to could be on the PPAC. Out of 35 teachers, 26 were on the PPAC. A first-grade teacher was elected chair. It seemed that there was interest and commitment to becoming a part of the reform effort on the part of the teachers.

Sustaining faculty interest was difficult. The PPAC had no clear vision of what to discuss and what issues to deal with. They knew that their role was to be an advisory one to the council, but there were no mechanisms in place for them to give their advice, and in fact they were unable to participate in council meetings except at the end of the meetings. A larger issue, however, was a lack of faith in the reform plan and shared decision making. At Jackson, the decisions were made without any faculty input, and then faculty had no reason to believe that things would change. One teacher in discussing the lack of enthusiasm of faculty and lack of participation on the PPAC likened the situation to that of freedom from slavery:

> It's like we're newly freed slaves. If you put a whip to my back every day for 50 years, why would I think it would not happen tomorrow? Teachers don't believe in or trust reform, and the top-down administrative style has caused teachers to pull back into their classrooms.

According to one of the teachers on the LSC, "classrooms are the true domains of authority, the bastions of autonomy. The council depends on us to guide them and the faculty thinks we can get their wishes through. We are stuck in the middle."

The PPAC meetings became less frequent as the year wore on, and when it did meet, it was in response to something negative that had happened. According to one teacher:

> Being on the PPAC has been frustrating. I thought there would be more working together toward something. Most of the time meetings turned into gripe sessions. Meetings were held less and less frequently. It was frustrating that we didn't receive our training. When the research-practitioner mentioned to the PPAC that sessions could be held on Saturdays, they went nuts. Teachers need to buy into the PPAC before it can work.

It began to appear that the PPAC was not a functional body at Jackson. However, in March, two things happened that pushed the PPAC to activate itself: First, the faculty reacted strongly to the results of a needs assessment that clearly pointed out many glaring problems at Jackson, and second, one of the teachers on the council, Mr. Morris, assumed a strong leadership role in the PPAC and in the faculty in general.

At a faculty meeting that was held at 8:00 AM in April, the Jackson counselor presented information to the faculty. The information presented came for two sources. First, there were results from a short needs assessment that the board had disseminated, to be administered to parents and teachers at Jackson. Second, there were results from the Iowa test that was given the previous year. The board-developed needs assessment was poorly designed. However, the results did expose some pervasive issues of poor climate at Jackson. The discussion highlighted three particular statements to which the respondents had to indicate agreement or disagreement:

	Jackson		Citywide	
	Teachers	Parents	Teachers	Parents
You have high expectations for student learning.	63%	83%	85%	90%
The educational program is of high quality.	37%	55%	72%	68%
The program meets student needs.	22%	58%	67%	72%

The discrepancy between citywide and Jackson percentages was great. Even more alarming was that parents at Jackson were more optimistic about the educational program than were the teachers who were delivering the program. In addition, the Iowa test scores were very low, and at sixth grade there was not one student reading on grade level.

This information was met with much discussion from the faculty both in a meeting and informally in the teachers' lunch room. Teachers identified the problem as one involving the climate for both teachers and students at Jackson. Teachers had been aware of dissatisfaction among their peers, but the information that only 37% of the teachers thought that the educational program was of a high quality was startling. Teachers began to discuss what it would take to make Jackson a more pleasant place in which to teach and learn—what it would take to raise the quality of the instructional program and the faculty perceptions concerning the program. In these discussions, the issue of what happens instructionally in classes was generally avoided. Teachers knew that they were dissatisfied, but they had little idea of how to rectify the situation.

Out of this dissatisfaction, Mr. Morris, an eighth-grade teacher, came up with the kernel of a plan. Mr. Morris proposed to the faculty that the school examine the issue of departmentalization and present a plan to Ms. Morgan about how this would work and how it would be a factor in correcting some of the problems at Jackson. Mr. Morris believed that this would be an issue that would unite the faculty, which was divided. He also believed that the faculty and the PPAC needed to assume its advisory role and enable itself in designing a plan.

Jackson was one of the few schools in the city that did not have a departmentalization program in the seventh and eighth grades. In fact, as of the 1988–1989 school year, the board mandated that all schools would departmentalize in those grades. At Jackson, this plan was not implemented. When Ms. Morgan took over as principal of Jackson, the seventh and eighth grades were departmentalized. One of her first changes was to eliminate that program. Her objections were mainly in the area of management. The halls were very noisy during passing time, and teachers were not getting quickly down to instruction, which created a great deal of transition time.

The ending of the departmentalization during the "clean-up" process established Ms. Morgan's tight control over classroom organization. However, when the board mandated departmentalization and it was not implemented at Jackson, a message was conveyed to the upper-grade teachers that instructional decision making would continue to be kept under a tight rein.

Mr. Morris believed that the teachers needed an issue and a leader to ignite them. In a conversation at the beginning of April, he said:

We need someone to come in and light a fire under the teachers. Teachers only think of what goes on in their own classrooms. I think if you teach one kid, you teach all kids in the school. There is such complacency—no investment. I've been involved with my church and they once in a while have a drive for an organ or a roof and it unites the whole congregation. I think we need a band.

Mr. Morris believed that departmentalization could be the "band" that they needed. Mr. Morris called a PPAC meeting so that they could discuss what could be done to rectify the situation that the needs assessment uncovered. The ideas that were discussed were pull-out programs, individualized instruction, tracking, and departmentalization/team teaching. Discussion focused on many of the negative aspects of pullout programs that had been tried without much good results. Many teachers complained about students being taken away from the classroom instruction that they needed. The negative effects of tracking on children's self-concepts were also discussed.

Many of the faculty described positive experiences with departmentalization both at Jackson and at other schools in which they had taught, attended, or were familiar with. The assistant principal spoke of her own elementary school education and how it had been departmentalized throughout the grades beginning with first grade. She believed it to be a positive experience that contributed to student independence from an early age. The meeting ended on a positive note with Mr. Morris suggesting that the PPAC meet twice a week, on Tuesdays and Thursdays, before school, from 8:00 AM to 9:00 AM. It was agreed upon and the teachers left the meeting expressing enthusiasm about developing a plan.

The meetings were held and most of the faculty attended. According to one of the teachers, "five or six don't come. They don't want to be part of the family." As the meetings proceeded, even the few who never came began to attend. Some faculty rallied behind Mr. Morris's plan for departmentalization, the faculty prematurely took a vote, and the majority were in support of the plan. Several faculty members, especially four people who rarely attended any meetings, became particularly vocal against the departmentalization plan. The primary department expressed grave concerns and did not want to be included in the plan. Several intermediate teachers stated that they didn't want their students to be in classes with "incompetent teachers." A schism was created among the faculty.

Several models for departmentalization were considered, and some of the major proponents of the plan wanted to departmentalize across all of the grades. The more conservative among the prodepartmentalization group advocated beginning with the seventh and eighth grades in order to test the waters. The issue became very volatile. It was finally agreed upon by the PPAC that the plan would begin in the sixth, seventh, and eighth grades. Mr. Morris presented the plan to Ms. Morgan. She refused to allow them to implement their plan. According to Ms. Morgan:

> The plan that I received was nothing but some jottings. If students are going to be walking around Jackson, there is going to have to be a good reason for it, and everyone is going to have to know what that reason is. They were not ready to implement the plan, so I asked them to take more time in planning. The situation almost got out of hand. The school was very divided over the plan, and one of the teachers threatened to take the issue to the council. Reason prevailed, and they went back to the drawing board.

The tension between the faculty and the principal grew as the year progressed. This issue was one of the key factors in exacerbating that tension. On this issue, there were no winners. The faculty became divided, and the relations with the principal became further strained. The worst outcome, however, was that the PPAC was unable to successfully empower themselves around an issue. The principal was probably correct in her assessment that the faculty had not taken enough time to carefully plan and present a well-thought-out design. On the other hand, the faculty took interest in an issue that concerned the school and were not allowed to take action. The message conveyed by Ms. Morgan was that the faculty were not going to share in the decision-making processes of the school; thus, the PPAC's advisory role was less than meaningful.

According to the chair of the PPAC:

> It started with high hopes. People seemed to buy reform. However, people want others to do the work. The teachers at Jackson didn't want to change. I think there should be a closer relationship between the PPAC and the LSC, more interaction between councils. The vote of the PPAC on academic issues should have a great deal of weight. None of this has happened.

The role of the PPAC at Jackson had not been established. Their one effort at exerting influence was aborted. It was questionable whether teachers at Jackson would be willing to give it another try.

In sum, the departmentalization issue at Jackson represented a bid by the faculty, to shift the power base. The faculty led by Mr. Morris, attempted to accept a portion of the responsibility for making decisions that the legislation had given them. The power remained clearly in the hands of the administration leaving the faculty angry and frustrated.

Shared Decision Making and the School Improvement Plan

The process of shared decision making is based on respect and trust, and at Jackson respect and trust were major problems. The principal acted in ways that indicated to the entire school community that she did not trust them to make good decisions. She did not hold faculty meetings; instead, she tended to communicate in written form or give directives over the PA (public address) system. She seemed to be uncomfortable with open meetings. There was always the notion of "keeping a lid on it."

At one early all-school in-service meeting dealing with the idea of site-based management, a facilitator asked the faculty to brainstorm ideas of what a good school should look like. The teachers shared thoughts for 45 minutes and the facilitator guided them into beginning to think about a vision for Jackson. The teachers were all talking animatedly when they left the room, and their evaluations of the experience were uniformly positive with many expressing the thought that this session was a good beginning of a process that should be ongoing. Ms. Morgan sat through the session and told the facilitator that she was very uncomfortable with the session. The facilitator was surprised and asked Ms. Morgan what she thought had gone wrong. Ms. Morgan said that some of the teachers had expressed negative thoughts about the school, and she didn't think that this should be a forum for any negative comments. The facilitator responded that she trusted the teachers to get out some of their negative thoughts so that they could move on to treating issues in a more positive fashion. Underlying the issue of trust is the issue of respect. Members of the Jackson community complained that the principal's indicated a lack of respect for both teachers and parents.

According to the legislation, a school improvement plan was to be developed by the principal with the advice of the PPAC, the body that represented the teachers, and approved by the LSC, the body that represented the parents and the community. The legislation specified that there be two open hearings for the community to respond to the plan. Clearly, the tone of the law was that the plan was to be the result of a collaborative process based on the results of the comprehensive needs assessment that was to have been carried out. The nature and scope of the task was made all the more difficult because of two factors. First, there was not enough time to do the job well—the needs assessment was to be finished at the end of March and the plan was due in the middle of May—and second, none of the participants in the process had ever been involved in this kind of comprehensive planning for a whole school plan.

Of the 541 schools that were to engage in this process, 200 schools did not even turn in plans. According to an outside consultant to the board who was hired to evaluate the plans, there was a great deal of diversity in the kinds of plans that were turned in, and very few of them indicated a vision for their schools. Indeed, many of them were merely a series of stated goals without much thought to how these goals would be implemented, let alone integrated into a comprehensive plan.

Jackson did turn in a plan. Although there was an attempt to involve teachers in the process of developing the plan, it was in the end written by three teachers who were released from their duties for 3 weeks to accomplish the task. The teachers at Jackson, like teachers at most schools, had never before had an opportunity to talk or think about what they wanted their school to look like. Decisions about curriculum, programs, and budget were made by the principal without any input from the faculty and staff. As one teacher at Jackson put it, "classrooms are the teacher's bastion of autonomy." At Jackson, this was particularly true because the school is a "closed campus." This means that the students are dismissed at 2:30 PM, and there is no lunch hour for teachers. Both teachers and students eat lunch together and have 20 minutes to eat. This plan was developed in the 1970s and implemented in areas where it was believed that it was dangerous, because of crime and gang violence, for students to be outside of their schools for the lunch hour. Closed-campus schools have contributed to teacher isolation, because teachers do not even have time to talk to each other during lunch. One upper-grade teacher at Jackson, when asked if Jackson had full-day kindergarten, said that she had "no idea what went on the first floor."

Clearly, the faculty, community, and administration did not have a shared view of what was in existence at Jackson, let alone a shared vision for what Jackson should become. It was in this vacuum of knowledge and experience that Jackson undertook to develop a comprehensive 3-year school improvement plan. Sylvia Smith, from the Center for School Improvement, helped the principal and faculty to design a plan to examine the school's needs and to develop a plan to meet those needs. The legislation clearly specified areas that each school improvement plan should address: reading, writing, mathematics, staff development, parent involvement, truancy, and transition into life. Sylvia helped the faculty to break into committees for each of these areas in order to examine the strengths and weaknesses in order to begin to make recommendations for the school improvement plan.

When each of the groups met for the first time to compile a list of strengths and weaknesses, the discussion of weaknesses centered around the students, the parents, and the community. For example, in the reading committee, the teachers spoke about the absence of books in the home, the lack of positive role models, the limited opportunities that the children have to express themselves orally, the lack of space and time for doing homework, the late hours that children kept, and the lack of support from

parents around homework and discipline. Ms. Smith responded to all of these legitimate concerns and attempted to guide the teachers into a discussion of their own instructional needs and weaknesses. At the first meeting of the reading committee, the
teachers did not discuss one area of weakness in their own instruction.

The second meeting of the reading committee was held the following week with
much the same kind of discussion. Ms. Morgan was present at this meeting and sat
with her face impassive as Ms. Smith again attempted to guide the teachers into a
discussion of the areas of weakness in which they could use some assistance.
Teachers finally began talking about pullout programs and whether or not they were
effective. Teachers complained of disruption in student learning and lack of improvement for the children who participated in the programs. Finally, Ms. Morgan
asked teachers to think about their own strengths and weaknesses. One teacher responded that she would like to update her instruction and would like to learn about
the whole-language approach. This was the only comment in the two initial meetings that clearly dealt with the teacher's own instruction.

The teachers at Jackson were unwilling to accept much responsibility for the students' lack of achievement. This unwillingness coupled with their lack of knowledge about the school, lack of shared vision for the school, and lack of experience in
comprehensive planning resulted in committees making several shallow,
decontextualized recommendations for the school improvement plan. After the
first two early morning meetings, the entire school spent one afternoon, which was
one of four board-mandated in-service days, working in their committees. Their
recommendations were sent to Ms. Morgan.

The deadline for turning in the plans was quickly approaching. By this time in
the year, Ms. Morgan was showing signs of strain from the year. She was out sick for 2
weeks and feared that reform was making her sick. In her absence, Ms. Morgan assigned three teachers the task of writing the plan with the input of the recommendations of the committees. None of these women were classroom teachers, and they
were released from their duties, given a place to work, given the guidelines from the
board and the committee recommendations, and asked to complete the plan.

The legislation was calling for a very different process and product. The plan was
to be a living document that had input from participants and that was known and
understood by everyone. Of the three teachers asked to actually write the document, only one had ever done such a task before, and the plan that she wrote the
previous year was written only to comply with a board requirement and had nothing
to do with the instructional program at Jackson.

It took the teachers 3 weeks to write the plan, and the document that was completed and turned in to the board was merely lists of goals and activities for each
mandated area of the plan. The plan did not deal in any way with how these goals
and objectives would be implemented, monitored, or evaluated.

The legislation mandated that there be two open meetings in which the plan would be presented to the council and the community for approval. As of the end of the school year, these meetings were not held, and none of the faculty had received copies of the plan. When Ms. Morgan was asked about how the plan had turned out, she said:

> The plan will need lots of work. The teachers did what they could, and I was too sick to help them. We turned it into the district, but I am not happy with it. I hope that we can work on it over the summer and then show it to the council.

Although the plan was lacking in focus and vision, and the process was less than successful, the outcome is predictable considering the variables. The lack of time for reflection and writing seemed to doom the process at the outset. Also, the teachers had no experience with planning and rarely even considered anything that occurred in the school outside the purview of their own classrooms. There was almost no time given to the concept of building a shared vision, and teachers were very defensive about looking honestly at their own instruction and weaknesses. Perhaps most important, there was a history of school improvement plans being meaningless pieces of paper. Why would teachers be convinced that this plan would be different?

According to one teacher, "One of the greatest problems at Jackson is getting teachers to look more globally at the school and not just look at their own room." The climate at Jackson contributed to this problem. Teachers who were unhappy and felt that they were not trusted retreated to their classrooms. This survival strategy increased the level of difficulty in developing a comprehensive plan.

A shared-decision making process at Jackson had not been established in the first year of reform. Decisions continued to be made by the principal without much attempt to get faculty or parent input. Some of the teachers who were close to Ms. Morgan had an idea about just how hard it was for her to relinquish control, but were hopeful that it would eventually happen. According to one teacher who was very close to Ms. Morgan, "Shared decision making is not a reality yet, but we're on the road to it. Teachers are trying to share and Ms. Morgan is making a definite effort to share." Another teacher also thought shared decision making "is coming, but it won't be easy. We're going to have to force her gently. She has a hard time delegating."

Postscript

Ms. Morgan is no longer at Jackson. As described in the case, she was elected by the council in the first year of reform and given the 4-year term of office stipulated by the law. Those 4 years were tense transition years at Jackson. As described, her election was supported by the two teachers on the council and she was given several recommendations for changes that should be made. She stayed in the position for 4 years and then took the early retirement plan that the board was offering, which was referred to as Five Plus Five. Ms. Morgan was followed by the current principal, Sarah Shapiro.

Ms. Shapiro worked at Jackson for 25 years before becoming principal. She held positions as a classroom teacher, a learning disability specialist, a released reading improvement teacher, and assistant principal under Ms. Morgan. Ms. Shapiro is White, and Jackson is located in a highly visible Black community that is supported by many Black community groups. Her selection to serve as principal in 1993 was a huge vote of confidence, and an affirmation of her work at Jackson over the past years.

Ms. Shapiro has retained the order of the building, and has placed her own definite stamp on the school. Having been a teacher for so many years at the school, and having worked alongside most of the teachers, she continued the collegial working relationships that she had always enjoyed. The teachers all continue to refer to her as "Sarah," and she has managed to evolve a personal leadership style that has created better relations among the faculty and that succeeds in focusing on instructional issues.

Analysis of Leadership

This first year of the implementation of SB1840 does not tell the complete story of the restructuring of Chicago schools. It does, however, provide some insight into the transition from a bureaucratic, centralized governance scheme to one of decentralization and site-based management. The period of transition in many Chicago schools was turbulent and political with councils exercising power merely because they could. About 42 schools lost principals. Jackson experienced a much less outwardly dramatic transition period, but nevertheless dynamic.

This case is of interest in that the participants in the process at Jackson had no visible political agenda. There were no outside forces exerting influence on the participants and therefore the case can be examined as a way of observing the process at work in a context that is free of arbiters of special interests.

In this context, the role of leadership is perhaps the major theme that bears examining: leadership as it is exerted by the school principal, and leadership as it emerges among the professional staff. These leadership issues influence the balance of power as it plays out over the course of the year.

Jackson operated in a hierarchical manner with clear and formal role differentiation and leadership that originated from the top. This form of organization, and the culture that emerged from it, worked against the new site-based governance scheme that was imposed upon the schools as a result of the reform legislation. The principal at Jackson was clearly operating in a culture that understood and supported an authoritarian leadership style, as faculty were rarely consulted in the decision-making process in either the areas of governance or curriculum. The teachers defined their roles narrowly, and their patterns of interaction were in keeping with the formal, hierarchical culture of the school. The principal was comfortable with her institutionally sanctioned role. Viewed from a cultural leadership point of view, the absence of trust and respect may have accounted for the relative failure of the change effort.

In order to share or relinquish power, it is necessary for the leader to trust those with whom the power will be shared. Administrative resistance can create major obstacles to the organization and implementation of shared decision making. Resistance can occur for reasons of lack of trust and respect for the constituencies in the school community. At Jackson, teachers complained that the principal did not trust them, and parents complained that she did not respect them. Indeed, many of her actions seemed to confirm these concerns.

The perceived lack of administrative trust and respect had permeated the culture of the building. Jackson was not a supportive place to work for many of the faculty. There existed an inner circle for whom the working climate was not as negative, but even some of them reported that many of the faculty felt alienated. The board's needs assessment measure uncovered the data that only a small percentage of the faculty were satisfied with the instructional program at Jackson. The absence of administrative trust did not encourage teachers to become involved in the process of assuming greater responsibility in either governance or curricular matters. Instead, it encouraged teachers to retreat to their classrooms, which are, in the words of one of the Jackson teachers, their "bastions of autonomy."

Indeed, the principal's task of "cleaning up the school" was one that did not help her to communicate her personal attributes for leadership. She came into the school because of a deplorable situation that had left the school in a leadership vacuum. She was faced by a veteran faculty who had become comfortable with a laissez-faire style of leadership and were not open to the change of style. For her part, Ms. Morgan perceived that many of the faculty had to have been aware of what was occurring at Jackson. This, combined with the total disrepair of the physical plant, left her with very negative feelings about the faculty that she was to lead. In fact, many faculty left because of the new regime, and teachers reported that she "came on too strong especially with such a veteran faculty."

The lack of trust was reciprocated by the faculty. Their lack of participation on the PPAC until an issue united them was reflective of their collective attitude. To use the plantation metaphor that one teacher so eloquently used, the teachers had no reason to believe that the slaves had been freed. One faculty member said that she would not do anything that might make Morgan look good. In fact, their one attempt at involvement, around the issue of departmentalization, was suppressed as "not well thought out."

At Jackson, the lack of trust and respect was entrenched in the culture and inhibited the transition process of attempting to become a community of professionals sharing the decision making for the school. Ms. Morgan was the wrong leader for that time.

EXTENDING THINKING

Questions

1. At Jackson Elementary, what forces within the school and within the district operated against the principal establishing a supportive school culture?
2. Shared leadership did not become a reality at Jackson. What could have been done differently by the principal, the teachers, and the parents to achieve this goal?
3. Consider the role of the principal. How did she define her role in relation to professional development and curriculum and instruction?
4. Consider the issue of the PPAC's proposal to begin departmentalization. Reflect upon the issues that this event brought to the surface. Look at this event from the perspectives of all the constituencies: principal, teachers, parents, council, and students.

Activity

1. Attend a school board or LSC meeting. What issues are dealt with? Who writes the agenda? Whose voices are heard? How is audience participation handled?

CASE 2

The Chicago School Reform at Maria Saucedo Scholastic Academy

Karen L. Morris
Maria Saucedo Scholastic Academy

Joseph C. Fischer
National-Louis University

Background

Maria Saucedo Scholastic Academy is a young school, founded in 1983 as a fourth- to eighth-grade elementary school and occupying the building that had previously been Harrison High School, which had closed. It was then called Maria Saucedo Magnet School and was part of the desegregation plan for the Chicago Public Schools (CPS). Before the reform, in 1984 when Karen Morris became principal, parents were involved in the schooling of their children (especially through Head Start, the parent–teacher organization [PTO], and the Local School Improvement Council [LSIC]), and teachers worked together on curriculum innovation and professional development activities.

Since 1985, Saucedo and National-Louis University have worked in partnership on staff development and curriculum innovation projects. Some of the school-based curriculum development included the beginning of a process writing program, integration of subjects, hands-on science and math, computer labs, and teacher collaboration. Working with National-Louis University faculty, teachers attended Saturday workshops, had teaching demonstrations in their classrooms, and formed teams to discuss curriculum and instructional practice. As is described further in this case, Saucedo became a pre-K to eighth-grade neighborhood school in 1989, through the leadership of Karen Morris.

Saucedo is a large school with more than 1,300 students, 95% minority (mainly Mexican) who are from low-income families (96% in the free-lunch program). It is located in a neighborhood where poverty, gangs, and crime threaten families and compete with the school's efforts to educate children and prepare them for a hopeful future.

Saucedo heroically offers these children a safe and caring haven for learning and grow-ing. The struggle between the streets and the school plays out each day, providing a so-bering context for the visions and ideals of the Chicago school reform.

THE CASE

The case description is divided into five sections or themes that interconnect: (a) Reflection on Reform, (b) Building a Neighborhood School, (c) A Guiding Philosophy, (d) Creating a Teaching/Learning Community, and (e) Hopes for the Future, Work Still to Be Done. Much of the story of reform at Saucedo can-not be told in this limited space, but the main threads and themes are clearly vis-ible. The perspective here is that of Karen Morris, the principal, told to Joseph Fischer, a colleague from National-Louis University who has had the good for-tune to be a part of the Saucedo story since 1985.

Reflection on Reform

KM: The key component to reform is that we have discretionary monies from state Chapter I that allow us to build programs to meet the needs of our stu-dents. Reform also formalizes parental input. It has given teachers the opportu-nity to develop curriculum, to look at the curricula that they are using to determine if it is effective and to become more professional. Before reform, cur-riculum was handed down from the central office in a "one-size-fits-all format."

Reform has given schools more opportunities in response to the State of Il-linois educational outcomes and the accreditation process. Saucedo staff has been examining curriculum and developing instructional units. We have been spending time and money on the development of meaningful assessments that are linked to instruction and trying to make certain that all teachers have the same base of knowledge of what they are expected to teach. How they are go-ing to teach the concepts is at the professional discretion of the grade-level team. The assessments across the grade level are the same, but the methods of teaching may differ. One of the things that was wrong with the curriculum that was handed down from the central office was it did not allow the teachers the opportunity for creativity. Reform has allowed teachers to be more cre-ative in their teaching. It has allowed schools to build on the creativity by hav-ing the funds to buy materials for the teachers. Before reform, if you had a box of crayons in your room, you were rich! Now, here at Saucedo, because we have discretionary funds, teachers have the materials they need in order to implement the curricula.

JF: Trying to build a faculty that is creative, that is concerned with students, and using the classroom as the source of building the curriculum has always been a concern of yours even before reform. How to help a group of teachers help children—doesn't that seem to be the bottom line of a principal?

KM: My personal bias, Joe, has always been . . . I love working with teachers and children. All of this other stuff is something I really don't enjoy. I became a principal because I like to work with teachers and children . . . impacting on instruction in the classroom. I have been forced since reform to make a lot of compromises in style because I have to spend so much time on budget and administrative-related items, making sure that proposals are written . . . there are a lot of other extraneous things . . . a raft of meetings. I have always enjoyed working with parents too. When I was a classroom teacher, I knew the parents were very important. Reform has caused us to make certain that we are spending money wisely to benefit the children. We meet with parents, staff, and community members, and make sure that we are planning and implementing instructional programs that will impact students.

I think the key to the reform is teacher and parent involvement. Parents should feel comfortable in speaking up and letting us know if we are not meeting their children's needs. And if we are not, we should not take the criticism personally and get all bent out of shape. That has been difficult for myself and for some others on the staff. To look at what we are doing, you know, children are changing. Children are very different from when I first started teaching. Even since I first became a principal. Society has changed. What I tell my staff is: "We always need to learn something new. When we stop learning, we should stop teaching." We are constantly looking for new things, picking people's brains. Not feeling ashamed to go to someone and say, "What I did is not working in the classroom, what do you suggest?"

I know that small schools are kind of in vogue now; the new board is going to have small schools and year-round classes. I started to think, although we don't call them small schools, I think we have done that here at Saucedo in that we have grade-level teams. Teams give teachers a more manageable group with which to interact. We bring them together to discuss and coalesce on points. On a day-to-day basis, the planning takes place in the grade-level teams. For instance, five kindergarten teachers get together and discuss and critique their program: the children they are working with, what is working and what is not working, and the materials they need to implement the program. They write a short agenda, do minutes of their meeting and any concerns/problems they are experiencing, and turn it in to me. I respond to the agenda and concerns. It makes a large school more manageable for me. I cannot attend all of the meetings. If teams have a question or concern, I respond with a note and ask to come to their next meeting.

JF: So, they had a sense they could do their own curriculum talking together knowing what is good for the children.

KM: Yes. Teachers know what they are expected to teach, because that is a given. You need to have focus. There is a body of knowledge that all teachers at Saucedo must teach, but they know that not every child is going to master that in a given year. However, all students are expected to master the curricula prior to graduation from eighth grade.

A concern that we have is we are not at national norms on the Iowa Test of Basic Skills (ITBS). Since 1989, we have very different children. Before reform, we were about 35% nonminority/middle-class students. We are now probably 6% nonminority. Since reform, we have taken most of the students from our neighborhood, and their first language is not English, and income levels are low. If you stacked us against other schools in the neighborhood, we are doing very well on standardized scores. Much of it has to do with stability. Students can stay here at Saucedo. We lose very few students to transfers. I also expect staff to give 100%. Hard work is a given for Saucedo staff, parents, and students.

We chart students' standard test scores. We are getting an average of a year's gain for every year of instruction in reading and mathematics. But, some children start out very low. In first-grade, we are still not there. I was a first grade teacher, so that worries me a lot. But many of our primary-grade students need vocabulary development, concept development, and basic skills that suburban children have before they enter school. Once our students get to third grade, we are seeing the growth. Thanks to reform and state Chapter I funds, we have pre-school programs and smaller class size in primary grades.

We've really made an extra commitment to work with the parents of the younger children. We have been doing every other Friday "parent workshops." Not "in service," but workshops, where they can talk to each other. Sharing. Some of the parents who are more successful can help the other parents. We have a number of parents, like Hilda, our [Local School Council] LSC chairperson, who has come a long way since 1988. Hilda would not speak during the first couple of LSC meetings, and now she is really a leader. Her boys are doing well. She has a lot of influence on parents, not only for local school governance but also parenting. She has suggestions. I have a number of parents who are role models for others.

I think the key to reform has been parent and teacher involvement. Allowing them to be involved. I don't feel threatened by people taking charge of meetings. I am very glad if someone will carry some of the load. Our Professional Personnel Advisory Committee (PPAC), has worked very well. They are an active and involved group. Although, theoretically, the principal is not a part of that group, I am included in discussions. We have dialogues about our school and how to improve programs. When the two teacher LSC representatives come to the LSC with suggestions, it is usually they are not springing anything on me, like "I gotcha." It is usually things we have talked about in staff meetings. We don't always agree on everything. Some of the things I think are wonderful, they hate. We come to a compromise. We argue and have professional disagreements, but I think that makes us stronger.

JF: It is a democratic leadership style that you feel most comfortable with, isn't it?

KM: We have all kinds of committees, and they are active committees: the language arts committee, the math committee, a social studies committee, science committee, and a conflict resolution. People are on committees; they provide feedback; they provide ideas; they carry out programs. I give staff a lot of responsibility. When we do science fair, young authors, geography bee . . . that is their baby. All they need to clear with me is the date, so we can get it on the calendar. The expectations are to carry out things on their own. I don't do a lot of checking up on them. Saucedo staff are super achievers. If somebody does a young authors conference and does a beautiful job, then the person who does the geography bee has to top that. It is just like assemblies. I don't require this big, elaborate assembly, but everybody feels they have to put on a big, elaborate assembly, "Because the fourth-grade teachers did this beautiful thing, and I don't want to look like . . ."

JF: Perhaps we could talk about your role as principal during these times . . . share your thoughts about your experiences, the pros and cons.

KM: Well, I think one of the unfortunate things that has happened in reform (I was speaking to some of the people on my council about this a few months ago) when I first became a principal, I had a lot more time to be the instruction leader, and that is what I really like to do. I really like to work in classrooms. I really like to work with teachers. I really like to plan curriculum. I really like to work on programs. Since reform, especially in the last couple of years, I have become a bureaucrat. I don't like to use the word *bureaucrat* because I don't like the words' negative connotation, because I spend so much time at meetings, planning programs, and doing budget things, I think, at the expense of being the instructional leader. I think that is unfortunate.

I try to spend as much time as I can in classrooms, but there are some days when I never get out of the office, and that makes me upset. We have 1,350 students. Most of my suburban colleagues cannot believe there is one school that has 1,350 students. Because we've got more children from the neighborhood, we have many more social problems now than we have ever had in the past. And, I think, society generally is having a lot more social problems with children—abuse, families that are not cohesive because of poverty, broken homes. Those things are causing us to spend more time on social problems rather than building educational programs.

So, before reform, I prided myself on being an instructional leader. I think in the last 5 years, I have become less an instructional leader and more a manager, and I think to the detriment of, at least in my opinion, my school. I think that my strength is in curriculum and instruction. I really don't enjoy doing the other things. As a matter of fact, I usually save them for after school or vacation days. And, I spend a lot of Sundays on paperwork. I guess that is the trade-off. I don't know that it has been a positive trade-off.

JF: In the old days that stuff would have been handled by the district.

KM: Right. Right now at Saucedo, we have almost $1 million in state Chapter I money that is at our discretion and another $500,000 in IASA (Improving America's Schools Act) money, and then the board money that is based on a formula—probably another $75,000. So, you are talking $1.6 million to $1.7 million that I am held accountable for making sure that plans are made and that the money is being spent correctly and that all the paperwork is done. It is a big responsibility.

JF: It was a gift given to you in some ways, but to manage that takes time away from academic needs.

KM: We have hired people and built programs; hopefully we have been spending the money wisely for the children, but it also requires a lot of time to meet with people. Teachers and staff members resent the time it takes away from classroom instructional time. We have had to do a lot of things before school, after school, on weekends. Many times you think that you are never going to get out of a meeting. You start meetings at 7:00 AM and at 8:00 PM. You are still meeting about how you are going to spend this money. Making sure that everyone agrees how you spend the money. Sometimes you never get everybody to agree because a lot of people only see what they need in their program. And really as the principal, you have to see the whole picture.

JF: The problem seems to be with helping the principal meet the instructional leadership needs of the school while at the same time meeting all of the new administrative and organizational demands.

KM: Supposedly the reform was giving the principal more authority, more accountability, and a 4-year contract. This was going to solve all of the problems. There were a lot of principals prior to reform who were part of the "good old boys network," and probably should have been removed. But, I think there should have been a phase-in, and there needs to be more meaningful training of council and principals. I mean these new principals coming in . . . I feel so sorry for them. Because, they are being dumped into something . . . at least I had the benefit of being a principal before reform.

Many of the new principals are coming right out of the classrooms, and they are being dumped right into school—sometimes some of the toughest schools in the city with discretionary money and no training. They are giving them some training at the central office, but the people doing the training are people who have never been principals in reform. There is really no uniform, consistent training of principals and LSCs as to their rights and responsibilities. A lot of people want to be on their LSC, because they have a lot of personal agendas. The agendas are not always, "What are we going to do to make sure these children are prepared when they leave our schools."

JF: Some people say of the reform that they created hundreds of little boards of education. Do you see it this way? Was this politicizing the system more than it was?

KM: Well, the CPS have always been political. I have been working in them since 1964, and it has always been very political. My supposition of the bottom line of school reform was to involve more parents in the decision making at the local school, which is a great idea. But, I don't think in many cases that all LSCs have involved parents. It has put too much of the recruitment of parents at the local school. There really are not a lot of resources out there to actually do that. I think some schools have been very fortunate. They have gotten some very committed, active parents to come in and really work with the LSC. Other schools, which are probably very, very needy, are still struggling. As I say, I think the key to anything is training—staff training, parent training, and commitment from the community as a whole. I think even though the Chicago business community really jumped on board with this reform, they have rapidly jumped off board. The first couple of years it was the "in thing" to do for all these big companies. They were doing all these things with reform. They have not continued that commitment in my opinion. A few of them have. But the majority have not. The business community has pretty much left us again. I don't think it is money that we are after. I need people. And I need committed people who would be willing to come in and talk to my parents, do some job training, some human development, and most important, work with children.

The schools where they had active councils and a lot of things going on are the schools that are the most successful. The least successful schools are schools that were unsuccessful before reform. Although they can hire their principal, if they do not have a group of committed parents, committed community, and committed staff, they are probably not making a whole lot of headway.

JF: Where is Saucedo in this active council, committed parents and staff? Where does Saucedo fall?

KM: We have a core of very committed parents, but certainly not as many as I would like to see. We are continually trying to develop programs and committing some of our budget to parent development activities. I have seen over the years that I have been at Saucedo a lot of positive growth with parents. A lot of the parents, who came to us and took GED (general equivalency diploma) and ESL (English as a second language) classes have become active members of our PTO and our LSC, now are going to college or have gotten a job or done something to better their families. But, I still don't see the kind of commitment that I would like to see. We don't have a lot of parents on public aid. We do have a lot of low-income parents. In many cases, these parents leave in the morning before the children go to school. They come home at 6:30 or 7:00 at night. They are really tired. They just don't feel that they have enough time or energy to give to their children. The solution to that may be some kind of a lighted schoolhouse concept. We have developed a lot of after-school programs for the students. However, you would almost have to get a whole new staff to be willing or at least a core staff who would be willing to stay late in the evening. Teachers also get very tired. Teaching is an exhausting job if you are doing a good job.

JF: Has the reform helped you address some of these concerns? What are some things you have done to help parents get involved?

KM: We have done a lot of things with our discretionary funds. We are entitled by formula to 1.5 counselors. We bought another .5 counselor, so we have two full-time school counselors now. We have also bought a full-time social worker who works only with our school. We've given funds to a parent center and hired a parent to work in the parent center to, for example, lend out materials, books, games and videos, and things that the parents can take home to use with their children. The room is available for parent workshops. We have a parent workshop every other Friday with different speakers. Parents plan the workshops.

A key to a successful school is parents who are actively involved and who have some education skills. So, we really have to walk a real thin line between providing support for the parents and doing programs for children. The other component is staff; prepare staff at the university to teach in urban areas. I think they are getting better at it. We have had student teachers from the University of Illinois at Chicago. They have a practicum program where students come in before they student teach and act as teacher aides before they student teach, so they have an opportunity to interact with students in urban schools. I really feel that there is not adequate training for teachers in urban schools. Preparing teachers to meet a lot of the challenges as far as social issues, discipline issues, and the academic issues in urban settings. They are still training them to be teachers for suburban children. And there is still a real dearth of trained teachers, especially teachers for urban middle schools.

JF: Would you go back to the old way? Prereform?

KM: I think that with the added funds the schools have been able to do some very super things for children that we would not have been able to do prior to reform. Monies that previously had been kept at the central and district offices, now are at our school. So, now, our teachers have adequate materials. They do not have a proliferation, but certainly teachers can give me a list of wish things—I mean, get together as a grade-level team and say this is how it would benefit the children. The PPAC, the LSC, can look at it and say this is how it is going to benefit the children and we can fund it.

We have been able to expand our curriculum and hire people who have special expertise, who can come in and act as a consultant to our staff. We can run after-school programs. We can run summer school. We are not beholden on the district to decide. We are more accountable and can plan things that benefit our school rather than depending on the district superintendent to do that. So, now if we have the need for an after-school program or if we need to buy new math books, or we need to buy new social studies books, or maps or something, it is up to us. We know what our pot of money is, and we have to set priorities. But, I think we have over the past 5 years used our money wisely. We have textbooks now that are current—that aren't 15 years old. We've got a new reading series for all of our children. They all have new readers and new math books. We have been getting new maps and new globes. By the end of this year, we hope every classroom will have a Macintosh computer and printer. We have done a lot of staff development. We still have a long way to go.

Building a Neighborhood School

KM: When I first came to Saucedo in 1985, there was an organization called LSIC, which was like an "advisory group," but it was very loosely put together. We would sit and talk, but it was not about instruction. Once in a while we would ask their opinion about something, but it was very loosely knit. We began working on the PTO, which is a service organization to the school, trying to get parents into the school. We began doing parent workshops: reading at home, studying at home. We were doing a lot of parent training; trying to get parents to come into the school; trying to get parents to work with their children at home.

So, the major purpose was getting parents to come in and to start feeling comfortable. There were some advisory things, but it wasn't anything major. We did not have any money. It was mainly just talking together. I encouraged those parents to run for the LSC who were involved in the PTO at school or involved in some of the classes and who already knew something about the school.

In the first council (1989), it was really very gratifying to look at the election. In the first election, there were people coming out of the woodwork from all over the city to run as community members. People thought this was the thing to do. It was really gratifying to see that the people who were elected here, were people who had been here before reform and that the parents recognized. Voters were not fooled by some of the names of the people who have never been to the school, who all of a sudden decided they were very interested in the school. So, the parents were not fooled by somebody just because they got up on the stage and said they had a university degree but had actually never done anything in the school. So, the people who were elected in the first council were people who knew about our school, who had been involved in our PTO who had attended the different classes that we had here, who had been working as classroom volunteers. We really had to struggle with making decisions as a council, because most of our parents did not understand parliamentary procedures and did not feel comfortable standing up to express their opinions.

JF: This progression from advisory, taking responsibility, really parallels what the teachers went through too. They get involved in their children' s education and making choices that create an environment for their children to learn and to support teachers and schools in this process. This is a story of many people building a neighborhood school. How did this come about?

KM: When I first came here it was fourth- to eighth-grade. We were a magnet school. We spent a lot of time on recruitment of children. We were supposed to have 35% nonminority White children in order to be a magnet school. So, I had teams of people out visiting schools, making mailings, and doing all of these things, and had a lot of children who lived outside the neighborhood—spent a lot of time on busing and recruiting.

We really had a more racially diverse school at that time, but many of the students came from outside of the area of the neighborhood. I think back then one of the things was because the parents lived so far away, we did not have as much parent involvement. The parents worked, and they did not live close enough to the school to be really involved. As time went on, especially after the first LSC election, we started looking at that and deciding if we were using this school building in the most efficient manner to serve this community. Many of our parents who were on the first council were community residents. They knew about the schools in the area that were very overcrowded: Hammond, Burns, Whitney, Spry. Why are we spending all of this time on recruitment when there are so many children in this area who are in very overcrowded schools—40 to 50 children in a room and who were on the waiting list at Saucedo. We had a long waiting list of Hispanics and a very short, if any, waiting list for Whites.

That was why we decided to ask the board what would happen if we did not want to be a magnet school. We found out that not much was going to happen. We needed a board report saying that we would give preference to children coming from surrounding Hispanic schools, mainly Spry and Hammond.

JF: And you went from a fourth- to eighth school to a pre-K-eighth.

KM: Right. We did this because we felt that when we received children at the fourth grade, there were a lot of them who could not read. At fourth grade they are 9 to 10 years old, and it is very difficult to have them go back and become beginning readers. So, we wanted to provide the kinds of background and skills that students need in order to be readers. In order to do that, you have to have them as early as possible.

Now, we didn't do it all at once. What we did is add kindergarten first, so we built each year. We are pretty much where we want to be. We have five seventh grades this year. We will have five eighth grades next year as opposed to eight. This year we took no new eighth-graders. All the eighth-graders are students we had last year. I know that it is an ideal. A lot of my colleagues don't have that. Because we are a scholastic academy, we have a pretty stable population. I know that with many of my colleagues, the children who start with them in September are gone by June. They have a whole new group. So, I know we have a lot of things my colleagues do not.

JF: Why are your enrollments stable, and many other schools' are not?

KM: Well, because if a child moves, as long as he stays in Chicago, he can stay here. If we do not have transportation—as long as they move within a reasonable distance or the parents say they will bring them.

JF: That means you have continuity. You can get to know the children. They are there. The parents are committed to this building, so the community is really a strong community. Here teachers get to know the children, the families.

KM: I think the key since we have changed our grade structure is that we are seeing a year's growth for a year's teaching as a mean. The children are moving; they are achieving. Parents are becoming much more on top of it and much more attuned to what we expect. It is making it easier for us. It is always hard in an urban area where a large percent are on free/reduced-priced lunch, which means that your children are not affluent. I think now we are more in tune with servicing our community, and I think we have a reputation in the community that this is a school that people want to go to.

Aida Latona-Lozano, assistant principal, asked a student the other day: "Well, why does your mother want you to come to Saucedo?" The kid said, "Because it is a good school." I think we have a reputation of being a good school that will move their children forward.

JF: But you have become . . .

KM: A school of choice.

JF: Of choice for the neighborhood. And these are inner-city children.

KM: We do not select anybody. It is strictly a random lottery. I think that is something we need to say. We do not pick only the best students. But, it is strictly a random lottery, and we know nothing about the children other than name, address, and age. We have a waiting list from the random lottery.

JF: But you try to keep families together.

KM: As much as possible siblings—but we cannot promise. We are on the second generation. Over the past 10 years, those children who were in seventh or eighth grade, now have children who are in the early primary grades.

JF: That is an added sense of stability here. As far as children making more choices about their learning, children getting more involved in their learning, children being more responsible. How does that play out?

KM: I think children like it, because we have more things here than they do in a lot of schools. That is always a big thing for children. We have a swimming pool. We try to have more activities and more things that are related to children, and I think they like choices. We are very structured at Saucedo. I think most children like that, but there are some children who are a little rebellious, but they still do it. One of our claims to fame is that we are well disciplined. Parents like that.

JF: It is a safe place.

KM: I think children ultimately like that.

JF: They want to be free, but they also want predictability and not to get messed with.

KM: We try to let them know what our expectations are and not decide just on the spur of the moment. We do not make up the rules as we go along.

JF: Do children get to help make the rules?

KM: Yes, we have a student council. We now have a lunchroom advisory group. Maybe not as much as we would like, but this is an elementary school; but we will listen. One of our big fights now is uniforms. This year we have really put the clamps on it. Up to now, we have been a little looser, but this year we have said 100%—no excuses. We have attached some consequences to people who do not wear them and some rewards to people who do. They are doing real good. Today is School Spirit Day, so they don't have to wear their uniforms.

JF: But that takes another pressure off them. There are no gang things.

KM: The parents really like it. You fight with the older children—the seventh- and eighth-graders. I can understand their feelings about it being restrictive, but on the other hand, I think the neighborhood where we work . . . it alleviates; it really makes the children calmer. Because they are not wearing all of this weird stuff that is gang related. They do not have to worry about it. The teachers don't have to worry about it, and I don't have to worry about it. Aida does not have to worry about it. We do not have to spend a lot of time on something that has nothing to do with educational goals, although I realize it is restrictive for some children.

I think it was 2 years ago when we voted on uniforms. The parents voted 70% in favor, so we went with the uniforms. But, we still have some parents, 30%, who were not sold on it. So, we started working with the uniforms and giving people time to learn about it.

JF: Let's talk about your faculty and how they benefited from the reform.

KM: The first couple of years we spent a great deal of time on staff development and meeting together and developing our language arts program. As you remember, we started with the writing with yourself and B. J. Wagner, and we had a lot of computers here. They were using the computers for prescription learning when I came. I just felt that computers could be used more creatively for instruction. Then I started working with National-Louis University, yourself and B. J. Wagner. We started working on the writing. We did a lot of things at the Teacher's Center the first couple of years and that was prereform. We did a lot of things with the extended day. The teachers did not get paid. We paid the consultant's fee but all the teachers gave all their Saturdays. I can remember a couple of year's worth of Saturdays, once or twice a month. That is how we got started. The teachers began to see more of a commitment to professional development. I went with them and did whatever they did. We worked a lot with you and B. J. Wagner, Sandy Turner, Linda Tafel, and Jura Harris.

We began to talk about writing and vocabulary, which are two of the critical things for nonEnglish speakers. We began to look at what we were doing and if teacher-based instruction was still the most effective way. A lot of the teachers began to change their classroom environment to be more open and to allow children to work in groups. We had a lot of people from your staff who came and worked with teachers and children right in their rooms. A lot of it had to do with providing support. It was not just having a workshop and saying OK, tomorrow we are going to do this. Saucedo and National-Louis had an ongoing relationship for several years.

JF: Your work with teacher development started prereform. You looked at the curriculum and tried to do things in a different way. Some of the teachers, who were not necessarily primary teachers, had to teach like primary teachers. And, you started where there was the greatest need—fourth-grade reading.

KM: When I first came here, there were no primary teachers and fourth-grade students came to us with abysmal reading scores. We had "a cast of thousands of nonreaders" in fourth grade. Luckily, I was a primary reading teacher, so I knew a lot about teaching beginning reading. I had also done a lot with remedial reading with older children. So, reading was kind of my area of expertise. I won't say expertise, because I don't think anyone is ever an expert in reading. I think every kid learns in a slightly different way. I always tell the teachers: I will not be satisfied until we get all of the students where they should be. I think all children are smart.

JF: What guided you in helping teachers change their reading strategies? How did you involve the teachers and your council?

KM: We were spending a lot of time on remedial reading. My premise was that if we had the opportunity to get children younger, we could do some of the things we felt were important for early learning. Before reform, we had approached the desegregation program about dropping out of the magnet school. They were not real receptive to it. But after reform, when we were starting to talk about it, and especially after we had gotten Headstart at our school, I had parents who were very upset, because after Headstart they had to leave us until fourth grade.

Then, a couple of the parents were elected to the council while their children were pre-K and Headstart children. So, when we really started talking after reform, we just came together and said this is what we are going to do. What were our options? Then, the board pretty much said we could become a scholastic academy as long as we would agree to give preference in the lottery to children from Spry and Hammond in order to relieve overcrowding. So, that's what our board report stated in 1989. That we would give preference to Spry and Hammond and children in surrounding Hispanic schools that were over-crowded. We completely dropped the recruiting, because we can get enough by word of mouth. We sent a letter to the principals at Hammond and Spry and the surrounding schools and said: We will be accepting applications. Then, they just sent us the applications.

I think that at Saucedo we didn't see a big difference when reform came in, because prior to reform we had LSIC, which was an advisory board. We had a strong parent advisory board before reform and a lot of active parents. So, those parents just folded right into the reform. The reform was not like at a lot of schools where parents had no input before. I think it was very traumatic at some schools. It was not that traumatic, because we had teachers who were actively involved in curriculum development and those kinds of things.

JF: Parental leaders—how to get them? You mentioned that you had the first council, then the second, now the third council.

KM: We had to grow our own. As I said, on the first council we had several par-ents who were a part of our Headstart program. The Headstart program and pre-K program are excellent in that they demand that the parents volunteer in those programs. It really sets a precedent for the parents that they need to be in the school. When we had the first election, a couple of those people were elected to the council. They were instrumental in Saucedo becoming a pre-K to eight school. Over the years, through our PTO and LSC bilingual advisory council, IABA council, we have kind of grown our own parent leaders. Just by coming to meetings, providing input, going to workshops, acting as volunteers, they have become much more confident.

On the first council we had—no one wanted to say anything. Now if we can finish a meeting in 2½ hours, I am thrilled to death. No one feels real hesitant about speaking up and speaking their mind. Although many of our council meet-ings probably are not exactly according to Robert's *Rules of Order*, we do have an agenda, and we do make motions and those kinds of things. But, we accept more input from the audience than we probably should. But, frequently we do have a public presentation if we are talking about an issue and somebody from the audi-ence wants to say something, we usually allow them to do so. Many of those peo-ple then come back; and then they act as volunteers; and then they become more active in the school. I think that school reform has made my parents become much more confident in their abilities to do things and take charge of what is happening in their lives. The bulk of the people who are active participants at my school are Hispanic females and for them it was a real difficult transition, because they were not used to voicing their opinions. It was something that did not come easily to them. Sometimes people have shot some arrows at them. If they have done some things, they have had to learn to develop kind of an armor about criticism. This was not easy for them. In many cases, it still is not easy for them when people do not agree with them or do not agree with the decision they make. It has been very difficult for some. I think it is difficult for any parent. It is very difficult to make a decision and have people tell you that it was a stupid decision and not to back down if you feel it is something that is right. I think a lot of my parents have grown a great deal that way. They have made a decision, and once it was made they have been willing to stand up for this decision they have made in the face of people who do not agree with them. I think for Latino, Hispanic females particularly, it's been an education, an evolution.

JF: The first council did the pre-K change. That was the big change. And moving from a magnet school to predominantly a neighborhood school. Also, I suppose becoming a council and being concerned with school and making a positive contribution to the school. Those were elements too, weren't they? Second council: Were there some highlights there that you can think of?

KM: Well, with the second council we started thinking of looking at programmatic things . . . for instance, we started adding the full-time social worker. We added the other counselor. We expanded our gym program. We expanded our library program. We started looking at different kinds of programs we wanted to add. So, I think, the first council looked at the organization of the school. The second one we really started working more on individual programs and consolidating programs and making sure that we were spending the money to benefit the children. And, providing something for every child, not just for the remedial students or the best students, but that we were looking at all the students. And we really started firming up our primary program, giving more resources. When we started those programs, the board only gave us a teacher. Books, equipment, supplies all had to be written in our budget, and we had to purchase it. Those things were all our own doing. So, with that second council we really got a lot of the programmatic things for the educational program.

JF: And some of those on the second council were on the first council, no?

KM: Right. I have some who are serving their third term.

JF: They have a continuity that goes through here.

KM: I have three who have been on since the first council. Maria Elena Garcia was a parent of children at Saucedo. All four of her children have graduated from Saucedo. Her two daughters are now in college studying to be teachers. Her two boys have gone either to college or a trade school. So although she doesn't have any children at Saucedo any longer, she certainly does have a history at Saucedo and can tell you something about what has happened.

It would probably be nice to get a couple of graduates to talk about what the school has meant to them. Some of the students we have had to really "work with" will come back to us and say: "Oh, Mrs. Morris, can we come back to visit." I think one of the things we pride ourselves on is although we have 1,350 children, we try to treat each kid as an individual and, as much as possible, to learn as much as possible about the children. The administrative team I have are all people who are really committed and not afraid to work hard, and so among the six of us, I think we know every child.

It is important to parents to think that you know their child. If they come in and start talking about their child and you don't know anything about them, I would not have a great deal of confidence in the school that treated my child like they were a number or a digit. I try to know as many as I can. I obviously don't know every single one of them. Most of the children who are having a great deal of difficulty, I know them. But, you know, Tanya knows a lot of them, Kathy knows a lot of them, and Lucy and Aida and we talk about them and try to see them all as individuals.

I think that probably the ideal school size would be no more than 500. Because then you could know every child and every teacher, and you have the opportunity to interact with those teachers. I have 75 teachers and if I spend 1 minute with them a day—you know. I don't like to sit in my office. During the school day I am very seldom in my office. Many people get mad at me, because they can't reach me in the office. They have to leave messages, because I am not comfortable sitting there. I like to go out. One way I get to know students is in the morning when the children are outside on the playground. I go out and I talk to them and at the lunchroom. You get to know a lot about children, and you get to hear what their problems are, what their successes are, and all those things. Everyone on my administrative team has lunch duty, has outside duty. We don't have any administrators who just sit at their desks.

I think it is important that we keep in touch with what is happening with children and with staff. I don't ask staff to do anything that I don't do myself. If they are out on the playground, if it is cold and it is raining, I am going to be out there too. I think it is important that you are visible and that you are out there and that the parents know you care about their children. The boulevard is not the safest place in the world outside of my school. So, I make a point every day at dismissal time, which is always a kind of chancy time as far as gang activity, that I am out there and that I keep my eyes open. If anything happens, parents know that I will react to it.

JF: So, the gangs are recruiting—the gangs are there.

KM: They are not on our property. Usually, they are across the boulevard. They can be very intimidating. The gang activity in the neighborhood, as a whole, has increased. Well, it has been there ever since I have been there. I think that the gangs probably are becoming bolder. It is something that we continue to have to work on in the building. One of the reasons that last year there was a strong recommendation to go to school uniforms to get away from a lot of the gang colors and gang clothing and things that interferes with children's ability to concentrate on school work, because they are more interested in things from outside.

We are really very structured as far as our expectations for students; but you are very aware of pressures of a lot of our children and when you talk to children who are having academic and social problems inside the school, a lot of it will be based on the fact that then they walk across the boulevard on their way home, there are children hanging around trying to recruit them and on the weekends or in the evening, "We can't go to the Boy's Club, we can't go here." A lot of our children can't walk off their block, especially the Hispanic males over the age of 10 or 11. I will say to one of my young men, "Well, just go over to Toys R Us." And, they will say, "I can't go over there."

A Guiding Philosophy

KM: The two things which I feel are the real challenges are: *Getting teachers to understand children.* It is a constant thing that we need to work on as educators. Children are not a finished product. We can't blame everybody outside. As educators we tend to say it is this guy, that guy. They are ours for 6 hours, and we do the best we can. We try to communicate with parents. We continue to work on it. There are a lot of parents we cannot reach. They don't have phones. They are never home; every excuse in the book. I tell the teachers that is just an excuse. If we can't reach the parents, OK. We can't give up on the children. We still have to take care of this child. And, second, if we know he has all of these extraordinary needs, our job is to figure out how to make it better for him. I am not saying it is going to be perfect. Our major theme ought to be *we are going to try and make this life a little better and educate this child as best we can.* We are probably not going to do as well as with cooperative parents. When you look at the children who are really having extraordinary problems, it is because when you look at the whole child, I mean you almost want to cry. You sit here and you think, my God, this kid is doing pretty good. When you look at all the things, "Wow." You start with the positives! *Focus on positive things.* I think sometimes as adults that is real hard for us to do.

JF: You do look at the positive in every single child.

KM: Yes. It is so frustrating sometimes. But, if you look at the whole child, you find out he is not doing too bad. With all of the things going on in the world. You just never give up. I keep hitting and hitting and hitting and hitting. And sometimes you have successes and sometimes you don't, but you can't give up.

JF: Getting teachers to understand children—that is one of the main challenges.

KM: Well, to understand a little bit about the whole child, the time that they are here is only a part of their day. There are a lot of things going on outside—not to excuse. Don't use these things as excuses for the child not doing their work, but to understand what is happening and then develop some plan of attack that will help chip away at the things that are hampering the child's education achievement. Most teachers in the whole country—we are very middle-class.

JF: Just to understand where the child sleeps at night and gets up in the morning; and to understand what it takes for that child just to make it to school.

KM: And to understand parents too. As I say, teachers are very middle-class people. We need to constantly be reminded, at least in urban settings, that our children are not in most cases middle-class. So, we are expecting X, Y, and Z. We are expecting parents to come home and read with their children. Well, if you leave for work at 5 o'clock in the morning and get home at 7 o'clock at night, you still have to make dinner and do your chores around the house. So, reading with your children or checking their homework—sometimes we forget that not everybody gets out at 2:30.

JF: How do we help teachers understand this?

KM: Really working with teachers; talking with teachers; trying to give them more information. We have a full-time social worker now. We have school community representatives now who go out and talk to parents. Doing staff development. Doing a little bit about what our community is like. I don't want teachers to lower their expectations. You are walking a very thin line between understanding the whole child and saying oh, you poor child, you can't do anything. I would really be upset if someone said, "Well, his mother drinks and his father does this. Therefore, we don't have any expectations for this child."

JF: Those were the two challenges you were talking about. Both to understand and still have high expectations for learning and, to continue to find ways to help the child learn.

KM: Expect this child to learn. Expect this child to do good work, but realize that sometimes it is not going to get done; and it might not be the child's fault. A lot of my teachers stay late and work with students after school and come in early. We have programs, or we have homework center. We have a lot of things to help those children who maybe don't have someone at home to help them. My teachers, many of them, are wonderful about giving their own time to stay after school to work with children. They don't do it for brownie points, because unless I happen to be looking for that teacher, I don't always know they are up there with children. They don't make a big deal out of it.

JF: The sense of community—that we are all in this together even though we are 1,300—we are still a community of a kind of family.

KM: In seventh and eighth grade, we have pods. The pods consist of three classrooms that share tecahers. We try to create a sense that they do belong to someone, so if they have a particular concern, there is someone who knows them and can talk to them and be their advocate. In most cases, teachers who taught their children in second grade and sent them to third grade are still strong advocates of those children even in third grade.

JF: You mentioned that you were reading Roland Bath's book, *Run School Run*. What strikes you about the book?

KM: When I read books, in many cases, I am looking for suggestions for improvement or affirmation of what I am doing. Probably I am looking at a lot of things he has done. I am thinking did I do that; did I not do that. I do not think there is a right or wrong way to do a lot of things in education. Most of the things we do have to fit our style. I don't think you can pretend. If you do, you are probably going to be too wishy-washy. And in this job, you cannot be wishy-washy. You have to have some principles that you feel are very important for learning. Although you can grow in those principles and learn a lot of things that fit your style.

I don't think there can be cookie-cutter teachers or cookie-cutter principals. Number one, it depends on where you are, who you have to work with. I think that is one of the problems that the board of education is going to have now. There are 149 schools who are not meeting state standards and who are on this watch list. They are going to have to do some kind of retraining with these staffs. They are going to have to be very careful about how prescriptive they are with those 149 schools. Every one of them is different. Every one of them has a different staff, a different group of students. I hope they are careful with the idea, that just because you do X, Y, and Z, does not guarantee success. It has to be more personalized than that. Certainly there are some basic tenets for running a good school. Probably the major one is that you like children and that you understand basically how children learn; and that you are open to ideas; and the staff is willing to help. Maybe in those 149 schools there has to be some major shifts of staff or administration. There are probably a lot of really good people in every one of those schools.

JF: A theme at Saucedo is that students are central, that you care about children. This is part of the reason we went into teaching, isn't it? It is the reason you became a principal. There are principles that you keep and continue to fight for and bring about.

KM: I think the key is we care about children. Students are first. I care very much about my staff and their professional development and helping them become more capable teachers. Parents are very valuable partners in education. As much as possible, enlist their help. You are going to have some successes in all three areas. Some teachers are not going to jump on the bandwagon, and you are going to lose some of those people who do not want to work that hard. I have been very fortunate that most teachers who have left Saucedo have gone on to get a promotion at another school or board office.

JF: Leadership style comes with time, and yet it is always there. Because it is your personality and your personality develops over a long period of time—from the time you were a student in elementary school, to college, to your first year teaching. If you had to talk about your style, do you have words to describe this style?

KM: I think I already have. The first thing is: I really like children. And children need the opportunity to grow, and I try always to think about how I could make education more exciting, more fun, more productive for students. Then, I try to facilitate that through my staff, myself, the parents, the community. I was pretty lucky when I was in school, I liked school. I was a pretty successful student. I think most teachers were. That is why we went into teaching. But, I have had a lot of students I went to school with who are not real successful.

Another reason why I probably went into teaching, I did a lot of tutoring with those children who were not so successful. When I was pretty young, I went to a two-room school. When you go to a two-room school where a teacher has four grades in the room, the teacher uses other students in the room. Nowadays, we call that cooperative learning. Back then we did not know cooperative learning or peer tutoring. We did not know anything like that, but the teacher would say to some of us who caught on to things fast, "You go over and help Jimmy and Johnny with social studies or math or whatever it was." And, so I saw children who really struggled a lot. That is why I wanted to become a teacher. If you worked with them long enough, they began to catch on, and you began to see that little light to on in their faces. That is what made me want to become a teacher. After I became a teacher, I was a first-grade teacher most of my career, I worked real hard on reading with children and saw the same kind of light go on. That is what I like to do as a principal—to see if we can maximize the children where that little light goes on saying, "Oh, God, I've got it." So, it is more a facilitator trying to maximize the potential of all these children. If you like children you want them to be successful. We have had a lot of successes. We have had our failures too. They hurt a lot, but you cannot dwell on the failures. You kind of glory in the success and pray a lot that your children are going to make it.

I think many times we forget. I tell the teachers, "These children are the people who are going to value and support us in our golden years." If we don't educate these children, our golden years are going to be a little tinny. I do whatever I can to make children's lives better. I do not accept the fact that children are getting beaten up, or they are not being fed or they are not coming to school as a reason for not teaching that child. I continually try to get my staff and community to do whatever we can to make these kids' lives better.

I try to know all of our students. I make a point of—I might not know every single child's name, but I know a lot about every single child even if I don't know their name. I know what room they are in, how they are doing. I make a point of looking at all report cards. Making children feel special—in a school of 1,350 is not an easy task. So, I try to make sure that I can say something to every kid. I have been very fortunate with the LSC over the years of reform, because they are very child oriented. They do not have big egos. The thing that probably concerns me most is the number of young people that I see as parents now. A lot of our students who have graduated, before they are 18, have children. They come back, and they share their babies with us. They are beautiful children, but when I look back at those children, and they probably were not very successful students in many cases, and now they are having children and I think this is something we need to improve. Very young parents need a lot of support.

JF: To be a teacher today poses huge challenges, doesn't it? And, yet, it brings all kinds of joy too. You are with them 6 hours, and I think that is what keeps you with it. You can see changes, can't you?

KM: That is what has kept me in the education business and certainly kept me in schools. The time I did work away from school I hated it. I knew that was not for me. In a few years I am going to retire, because I can't keep up this pace for many more years. I think I have found what I aspired to do. I really like what I am doing. If I didn't like it—something I also say to teachers, "If you do not like teaching then you had better get out of it and get another job." If it is not something you like, number one you are not going to be successful at it. Because no one can come here everyday and face a room of 30 six-year-olds and really hate it and be successful. Because the students are going to get the message that you are unhappy.

Creating a Teaching/Learning Community

KM: I think it is a good idea for schools to determine how they will achieve state educational outcomes. There are three or four levels of this task. The first are the state goals. Then, the next level down are the outcomes. Then the system-wide goals and objectives, which are more specific. The activities are the teacher's job. This is what children must know and be able to do. Now, how are we going to do it? We know what the State expects the students to be able to do. The teacher's major job as a professional is to develop meaningful activities for students in order to master the goals.

What we have really tried to do at Saucedo is integrate instruction. Our big project for the first quarter is a science fair. Every student in Grades 4 through 8 has to do a science fair project. When you do a science fair project you also do language arts, because you do a research paper and oral presentation.

All the K–4 teachers are responsible for the child in fourth-grade. Not just the fourth-grade teacher is responsible for the prior learnings. The fourth grade teacher cannot teach everything in 1 year. So, all of the K–4 teachers have to work together to make sure that by the time the child gets to fourth grade, they have mastered all the outcomes.

When I first started talking about state goals, outcomes, objectives, teachers would look at me and say, "What are you talking about?" They are becoming very good at goals, outcomes, and objectives now. I think they are feeling more confident, and they are much more independent. They are becoming very adept at developing instructional units and assessments.

JF: You have just talked about how the teachers in 1993–1994 looked at the state guidelines, outcomes, goals—how they learned the vocabulary and are taking over. I am wondering if we couldn't give an historical perspective.

KM: Well, I have always had very good teachers, but I think they looked much more to the principal for making decisions. After we got sizable amounts of money, we have really been able to work more on teacher-led activities, teacher-led curriculum, teacher-developed assessments; but also accountability for teachers along with doing all of these things; somebody has to be accountable. In the last few years, it has been more the principal as facilitator or the principal as partner. Facilitator might be a good word. Now they will come and say, "We want to do this but we need. . . ." It is up to me to see if we can find it. They have taken a lot more responsibility for what is happening in their grade level.

What I am really working on now is more responsibility to their colleagues. That is what I am talking about here. You are teaching kindergarten, but you have a block of this child's ultimate achievement. So, you can't be down here doing something that is not related at all. If you are not doing your job, we are never going to get the students where we want them to be. Rather than the teachers being accountable to me, they are accountable to their students and colleagues. That has been the progression. Where we were very autocratic, prescriptive, now we really allow teachers to be professional people who can sit down with each other and decide what works and what doesn't work. I have tried to build a schedule, so people have school time and can work together.

My teachers have five or six preps per week now—union contract calls for three. One of those preps, at least one or two a week, they spend on curriculum meetings, getting together talking about the assessments. Then, we are on this restructured day where we bring in students 10 minutes early in the morning, so that every other Friday the students leave at 12:40, and we have the afternoon to work together. What people don't realize is that if you are going to do curriculum work, you have to give teachers the time to do it. You can't expect them to do everything on their own time. They must do it at a time when everyone is together.

JF: Professionals have to build time in the day to meet together if they are to develop together. That is really one of the greatest progressions here, from being isolated to being professionals who work together and develop together.

KM: Hopefully, maybe I am seeing a glimmer of it—that teachers are actually taking more responsibility for children's learning rather than saying, "Central Office didn't send me . . . ," or "What are you going to do about it?"

JF: Now, teachers are in charge of integrating, of working together.

KM: You don't teach in isolation. For example, you don't just do computers. So, if a student comes in during the time that you are doing science fair projects, and you are the computer teacher, you might have those students typing their papers and doing word processing and those kinds of things. If they come into the library, then you have someplace with research books on science fair projects, and you are helping those students with their research skills.

JF: So, students begin to see the connectedness.

KM: Right. So, the idea of integration of curriculum—that if you are working on a project, you are not just responsible to just one person or one teacher. Teachers decide on themes based on what the system-wide goals and objectives are. They look at system-wide goals and objectives and kind of cluster them together saying, "These are pretty similar, so we can do this unit." Then, they look at the material they have available.

JF: How many themes do they have in a year?

KM: Probably four major ones by grade level, one per quarter. Although the science fair is a school-wide thing. Grades 4 through 8 the students all make an individual project and Grades K–3 it is a classroom project, but everyone is working on science fair. Science fair is a school-wide project. That is the first quarter. The third quarter we do young authors where everybody has to do their own book. So, those two things are school-wide. Sixth grade is now working on the westward movement, people going to the West. They are reading Laura Ingalls Wilder.

JF: So, the curriculum is less fragmented and is more interconnected. That is why teachers need the time. They need six prep periods to begin to say, "What are you doing? How am I doing? What can you reinforce? What does this scheme mean?"

KM: And what do you have in your room that I can use. Sharing materials and going on common field trips. There is a lot of planning and a lot of logistics. It is probably easier for everybody to do their own thing. Then, you only had yourself to worry about. If you have a common theme or something that you are doing, sure it requires a lot more time for teachers. But I think it is more effective. You are looking at materials that are available, getting feedback from other people on ways you might do this. When you are doing it in isolation, you revisit your mistakes over and over again. Giving teachers a chance to talk, "I did this, and it bombed out." And somebody says, "I did this, and it really worked"—giving each other some ideas on how we might do it.

JF: Because the community talks together.

KM: I think that has been a major plus and in a school this big, *you really have to look at how you can connect people together.* There is no way I could connect 75 teachers together effectively. We have a loose connection, but you certainly need somebody that you can go to today and say how do you do this? It helps the people who are new who come to us, because I don't need to spend my whole day orienting new people. They go to a team that is already there, a grade-level team that is already there. I don't need to sit down and explain procedures to them, because if there is a question or if they do something wrong, they are in a lunch with their team, they are at preps with their team, and they help each other solve problems.

Hopes for the Future, Work Still to Be Done

JF: Where would you want the Saucedo student to be in goals—let's say sixth, seventh, and eighth—about that time. What is it you would hope for in the future, what the Saucedo student would be?

KM: I want them to be able to make choices and not have choices made for them about what they are going to do. I want them to be able to make educated choices. To decide where he wants to go to high school or she wants to go to high school, what they want to be when they graduate from whatever level. I still feel we have too many students who are not finishing high school. It hurts me a lot when I see those students who are not finishing school, who drop out because they go to a high school where there are a lot of gangs or the girls get pregnant, or they have to go to work or for a variety of reasons. I would like to see us build our school community and help the students realize the value of an education. I think that is something we have to work on with parents too. We still have a number of parents who do not feel their children need a high school education. Then, the children stay home and hang around the house all day. I don't know why in the world parents wouldn't realize the harm a lack of education will do to their children.

I guess I will never feel like we are really successful until we have 100% who graduate from eighth grade and at least graduate from high school. We have started, and we are making gains. But, sometimes I think we are hitting the brick wall. We get so far and then bang. We need to talk about the programs we have, some of the things we have been doing with the discretionary money. Are we using the money effectively? We have done some major things with the reading program. We have been working on developing thematic units for instruction, making instruction more exciting and meaningful. Trying to get away from the textbook. But, all of that takes major staff planning and time. Time is probably the commodity that we have the least of. One of the things that we need to consider is a longer school day for students. 9:00 AM to 2:30 PM with a half-hour for lunch is not enough instructional time. Most of the suburban schools have 6 hours minimum. My grandchildren start school at 8:15 AM. They go until 3:30 PM. They have a half-hour lunch and a 15-minute recess. They still have more than an hour over and above what we have in Chicago. Sure you can have after-school programs, but in many cases you are not hitting those children who need it the most. So, I would like more time.

If the board is truly committed to reform, it ought to allow us more flexibility in the school calendar. For instance, the school calendar this year, I took a big hit on attendance in that we had to go until December 23 for Christmas. I had so many emergencies in Mexico starting the Friday before Christmas, the 16th, because everybody wanted to leave. They all wanted to be down there for Christmas, which meant they had to leave if they were going to drive—it takes 3 or 4 days. They wanted to see Mom and Dad. I can understand. You try to be open to their culture and understand things; but on the other hand, I am a school official, and I cannot say it is all right to leave 5 days early. We are still teaching, and your child is missing 5 days of school.

If I had discretion to say we are going to leave on the 16th, and we are going to tack an extra week on. . . . there has to be more flexibility. As long as we meet the number of days and the number of hours that the board of education prescribes, I am certain there are a number of schools that have a lot of Muslims or a lot of Jewish children where there might have to be other accommodations at different times of the year. We need a longer school day, and we need more discretion as far as what days we are going to do.

JF: Major parent and staff rejuvenation—that is quite a challenge, isn't it? The first council reorganization, the second council program and curriculum development, and it looks like the third council is really going to have to face even tougher issues.

KM: I think a lot of parents have aspirations of their children doing better than they are doing and being able to get better jobs. I see a lot of people who are not sure their children are going to be doing better than they are. There is not that upward mobility. A lot of people with high school and college degrees are now working for $6 an hour. A lot of them do expect their children to go to college, and I give them a lot of credit. They work awfully hard. They do motivate their children. A lot of the children who have gone to Saucedo have gone on to college. We have a lot of children who have dropped out too. Part of the problem in urban areas is the high school problem.

There are selected high schools like Whitney Young that are very successful. There are a few high schools that kids aspire to go to and parents really want their children to go to, but if they don't get into those schools, the motivation for a high school education diminishes. I think the high schools are too big and too impersonal. The key is holding onto a lot of these students, and I think the reason we are losing so many at the high school level is nobody really lets them know what the expectations are for success. There is too much freedom. Kids need freedom, but they also need to know that there are parameters to that freedom. Former students are always dropping by our schools in the middle of the day. I will say to them, "What are you doing here? Why aren't you in school?" It's, "We got out early because of this or that. . . ."

I worry about students who leave us. Some I know are going to make it in spite of what happens in high school. A lot of our more academically adept students go to parochial high schools or are fortunate enough to get into Whitney Young or Lane Tech or someplace where there is more structure. Some of them, because they can't get into high schools of their choice, don't go to school at all and nobody checks on them.

When children get older, there is more freedom to do things on your own. You know you have a lot of freedom when you are a teenager, but in many cases our children get too much freedom. I wasn't allowed to go out on school nights unless it was something related to school or the church. That is not the truth anymore. Children are out on the street doing a lot of things, because of the lack of a strong sense of family and educational values. No one is there to monitor homework or say you have to be in bed at 9:00 PM. I said to one child, "You ought to be in bed by 9 every night." He thought I was crazy.

When I first started teaching in the late 1960s, the Hispanics were just moving into Little Village; and you saw many more fathers who were strongly committed. You don't see that as much anymore. We see more broken families. I think it is particularly hard on children in the middle grades, especially the boys who don't have a father to really talk to. I think it is real hard. And, I sympathize with a lot of the young mothers too who are really throwing up their hands and saying: I don't know what to do. It is very difficult being out there trying to earn a living, going to work and coming home, and having a couple of teenagers to raise by yourself.

Analysis of Leadership

This dialogue presents both a portrait of the Chicago School Reform at Maria Saucedo Scholastic Academy and the story of many factors that coalesced in building a neighborhood school, and a community of learning for students and teachers. It is, foremost, a reflection on shared leadership among the principal, teachers, and parents that evolved over more than a decade to bring about improvement in student learning, teacher development, and community building. Moreover, continuity and stability in leadership, goals and mission, the school councils, the faculty, and the student body, were critical factors that supported the reform efforts, and remain essential conditions for helping the school develop a sense of community and achieve academic goals.

It is important to note that previous school improvement and instructional innovation efforts were already part of the school culture, thus permitting effective use of resources when the reform began. These helped local school governance, instructional leadership, and shared decision making to evolve and take hold. It is doubtful that, had these preconditions, school culture, and effective leadership not been present, the reform agenda would have made such progress. It is clear, too, that wider social and educational forces for change were having a profound impact on many teachers and school leaders, apart from the reform agenda.

The Chicago school reform experience at Maria Saucedo Scholastic Academy is a story both of opportunities and success, and of unfilled hopes and frustrations. The complexities and problems of educating students in a large urban setting remain. Great inequities in expenditures and support between urban and suburban schools persist. Good teachers are not rewarded adequately, financially or professionally, for what they do. Though Saucedo is an example to the contrary, teachers generally are not viewed as key instructional decision makers or educational leaders for school improvement. In fact, the Chicago school reform itself makes little mention of the leadership role of teachers, a very strange and unfortunate omission.

EXTENDING THINKING

Questions

1. Many of the changes imposed on the schools through the reform legislation were easily adapted to at Saucedo. What conditions were in place that enabled the changes to occur? Consider the idea of autonomy as a preimplementation condition.
2. Reflect on the idea of shared decision making at Saucedo. How were decisions made and what groups participated in the process? How was the voice of the parent community heard and affirmed?
3. The principal of Saucedo has both positive and negative feelings about what reform brought to her school. What were some of the ways the school was impacted both positively and negatively by reform?
4. Compare the working of the LSCs at Jackson and at Saucedo. Jackson's LSC operated mostly as a rubber stamp whereas Saucedo's was much more active. What factors do you think account for the differences?

Activity

1. The vision at Saucedo focuses on understanding children and helping to make their lives better. Examine your school, or a school with
   which you are familiar; what is the vision, is it shared among the
   members of the school community, and in what ways is it brought to
   life in the school?

Reflection on Cases 1 and 2

The Chicago school reform provided both challenges and opportunities. As these two cases show, the culture of the school—its values, goals, and ways of working—strongly influenced whether the opportunities of the reform could be acted on. On the one hand, just before the reform initiative, Jackson had faced severe internal problems and had selected a principal to effectively "clean up the mess." Yet, her autocratic style, lack of respect for teachers based on her suspicion that some were knowledgeable about the prior principals' misconduct, and lack of welcome for parents laid the basis for a frustrating first year of school reform. As the key events during that year reveal, much of her energy in working with the Local School Council (LSC) was focused on containment of their power: presetting the agenda, failing to schedule training for LSC members, and setting time limits on meetings. The two teachers on the council seemed to share the principal's skepticism about parents being equal to the task of council participation.

As discussed in Section 1, tensions might be expected to arise between the LSC and the principal. But such difficulties did not seem to occur at Jackson School. Indeed, no major reservations were expressed about the principal's leadership until the issue of the principal's contract renewal arose. And the LSC voted unanimously to renew the contract. There was, however, a long discussion during which the LSC members expressed concern about the principal's lack of openness regarding parents. They were concerned as well with her failure to show respect for student achievements through her attendance at some key school events.

The motivation of the teachers who influenced the council vote for renewal is more difficult to understand. Autocratic leadership may be seductive, encouraging selected teachers to reap benefits in return for supporting the leader.

The teachers acted as free agents, rather than as representatives of the school faculty, and the latter felt excluded from the process. This form of leadership served to divide a faculty into supportive and subversive factions.

Just as the work of the LSC was severely controlled, so was the interaction of the principal with the faculty. Far from being a community of learners, faculty were set to work on a task and then criticized when they failed to address issues in a way valued by the principal. She didn't seem to understand how to nurture teachers into more open and penetrating discussion. Because of her fear of negative comments and things getting out of control, she could not permit teachers the space they needed for growth. She held few faculty meetings and had only limited interaction with faculty and students. Philosophically, she expressed a commitment to "every child learning," but acknowledged that she had extreme difficulty sharing power. Morgan operated through institutionally sanctioned leadership, and she was expected by others to make the decisions to carry them all along. She lacked the skills to share her responsibilities, and there were no council members who had the personal characteristics to emerge as real leaders.

How might the decision-making structure have become reformed in Jackson School? The deliberative work of teachers does not suggest that they were ready or willing to grapple with the problems of the school. In their discussion of the low achievement of students and the low confidence of teachers in the quality of the instructional program, teachers seemed to be unable to focus on their own instruction as central to the problem. Yet, in a culture of evaluative judgment, few faculty would be inclined to risk critical evaluation of their work. In their attempt through the Professional Personnel Advisory Committee (PPAC) to find an issue around which they might coalesce, faculty selected the need for departmentalized instruction. However, because this issue pertained to the interests of only a limited number of the faculty (upper grades) and was one that the principal had previously not supported, its likelihood for success was limited. Perhaps the purpose was to goad the principal.

The postscript to the case suggests that a change in decision-making structure was possible with the selection of a new principal, one who already had the respect and trust of the faculty. Once a negative form of interaction becomes entrenched, even a major reform initiative may be of little positive consequence. Rather, major change in the role of at least one of the major participating groups seems to be needed.

The Saucedo case, in contrast, shows how a school already involved in shared decision making profited from the new resources made available through the reform initiative. It also makes clear the complexities involved in developing leadership on the part of teachers, parents, and community members. A strong principal, at the center of this school, modeled (a) attentive listening to the concerns of parents, teachers, students, and consultants, (b) an awareness that every person is always learning, (c) an understanding that time spent together is necessary for thoughtful deliberation, (d) a realization that things work best when administrators perform duties that others are asked to do, and (e) an orienting conviction that every child can and must learn. A pattern of respect pervaded her work, viewing teachers as capable of collectively determining the means of instruction. This same respect also penetrated her work with parents, community members, and teachers on the LSC.

To some extent the complex role of the principal is invisible in this case, but it seems clear that the principal was both a good manager and a strong leader. It fails to detail the numerous daily interactions with students, teachers, and parents. It doesn't show her work at home involved in organizing plans and possible versions of the budget to become aligned with the goals expressed by teachers or the LSC. It doesn't show the skill needed to sense serious problems and to take decisive action. It shows instead a well-crafted gyroscope of intersecting activities that the principal, with the help of others, keeps in balance—most of the time.

SECTION 3

Tensions Between the Local School Council and the Principal

The next two cases illustrate the tension that was created by the reform legislation, which stipulated the formation of a Local School Council (LSC) composed of teachers, parents, community members, and the principal. Key to the legislation was the attempt to build a partnership between parents and professional educators around issues of governance and curriculum and instruction. These partnerships were not easy to forge, and many of the school councils exercised power because they could, whereas others were unable to find their roles. The LSC was given the awesome power to hire and fire their principals, develop a budget for the school, and approve a school improvement plan. The school reform legislation challenged parents, teachers, and community members to come forward to help deal with problems affecting their children and their schools.

The third case, told by Nelda Hobbs, the former principal of Field School, reveals the conflict existing among factions on the council that affected all areas of the running of the school. The conflict at Field impeded change and created a climate where the most viable alternative for the new principal was leaving the school. In this personal reflection, Nelda Hobbs describes her ambivalent feelings and her unwillingness to be "manipulated" by people who were not professional educators. She was able to help the very large school organize into smaller schools, which still exist today, but was unable to find a way to work with the contentious council to support her instructional vision.

The fourth case in this section was written by Pete Leki, chair of the LSC at "W" School. The nature of the legislation was such that relative newcomers to the governance process were given a great deal of power. Some LSCs, like the one Pete chaired, went about their work in a thoughtful manner.

When their principal announced that he was going to retire, the LSC was forced into a nationwide search for a new principal. The chair and the members discovered the enormity of the task of changing a school, as well as the complexity of the journey.

CASE 3

Field of Dreams

Nelda Hobbs
Eugene Fields School Principal,
1991–1993

Background

The Eugene Field School is located at 7019 North Ashland Boulevard in East Rogers Park. The community is a cosmopolitan mix of many races and cultures, apartment dwellers and highly transient renters. There are many large apartments (two, three, or four bedrooms) and studio apartments but fewer homes. Homeowners' children do not attend Field School, but are bused out to other public schools or attend private schools in the city or the North Shore suburbs.

Rogers Park is a very political enclave, pursuing the best and the worst of whatever issue may be at stake. Even though the area has a rich history and background, it is presently losing those active leaders and their constituencies to immigrants, refugees, and others who do not have land, businesses, relatives, agendas, or anything else to protect. The community at one time had many resources and networks, but due to a shift in population, many resources are no longer there. People and programs that are replacing them are more vulnerable, with less expertise and fewer financial resources. The mobility of the community is also reflected in the school.

This case study traces the transitional activities of a newly selected principal serving a four-year tenure following the administration of the former principal . The personal narration of this new principal details the variety of issues facing urban schools. The case also traces the interaction between the Local School Council (LSC) and the principal during the period of reform in which a safer school environment was established and small schools within the school were created. The tensions between the principal and the LSC, from the perspective of the principal, suggest the problems inherent within the reform legislation.

As seen through the eyes of the new principal, the important participants in the school programs that were responsive to their needs. Among other participants are parents and other community members, which the principal views as being not well represented by the interests of the LSC. The LSC plays a pivotal role in defining the activities of the school, a role believed by the new principal to exceed their qualifications. Note as you read the case the role of the teachers, particularly in the development of the small schools. The dynamics within the school are strongly shaped by the interaction between the LSC, the principal, and the teachers.

THE CASE

Recruiting a Principal

Being a resident of the community and neighborhood, I had heard about the turbulence in Field School. I did attend some reform meetings to try to understand what the reform movement was and how it would really impact schools. It was during some of these meetings that I met parents and community people from Field School. Their discussions painted a picture of conflict and confrontation.

As I considered applying for the position of principal at Field, I talked with a parent and two teachers who were on the LSC. They were seriously committed to children, their safety, nurturing, growth, and support, and tried not to get involved in the politics between the principal and the LSC. It was their view that the LSC chairperson was interested in dominating the entire functioning of the school. Therefore all meetings tended to be confrontational. They described the LSC chair as controlling the LSC by always saying, "Well, I have seven votes."

According to these parents and teachers, the former principal did not have a chance to have any of his ideas implemented, because the control exercised by the LSC repeatedly placed him on the defensive on issues. There were a number of things that he wanted to do for children, but he was not allowed to voice his ideas, once the LSC had decided to get rid of him. Moreover, he wasn't a person to express himself freely; he was reserved. He had good rapport with students but never expressed his expectations for them. He respected parents, but was partial toward parents who were active in the school. Generally, he didn't try to please people, but did what he felt should be done for children. He had a viable PTA (parent–teacher association) room mother program, with parents engaging in fund raising, preparing lunches on records day, and sponsoring taffy apple sales, pizza day, and book fairs. When a new lunchroom manager ended the practice of selling prepared food, fund raisers ceased and parents became less active. Parents who replaced the parents moving out of the community did not have the same interest in the school. The former principal believed that the needs of students should assume top priority and that parents and teachers were of equal importance. He didn't deal with petty issues and had cultivated an acceptable relationship with parents, simply because he didn't have parents who wanted to "run" things before the LSC came into existence.

According to those with whom I spoke, the LSC chair was preoccupied with "petty" issues such as getting paperwork submitted to her in a timely manner and the details of purchasing—when an order was sent. In sum, the atmosphere before my coming was tense. According to the LSC members I interviewed, the LSC never focused on what the members of the LSC thought should be of concern. Instead, discussion was dominated by issues of concern to the LSC chair. LSC members spent more time fighting her agenda than spending time on fruitful issues relevant to students and programs. The persons discussing the 1989 to 1991 LSC activities reported that they would often cry over the way things were run. Even today they claim they are paying lingering emotional and physical costs for their involvement on the LSC.

On the subject of principal selection to replace the existing principal, who had served for approximately 3 years, the teachers and parents who discussed this issue stated that the LSC wanted somebody that they could control, but most parents wanted someone who would be impartial. Teachers on the council reviewed all guidelines, videos, and written material for principal selection, but the LSC had already made a decision. The council stated that they had nothing against the prior principal, but wanted to "open up" the process. The LSC had several priorities for a new principal. They stated that they were looking for:

1. One who would have good ideas and implement these ideas.
2. Someone to keep option programs, but put them under another name to retain the programs.
3. One who would be a good disciplinarian.
4. An applicant with elementary and classroom experience.
5. A Hispanic or Black person.

Bringing People Together

When I began my principalship on July 1, 1991, the Eugene Field Elementary School could be characterized by some of the indicators of a school in crisis published by the reform board of trustees in the fall of 1995. These included the following: The principal failed to implement (sign) the school improvement plan written by the LSC. The principal and LSC members were unable to resolve disputes and structure a program conducive to learning. The principal was unable to develop an effective working relationship with teachers, staff, and/or the LSC. As previously discussed, the failings of the principal arose, in part, because the LSC had a history of being adversarial, divisive, and controlling.

When I accepted the position in April, 1991 I began to question people in the community about the school and to talk to any teacher, staff member, or organization who wanted to talk to me. Council members would call individually and share tidbits of concerns about what they thought they wanted or about past experiences. Often they vented about what the previous principal did not accomplish. Teachers talked about the LSC and how they had taken over the school and created much tension. Parents wanted (a) to be included in the decision-making process about the safety issues of the school and community, (b) to feel accepted in the school, (c) to discuss issues related to quality education (high-yield/low-yield teachers, quality of instruction, varied materials), and (d) to have more parents involved in the total school operation.

Another tension existing in the school community was racism. The police, people in the community, and some staff had negative expectations of Black and Hispanic youngsters but Asians and Whites could do no wrong. I didn't, however, find as much of this racial tension between staff members, and I attribute that to their having worked together for so long. However, newcomers were treated as outsiders if they didn't share a close relationship with an established and accepted staff member.

Although safety and security emerged as the most prominent and evident need, an equally compelling need was to build positive, substantive, and sustaining relationships among the school buildings, with those persons and resources that had a direct relationship to the everyday operations of the school. This included those whose relationships were short term and sporadic. I discovered early on that there were many persons with connections to Field, and you could never be certain to whom you were talking. I learned early on to stay upbeat, focused, on the move, and to find a complimentary way to always be accommodating (as much as possible) and accepting of ideas as well as criticism.

This approach led to people in the neighborhood coming to the building and stopping me on the street to share their feelings about what they observed and wanted to see continue or discontinue. They always related to me that they had been told by someone that I was approachable, sincerely concerned about improving the school and the community, and eager for everyone's help.

Not only did I begin to see that there were many, many needs, but there were also many networks—some good, but some not so good. Every day, I had a new take on the lay of the land within the building and the school community. Daily, I tried to evaluate staff, student, parent, and programmatic issues in the building. I had to be guarded and discriminating about people, programs, projects, resources, and networks in the community. I had to learn through trial and error which ones were legitimate and sincere and which were purely political or out for money.

However, once my credibility and no-nonsense reputation spread through the neighborhood, some less sincere groups withdrew. Others persisted but found that I was focused on my stated vision that school existed for children and everyone involved must deliver quality and respectable services to children at all times. School is a business for children, not for adults. I developed a quick test that I communicated to people with requests: Tell me three things that you have tried to solve the problem or three ways that you have assisted in resolving any issue before coming to me with a plan in hand.

As time went on at a fast pace, I learned that the same procedure that worked inside the school also worked outside—using the same evaluative criteria procedures and tests. I remained focused, firm, fair, frank, and friendly—with some humor. Accepting everyone and listening to everyone earned me the reputation that I would listen, but not necessarily agree, and would continue to "play with and bounce around" their concerns. I constantly practiced and voiced options; I never wanted to say "no," and if I did, I would recommend more options that might be more doable that supported the "big picture" and the total school operation.

The student population at Field fluctuated between 1,150 and 1,250 students during the year. Some students would go to their respective countries for holidays. Some, when their relatives were ill, wouldn't attend school for long periods of time. Other children moved, ran away, or left with no forwarding address. Having a 50.2% transiency rate when I arrived said to me that half the students who enrolled left within that year. This was another signal to me to develop a very broad and challenging academic and social program between 8:30 AM and 3:30 PM. The goal of the program had to be to hold the interest of children and challenge them, please parents, and challenge teachers and staff to be the best that they could be.

Safety and Security

The LSC never presented me with a list of what they wanted. I deduced from conversations with LSC members, teachers, parents, and folks in the community that their top priority was safety and security inside and outside the school building. They were concerned about the entire attendance area, because of gang activity, drugs, an increase in violence, and hostility between factions of the community. There was an atmosphere of distrust—even the police were unkind toward the children. For example, I observed an officer slam a student, who was waiting to cross the street, against a light post. I just happened to see it. I approached the officer, told him who I was, and asked why he had done it. He refused to believe that I was the principal and said the student had broken the law. I escorted the young man home, got the badge number of the officer, called the district commander, and wrote a letter to the chief of police. The officer was removed. He reappeared 2 years later, as a crossing guard from time to time, but he was not hostile. This incident gave me a deeper understanding of the importance of safety and security. I then began to observe all officers in and around the school and neighborhood and asked other adults to do the same thing. I must admit that there were some difficult boys and girls at the school who were capable of instigating bad behavior, but the atmosphere of distrust placed an added layer of fear on top of an already fueled fire.

Tensions and adversity existed within and across school groups: LSC, staff, students, parents and the community. Little or no effort had been made to resolve these tensions and conflicts, or to move forward with a definite vision in the best interest of children. The LSC, however, became united enough to hire me, but remained for the most part adversarial.

Some perceived my coming as that of a "savior"; they expected me to bring a calm atmosphere, a vision for the school, and some resources. My own vision, along with the role I perceived, was to build a "mini–Notre Dame" for children ages 5 to 14. This school would be child centered with many programs, many partnerships, many networks, and job opportunities. I wanted to establish something that did not exist at the time, being the first school to establish schools-within-a-school (SWS) in Illinois. I hoped that these intricate connections would stabilize a transient and turbulent school, thus transforming the school into a "Field of Dreams."

During the first year, I tried to bring peace and stability to a volatile and unstable school environment. I knew that no educational programs could thrive in the existing conditions. I also knew that quality programs and student, staff, and community stability would build pride and respect. I asked teachers to tell me the subject(s) that were their favorites to teach and those they felt less comfortable teaching. I also asked about their hobbies and what after-school activity they would like to sponsor. This was done orally, informally, and matter-of-factly. Once I had their agreement, I developed a formal handout of offerings, time, places, descriptions, and sponsors of each activity for the after-school program.

Simultaneously, I was also prodding the staff and trying to find a way to restructure the curriculum and classes so that everyone (students, staff, parents, principal, and others) would be excited about teaching and learning, and all would take an active role in the adventure of change.

As I began to ask students, parents, staff, and people in the community what they would like, many wanted change but didn't know what should be changed or how to change it. Once I saw the "crack" created by their unclear vision, I knew that I had a chance to develop something different, exciting, and energizing with all of the players in the process. All would help to form the new model.

Not only did our plan have no name, but because it was newly created, there was no place from which to borrow game rules, political opinions, or players.

We forged our vision together. Those teachers who liked science formed a group; the language arts teachers grouped, and those who liked history, culture, and art formed a group. Those teachers in Headstart to Grade 3 grouped and all eighth-grade teachers grouped (because they didn't make any effort to join another grouping). These clusters were first called "options" in my mind, simply because there was an options program already in place in architecture, and I could foresee adding several other options with similar selection criteria and teaching expertise. These alternative clusters could work together because they had common concerns.

During my first year of administration as I was planting those seeds, I asked Dr. Linda Tafel and Dr. Al Bertani to serve as consultants in helping me to create a school that would stabilize and anchor the community. In my vision, because of the architecture of the building, Field would look like a mini–Notre Dame. I foresaw many buildings with many programs and activities, all focused on improving student academics and social performance, but ultimately stabilizing a transient and turbulent community. Moreover, the change and restructuring would provide some employment, partnership, and networking opportunities, thereby creating a child-centered place that was visible and impressive.

Drs. Bertani, Tafel, and I planned professional activities: teacher in-services, cooperative learning sessions at National-Louis University (NLU) taught by Tafel, problem-solving sessions at NLU, teacher-trainer sessions at NLU, and professional workshops at the FOCUS Conference of the Wilmette Public Schools. On staff development days, Dr. Bertani conducted sessions on restructuring, making change, building professional community, and options for reorganization. A weekend retreat was planned to take place at the beginning of the year. The retreat served two purposes: to get people to know each other outside of the school setting, and to expose them to current research on schools.

Creating Small Schools Within the School

After 1 year of working with the two consultants, the staff reviewed several readings given to them by Dr. Bertani, and discussed the pros and cons of the structure and day-to-day operations, as they related to Field School. The staff decided to try the SWS model. The model was presented to the LSC for approval, which, contrary to past actions, they granted with energy, excitement, and enthusiasm.

People who had previously had little respect for each other talked civilly to one another. When I asked my staff what was so exciting, they replied that they heard the word *autonomy* and that I was working with them as professionals, respecting them, and allowing them to take control of the school's destiny. I wanted my staff to have the comforts and space to discover and excel in a way that I did not have when I was a teacher. My request to them was to let me know what they needed in order to deliver quality services to our children and their families. The motto was: "We are one big family." I had extremely high expectations, lots of patience, and a lot of love to give. We were going to feel with our hearts, and to think and process issues as though all 1,300 of us live in this big overcrowded schoolhouse. I repeated the aforementioned statement daily to everyone with whom I spoke—be they students, parents, staff, community, police, firefighters, neighbors, whoever. I preached (with my missionary zeal) that those of us in the big schoolhouse had to earn the respect of our neighbors in the community by not littering, using profanity, or being destructive.

As staff became more and more excited about the SWS concept and reorganization, students became excited and parents began to ask more questions. We organized the schools in two ways. First, I asked them what they really liked to teach—where it was effortless and exiting, and for which subjects they had a certificate. Their responses fell along subject areas—English, social studies, and science. Second, I tried to find like-minded persons with whom they felt they could work (possibly four to five), learn to agree or disagree with, but work for the common good, and to name their school. The first school to form was classical (five people); the second was journalism (five people); then environmental science (five people), and high school prep (all eighth grade; five people). A bilingual classroom was included in each school.

To move from a traditional setting to SWS in 1992–1993 required that all classes had to be restructured. Classrooms had to be changed so that all persons in a school were located together in the same wing or location of the building. Classes were developed through a lottery with an even distribution of students performing at ability levels of $A < B < C < D < F$, special education, and discipline problems. This approach eliminated the existing arrangement of certain teachers having the brightest and least disruptive students, as well as low-yield teachers having the least able and the most disruptive students. Teachers chose which grades they wanted to teach and recommended to me the location in the building they preferred. I considered all requests as they related to the overall vision and the smooth operation of the total school.

As the time came closer to move from the old room to the new room, excitement, exuberance, and energy abounded. Students discussed why their school was better than another school. Teachers liked being organized together with common planning periods. Parents were enthusiastic because their children and teachers were happy. And I was happy because teachers, students, parents, and other staff were excited and happy. One teacher had been in one room for 38 years, but he was the first packed and ready to move. Moving was very exciting, somewhat traumatic, but successful. The tension in moving for me was understanding and coordinating the rules and policies of the movers from the board of education, the people, the spaces and things. Everyone was satisfied, no one was injured, no hostility was shown, and everyone felt safe. The move was successfully completed with the extraordinary help of the engineer and his entire crew.

After the move, curriculum, specialty school status, and student selection became our challenges. Student distribution was done by classes with the sending teacher, receiving teacher, assistant principal, and principal discussing the group on each class list, each student on the list, the composition of the class, and the needs of each challenged student so there would be no undue hardship on the classroom teacher in a heterogeneous setting. We hoped this arrangement would allow for more teaching, less interruptions, and more equity in materials, resources, and funding.

Some schools met during the summer of 1992 and developed camaraderie and a real sense of purpose, whereas other schools did not. The rate of growth was quite evident. Schools that had infighting reflected it. Therefore, when school opened in September 1992, all schools were operative but not functioning at the same level. My analogy was that I had six children and all of them were at different stages of development. From the most advanced to the least: classical, foundations, specials (art, music, computer, physical education), journalism, environmental science, and high school prep (all eighth grade). High school prep was disbanded after a few months and an eighth-grade class was added to each of the other schools.

Again, teachers were given the autonomy to choose which school and with whom they wanted to work, with my approval. All requests were granted. Another change occurred in the foundations school. It had previously included kindergarten through Grade 3. Due to first and second grade being located in the Annex and third grade in the main building, communication became a big problem and many decisions and issues had to be resolved at the teacher level. As a result, Grades K–2 and Headstart remained in the foundations school and Grade 3 became the transitions school. Why "transitions"? Teachers felt they provided a transition from the foundational skills to making an informed choice between classical, environmental science, or journalism. The transition curriculum became an introduction of information, themes, and activities of each of the three schools; some even shared information and activities with the respective school, so that at the end of the third-grade year, each third-grade student had some ideas about the school they wanted to enter.

The 1992–1993 year was busy but rewarding. My passing on much of the decision making to staff allowed me to become more a manager of funds, programs, resources, and grants between and across schools and grades and in the community. The long lines that formed at my office everyday from September 1991 to June 1992 were much, much shorter and lines were almost nonexistent by January 1994. The SWS arrangement reduced student discipline, student thievery, and student and teacher absenteeism. It brought a new excitement and energy that was observable in student–staff interaction. It raised the performance expectations of students and staff; it created greater involvement of students, teachers, staff, and parents in the planning and coordinating of activities and resources. The reorganization led to an increased and improved respect shown by others for everyone. I felt like I was the ringmaster of a 1,300-ring circus. I experienced joy and pain, but much more joy than pain.

It was a pleasure to see children bring their balls and jump ropes to the playground early in the morning (7 AM) to jump rope, play games, and share in fun rather than fighting with anger and hatred. It was a joy to see students come to the rescue of an ill or injured schoolmate; apologize and give a handshake of bonding when returning lost goods. It was a joy to see teachers recruit teachers, and parents recruit parents to the school because the school was good and the community was improving. It was a pleasure to have an early-morning meeting in my office and hear the joyful sounds of students, staff, and parents on the playground. On the playground, in the main office, and in the hallways, substantive conversations about issues affecting the school occurred in constructive ways. This was one of my most significant indicators that school safety was improving, even though I never let my guard down or took anything for granted when it came to safety. I enjoyed being invited to a meeting given by staff and being asked to see how they were doing business and conducting themselves. It was joy to see students mirror and monitor their teachers and teachers modeling each other for the better.

What was happening with curriculum? A new interdisciplinary literacy series became the basic resource for Grades 1 through 8. Every teacher was trained to use it, but encouraged to use it as a resource. One of my biggest challenges was to separate teachers from their teacher's guide and to encourage them to teach content based on their own knowledge and not from the teacher's edition. Some, however, never put the teacher's edition away, and some did poorly with or without the teacher's edition.

Consolidation and Confrontation

The 1993–1994 year was the smoothest of the 3 years, but not without problems. With regard to the LSC, there was less cooperation from the LSC and more tension over spending state Chapter I dollars. I sensed a basic dislike for the success of the school and misgivings about me because I could not be manipulated. With regard to the SWS concepts, several problems arose, including students and teachers wanting to switch from one school to another, and teachers wanting to move students from one school to another. Student selection criteria for each SWS needed to be developed and an application for specialty school status needed to be submitted to the Department of Desegregation. There were also disgruntled teachers who were displaced from old assignments and given challenges in the new SWS configuration that were in the best interest of children. Finally, community changes led to school problems: A growing student enrollment required more services, which was exacerbated by prior poor schooling and other social needs of students. Classes were overcrowded due to limited school space, and there was no place to form new classes.

In addition to these being the worst of times, they were in some ways the best of times. All indicators including academic achievement, attendance, safety, parent involvement, staff development, quality instructional program, personal relations, caring, strategic planning, and many other best practices were moving forward. Yet, while this was occurring, the LSC was never satisfied and remained confrontational. One disgruntled faction connected with another disgruntled faction on the council and decided they wanted to spend state Chapter I funds illegally. Be reminded that this LSC refused to be trained, refused the advice of the district superintendent, and refused my advice. They continued to pursue their desires, which eventually began to damage the calm and smooth operation of the school.

The thing that I continue to struggle with is how people with no citizenship, less than a third-grade education, and a limited understanding of the complex issues facing schools could make informed decisions about many issues, with many occurring simultaneously. A personal dilemma was posed for me. After spending years and years to qualify for a principalship, including having a Type 75 administrative certificate, "Was I to be led by a LSC that possessed limited expertise?" It is one thing to work collaboratively with others, but another to be constrained by a decision-making group that was unresponsive to the goal of delivering services to children. This would seem to be a betrayal of the public trust.

It became clear to me that the conflicts were worsening. The issues were about control and power, which I naively failed to see when I approached the role of principal with the dedication of a missionary. Given this variety of tensions, I looked closely into an early-retirement offer, and weighed this against having people on the LSC controlled by an angry, dominating community person. In the end, I decided it was time to leave while the school was working well. I took my lead from Michael Jordan, "Leave while you're on top or ahead."

This decision caused me to assess and reflect on what I had accomplished and to determine what I could do from 7 AM to 7 PM in a school that was resistant to basic changes. Principals need to be given legal authority, not more responsibility. LSC members should be required to be literate with some English language facility and be citizens with legal proof of residence. LSC meetings should be held in English, the dominant language of the nation. Responsibility for verifying addresses for LSC elections should be assigned to responsible and reputable agencies. The LSC should be given responsibility for community issues and getting parental support for school safety. Changes such as these in the legislation governing the roles and rights of the LSC and the principal would go some distance toward creating a viable position for principals and an appropriate involvement for parents.

My experience as principal of Field School gave me a perspective on the neighborhood society that I would otherwise never have had. It was a wonderful venture done from the heart. My only regret was leaving so many wonderful people who made so many sacrifices and contributions to turn a school around. I know that I made a difference. Schools can be successful if designed to meet the needs of children and family members, instead of being driven by the needs of the adults that inhabit them.

I came to represent a "savior" to students and their parents because I wanted to champion their rights to respect, security, and an education. Some comforting memorable remarks expressed to me include the following: "You were always there for me and always treated me with respect," "You gave all of us hope and light," "You were fair," "Children are definitely first at Field and everybody knows it," and "You cared about everybody and everybody knew it." It was a bittersweet departure.

Reflection on Accomplishments

As I said before, my immediate concern was to stabilize a community. By this I meant that I needed to put exciting and challenging programs in the school for all constituents—students, parents, and staff. These programs would bring stability and reduce the mobility. At a glance, the mobility rate or transiency rate (percentage of students leaving Field) did decrease from 50.4% in 1991–1992 to 45.9% in 1992–1993, and 43.7% in 1993–1994. Keep in mind that many students who left transferred less than eight blocks away because of a basic dislike for a teacher, a student, someone in their building or housing complex, or something related to paying rent or a housing-related issue.

Whereas transiency and mobility were decreasing, enrollment was increasing: 1,150 students in 1991–1992 and 1,158 in 1992–1993 to 1,214 in

1993–1994. With the increase in student enrollment came an increase in the number of students with limited English proficiency (LEP), necessitating broader programs to support LEP students. The newer enrollees were entering with far less schooling, coming from rural areas of Mexico, with some having had limited schooling and speaking no English. Their parents or relatives spoke no English, as well.

We knew that the existing bilingual program was insufficient in size and programmatic structure. Therefore, the bilingual teachers and other school staff decided to review the old program examining the number of LEP students who had been in the program over time, their success rate, who taught what to them and when, and how efficiently the program was monitored. We found that students entered the program but seldom exited. When they exited, many did not meet with success in mainstreamed classes. The students spoke well but could not translate speaking and listening skills to formal reading and writing activities from third through eighth grade. Therefore, we implemented an immersion program in English and Spanish where all bilingual teachers were paired with an English-speaking teacher. As a result, following a dual language program across the content areas in the classroom, at play, at lunch, and in assemblies, more students began to experience a more rigorous program in English for Spanish speakers as well as a more challenging experience in learning Spanish for English speakers.

Teachers then made recommendations to the bilingual coordinator and the principal to remove students from the bilingual program and place them in a regular program of instruction. Parents agreed to the new placement by submitting a letter of request for their child to make this change. Many students became successful but still experienced difficulty on the standardized achievement test. Tutorial support was put in place to aid those needing such help.

I considered this program one of my best successes because we saw students, regardless of their first language, assume more active roles in the school by volunteering for activities such as school patrol, playground patrol, teacher's aide, office aide, messenger, and many other specialties related to assemblies, special programs, and field trips. The same was true for Spanish parents. Although I hired more teachers and hired more supportive help for teachers, the more we tried to reduce class size, the more students came saying, "The bilingual program is a good program." Consequently, the pressure on class size was a continuing challenge.

Nevertheless, there was a decrease in class size as enrollment increased. This was accomplished, given a lack of space in the main building, by renting 10 classrooms from the archdiocese, dividing rooms, and using hallways (but never the auditorium).

Class Size	1991–1992	1992–1993	1993–1994
Grade 3	37.3	29.4	29.6
Grade 6	29.0	22.3	24.8
Grade 8	30	26.0	25.8

Our enrollment increase was heaviest in the primary grades. We had six sections of kindergarten, necessitating five or six first-grade classes, and in the first
year we had at least one split classroom for each grade level. The split arrangement (1991–1992) was hectic for students and teachers in terms of curriculum
and instruction. The following year we tried not to have split levels. In the
1992–1993 year, we had:

- Five first grades (three monolingual, two Spanish bilingual).
- Six second grade (four monolingual, two Spanish bilingual).
- Five third grade (three monolingual, two Spanish bilingual).
- Four fourth grades (three monolingual, one bilingual).
- Four fifth grades (three monolingual, one bilingual).
- Four sixth grades (three monolingual, one bilingual).
- Four seventh grades (no bilingual).
- Four eightth grade (bilingual pull-out support).

In the 1993–1994 year, first- and second-grade organization remained the same;
third-grade classes decreased from five teachers to four teachers (three monolingual, one bilingual), and fourth grade increased. This is evident in the following class chart showing the organization of schools within the school:

	Classical Rooms	Environmental Science Room	Journalism Room
4th	1	3(2 bl)	1
5th	1	1	2 (1 bl)
6th	2 (1 bl, 1 mon)	1	1
7th	1	L.5(.5 bl)	1
8th	1	1.5 (.5 bl)	2

Each grade level had a grade-level resource person to support teaching and learning in all activities such as field trips and assemblies. All teachers that were neither grade-level teachers nor resource persons were classified as "special," including special education, art, music, physical education, library, and computer. The teaching staff fluctuated between 59 and 60 persons, with an auxiliary staff of 31 to 32 persons, including security, teacher aides, lunchroom and custodial support.

Standardized scores show no clear pattern of change. However, where there were strong, committed, organized teachers who worked diligently with their colleagues, parents, and resource personnel, there was continuous growth (classical school). Where there was disharmony and a lack of cooperation, collaboration, commitment, and consensus, scores tended to drop. Some dips were also due to teachers who changed grade levels and were not familiar with new forms of teaching.

A Teacher's Perspective

In order to test some of my impressions, I asked the teacher-librarian to comment on her impressions of participants as they appeared before, during, and after my tenure. In addition to being a teacher and librarian, she was on the LSC, had an active role in the school, and was highly respected by school and community. Here are her remarks:

> *The PTA.* During the prior principal's tenure, we had a very viable PTA, which were involved as room mothers, in fund raising, as office help, etc. However, when the principal selected a Black parent as president, dissatisfaction arose and the PTA slowly dismantled. The PTA struggled to remain active during Ms. Hobbs' tenure with a few interested parents. They, too, became disinterested, and after Ms. Hobbs' departure, the PTA became nonexistent .

> *The LSC.* There were certain people who always seem to have a problem or a disagreement about something or somebody. However, these little arguments were never big enough to be considered stumbling blocks. Then the LSC was formed. The principal no longer had the right to come in and make the final decision and squash an argument with the best interest of everyone and the whole school in mind. This little side of power went straight to people's heads. It wasn't long before the whole school was divided and our principal retired. Then we finally chose a new principal (Ms. Hobbs' predecessor). The whole school was so torn apart that no principal could survive with the two sides constantly pulling in opposite directions. The stronger side (not necessarily stronger, just more devious) eventually ran all the opposing parents away. Even those who refused to take sides were forced to leave. With no one left to disagree with them, they began to find fault with the staff. The contract of the principal preceding Ms. Hobbs was up for renewal. The principal decided to stand behind his staff who all backed him 100%.

Unfortunately, they had no power and only two votes. Even the district superintendent couldn't find fault with the prior principal. He even said so to the closed council session where the final vote was taken. It became obvious that the LSC had a hidden agenda. Led by a parent who harbored bad feelings toward the principal dating back to the previous LSIC and PTA, she lead the charge to get rid of the principal. No matter what he suggested or tried to do, he was met with confrontation. The faculty became badly polarized. Finally, the LSC voted to not renew the prior principal's contract. There were a lot of tears and hateful arguments that night. Some staff left.

The smoke had not cleared when Ms. Hobbs took office. The problems that we were having about the time Ms. Hobbs came to us as principal were typical of a lot of Chicago Public Schools [CPS]. Overcrowding, not enough parent involvement, and low income with all the drawbacks that stem from that. We dealt with our problems on a day-to-day basis, one at a time. When Ms. Hobbs assumed the principalship, at first the atmosphere was very cheerful. The chair of the LSC was happy that she had selected a principal who would be at her beck and call. I think she even planned to move a desk into Ms. Hobbs' office! The honeymoon was short-lived. The LSC chair soon found out that she did not have the principal's ear. The final blow came when she lost control of the vote. The problems with the LSC did not just appear out of thin air. This was a council looking for an ax to grind. No one could have come into Field and kept this council happy. I know, because I was a part of it. Certain members used every underhanded trick in the book to make sure they got their way. Small differences of opinion were quickly turned into major grievances. It didn't take Ms. Hobbs long to realize what was going on and refuse to be manipulated. The showdown had begun. And when it was over and Field School had lost Ms. Hobbs, these people went on grinding axes in other places. Before the chair left the LSC, she planted seeds of deception and the council began to voice opposition and dissatisfaction with Ms. Hobbs. A new male community person, a friend of the former LSC chair, came on to the council to continue her fight. When Ms. Hobbs realized that she was not going to accomplish anything because of petty opposition, she opted for early retirement. The council is now in a state of rebuilding.

Faculty. The faculty prior to Ms. Hobbs' tenure had always been very stable. Everyone worked together but without much direction. However, the divisions on the LSC spilled over into the faculty. People took sides, often resulting in not speaking to each other. There was a lot of tension and back-biting. When Ms. Hobbs became principal, it was like a new beginning. Everyone was so tired of the way in which things were going, we greeted her with open arms! Her enthusiasm and cheerfulness caught on like fire! People began to talk to one another again. We listened to her plans in wonderment and thought, "Will we be able to do all of those things?" In October, we went on the first of two weekend retreats. During the workshops, staff relaxed, talked, and listened to each other—something which had not happened in a long time. There was a feeling of excitement which I think filtered down to the students. They seemed to be excited by the curriculum of their schools. After Ms. Hobbs left, we continued to follow the concept of small schools, but there has been no special training for teachers new to the school. Being in the library, I really don't get an opportunity to get involved in their planning . . . although I probably should since the library should be a resource for all of their programs.

Students. During the prior principal's tenure, because there was no general direction, the school just existed day-to-day. The students were involved in the regular school activities. When the prior principal came to Field, we still had a select group of students who were grouped together as gifted students. We also had an options for knowledge program that drew students from other neighborhood schools. However, this program and the cluster for Grades K–3 were declared discriminatory and were discontinued. There did not seem to be much discipline since the prior principal pretty much stayed in his office and did not make his presence felt around the school. During Ms. Hobbs' tenure, as I stated previously, the students seemed to catch excitement from their teachers about their school. Ms. Hobbs began her sweeps every day of the halls and playground after school. In this way, she not only kept abreast of what was going on in the school, both inside and out, but she was also able to forge a bond with the students. Ms. Hobbs enlisted the aid of the Guardian Angels in keeping the playground after school free from trouble. After her leaving, there appeared to be apathy among the majority of the students toward learning. This can be attributed to many factors. I don't know exactly what last year's test scores were, but both IGAP and ITBS (achievement tests) were extremely low.

The Staff and Community. The staff on board under the prior administration were unique because most of them had been in the system for 10 years or more. A majority of their time had been spent at Field. They knew the parents and families of most of the students because the neighborhood was a lot more stable at that time. These teachers called each other by first names, and often went to dinner at each other's houses. They knew each other's husbands and children. Most were Jewish and spent holidays together. Field school was like an extended family. There were no cliques, no ego problems, and plenty of dedication. There is a sharp difference between the students of this earlier administration and those of the following two. Most of the children enrolled at Field during the prior administration were of European ancestry. Most came from two-parent homes and lower-middle-class families. They were born right here in Rogers Park. They knew their neighbors and lived comfortably. They came to school well fed, well dressed, and eager to learn. As hard as I try I can think of no similarities.

A parent who is a long-time resident of the community, has four children in the school, has always been extremely active and involved in the school, and served as LSC chair for 2 years shared her views as follows:

The staff during Ms. Hobbs' term as principal were my favorite for so many reasons. This was the most energetic, motivated, self-starting staff I'd ever seen in any CPS. Their enthusiasm rubbed off on the entire building, and out into the community. It inspired the students to do and be their absolute best and take pride in being a part of Field School. This enthusiasm brought such a change over the whole school, aides, clerks, engineers, that it wasn't long before the parents and the community felt it too. They liked the change in the attitudes of the Field family and all wanted to be part of this winning team. Every day someone was off on some new venture. New programs, grants, and funding enabled anyone with a positive attitude and a plan to see it come true. We all felt like the whole world was watching. And it was, so we all did our absolute best. The community began changing at the same time the administration did. Many students came from lower income families. Most were transients and didn't care much about getting a good education. Some came only for the two meals a day. As the change came, it wasn't long before the student attitudes changed too. There were basketball games, cheerleading squads, and school programs that took the students and staff swimming twice a week. These were real incentives to thrive. Students started paying more attention to their studies because they envied all the attention being lavished on the new achievers. Discipline problems became role models. Achievers became overachievers. This was all because someone took the time to show they cared and taught them to show pride and be confident in all they did in life. It was a great feeling. I was proud to be a part of it.

After Ms. Hobbs' departure, the staff is playing a whole new ball game, these past 3 years at Field. Things have changed so much in the community that it's impossible to teach the way the staff did during the first administration. Only about one third of this staff has been at Field for 5 years or more. Most are sending resumes or inquiring about other positions all year round. Dedication and enthusiasm are low. Because of the changes at the CPS and the position cuts, job security is virtually nonexistent. This keeps everyone paranoid and on the defensive. Union representatives are kept busy with grievances. Many teachers work under a principal they have been to court with. After 3 years many of the staff still don't know each other's first names. Student differences, being in three different buildings doesn't help. It's difficult to work as a team. A lot has to be taken into consideration when you look at the change in the students at Field School. Many are from families supported through the Department of Children and Family Services (DCFS) or live with guardians other than their parents. They don't really make an effort to take advantage of the benefits of getting an education. I can't really say that they are given the incentives to try. The feeling they get now is more of distrust.

I asked some of the older students, "How do you think Field School feels about you and the people in your community?" Of the three most common answers, the first was: "I don't care and they don't care." Some said they feel like "everybody is just waiting for them to make a mistake so that they could get them in trouble." The last common response was that they didn't think "it was fair the same groups of students got special treatment." The staff has voiced the same concern.

In sum, over the past 5 to 7 years the school system has changed, the city has changed. Politics and corruption make it hard for anything run by the city government to thrive or prosper. Now classrooms are seriously overcrowded with very limited supplies to work with because there are almost no funds. At Field a teacher has to be parent, disciplinarian, and educator. The introduction of crack cocaine into the community has devastated it. DCFS has become the family of a lot of the students. Most of the parents that care work hard to move up and out of this community. Everything has changed so much it's impossible for us to come to school with the same attitude that we had 5 or 6 years ago. Today drug and sex education are just as important as history and math. Students today need survival and communication skills as much if not more than science. It's hard to say that one staff is better or worse than the other. If you took the 1986 staff and put them in a 1996 classroom, how long would they last? If you put the 1996 back into 1986, how would they react to students who come to school eager to learn?

Analysis of Leadership

The school and its community faced many of the problems of urban communities. A group of transient residents were replacing a more stable set of community members. As a result, there appeared to be less parental involvement in schools, along with an increasing school population with many new students who were not well prepared. Crime was high in the neighborhood, and the safety was of concern. The case study paints a portrait of a varied set of difficult community-based problems that impacted the school and that needed to be addressed by the principal.

The metaphor that most aptly represents the style of leadership shown by the principal is that of a "missionary" or "savior." This appears to be not only how she saw her own role, but also how she was perceived by teachers and parents. Her mission was to improve the schooling of children in terms of their physical safety, social development, and academic learning. The notion of small schools was an attempt to build on the interests of teachers and to empower them so that they would create learning communities in which children would thrive. Extremely ambitious, the plan required major changes and investments on the part of the teachers. The style of the principal seemed to be collaborative, tempered by expertise. That is, she was resentful of the LSC making decisions for which she believed that they were not qualified. Similarly, she wished to pass instructional and curricular control over to the teachers, but in some cases found them slow to assume responsibility. This form of leadership is informed by a coherent vision and demands considerable social skill in implementation. The principal's decision to not continue her mission appeared to have less to do with the hard conditions of the school and her work with teachers, than with the ongoing tensions in her dealings with the LSC. In the end, because of the LSC power to hire and fire principals, she was not in a position to follow her own guidance.

It is difficult in any case study written mainly from the perspective of three participants (principal, teacher-librarian, and parent) to reconstruct what might have been the perceptions of other participants. Yet, the comments by the teacher-librarian and parent suggest that the view of the principal was more generally accepted. Most clearly, the firing of the former principal after a 3-year term suggests that the LSC did wield power. Legalistic actions on the part of the chair of LSC in terms of contracts and other requests suggests that they did have the power to control the operations of the school. The potential misuse of Chapter I funds suggests either a lack of knowledge or a disregard of program requirements. In any case, the early resignation of the principal prior to consideration of contract renewal suggests that she suspected that her contract would not be renewed.

It is also hard to assess the perspectives of teachers and students, even with the comments from the teacher-librarian and the parent. The fact that the small-schools program built on the interests of teachers suggests their involvement and a responsiveness to their areas of expertise. Moreover, there seemed to be general enthusiasm for the program among many teachers and students. Yet, the plan represents a major departure from existing instructional approaches and this must have added stress to the lives of teachers. Learning to work collaboratively with other teachers and with students is a hard assignment. Such difficulties may well have led to a backlash among teachers that may have influenced the actions of teachers on the LSC.

EXTENDING THINKING

Questions

1. Consider the issues of power that existed between the LSC and their newly hired principal. What were some of the problems that arose immediately? How were these problems dealt with?
2. What steps did Nelda Hobbs take to create a school culture that was good for kids and was responsive to their needs and their safety? Would you consider her a manager or a leader?
3. Field School seemed to be operating without a clear vision. How did their decision for the creation of "small schools" come about and how did the schools work?
4. As the years went by, the principal had a more difficult time working with the LSC. Reflect upon the reasons for the difficulties from the standpoint of the legislation.

Activity

1. This case is a good example of a council or board exercising power because they could and not necessarily for the benefit of the students, and it illustrates the differences in perspective of the various constituencies. Identify an issue in your local school district, and interview a teacher and a parent about the issue and compare their points of view.

CASE 4

Yeah Yeah Boo Boo

Pete Leki
"W" School Local School Council Member,
1991–1996

Background

The "W" Elementary School is a neighborhood school located on the north side of Chicago. There are 650 children from grades pre-K through eighth grade. Eighty-five percent of the children are low income and receive free lunches. Seventy percent are Latino, 18% are European, 5% are African American, and 5% are Asian and mixed heritage, not specified. The diverse nature of the student body makes this a very interesting place to examine. Over the past 15 years, the neighborhood has changed from primarily European heritage to Latino. These factors of diversity have an effect on the implementation of the instructional program and the stability of the faculty.

In addition, this case examines W School during the transition period to site-based management when the principal announces that he is retiring. The process of finding a new principal challenges the council and the faculty to exercise very new powers. The awesome task of finding a new principal creates a tense atmosphere at W and brings to the surface many of the conflicts among the parents and teachers that had been dormant.

This case examines how one newly selected principal enacts leadership. The case calls into question the newly created council's ability to choose a leader. The council went through a very thorough process in attempting to find the right person for their school, and yet the principal that was chosen established his leadership in many unexpected ways. It is interesting to watch the new principal define his role and exercise his leadership style.

This case was written by a parent who was chair of the W Local School Council (LSC). It richly describes a best-case scenario of parent involvement in the democratic process of helping to run their local school. The most interesting aspect of this case is the large role that parents and community members take in gathering the knowledge they needed to do their jobs of writing the school improvement plan and finding a new principal. It seems that this kind of localized democracy is what the writers of the reform legislation envisioned. In this case, it is easy to see what a huge task it was to be a mem-

ber of an LSC and especially to be the chair. This case is notable because Pete, the au-thor, reflects honestly about his thoughts and feelings as he attempts to navigate the uncharted waters of reform.

THE CASE

At fourth grade, Jamal transferred into the local public school for nongifted, nonaccelerated, no-specialty, no-frills kids. W School is a red brick monolith from the first decade of the 20th century. Mr. W died in 1909, and his brethren in the Engineers' Union commissioned a bronze bas-relief of his face surrounded by pipe wrenches, calipers, and hammers that hangs on the entry wall near the office. Mr. S, the principal, walks around and around the school ground, the as-phalt prairie, nervous and bandy-legged. At five 'til he rings the school bell that he carries, like a Salvation Army Santa. The kids line up, boys and girls at sepa-rate entrances.

I went to see Jamal at lunchtime. First day at a tough school. We had worried. He was afraid it was dangerous. Too tough, too much swearing . . . right in front of Mr. S, without rebuke. I rode there on my bike, looking for Jamal. At one end of the schoolyard the pavement gives way to a dirt play lot shaded by giant oaks. There are so many kids. Obsidian black-haired kids. Mossy-cushioned, tousled kids. Round-headed kids and square heads. I ride around looking for a long-legged, silver-head Jamal.

A crowd by the playlot cheers, roars its approval. Then boooos. Two big men are there throwing a ball. "How nice of them to organize a game for the kids at lunch," I think. But I don't see Jamal. YEAH! BOOOO! Kids play soccer. Soft-balls, kickballs, basketballs are flying all around the place, transferring energy. Everywhere the Brownian motion of kids in a playground. But still no Jamal.

YEAH! BOOO! BOOO! YYYYEAH! I go closer. A big, pale man with a close-cropped, shrieking, Biff-type hairdo is yelling: "Hey! Hey! Yoooos kits get back. I tol'yus before. Get back behind dat si'ewalk."

"Mr. . . . Stan' unnerneat' an' tro' stray' up," one wise-guy, smiling boy pleads. The biff-men are throwing a softball at a hornet nest that hangs high, high up the tree. What a good idea!

"Hey I tol'yooos get back. Doze bees are gunna be mad when dey fall." The "bees" are already mad, swarming around the jolted nest. When the ball hits, the kids roar, the bees freak out. When the ball misses, Boooo.

Still no Jamal. There's Jamal! In the middle of the schoolyard sucking on a juice box.

"Hey. Where were ya', Jamal?" Suck. Suck.

"I was looking all over for you."

Suck. Shlooorp. "Went with a friend to Little Caesars. He got a pizza bread."

"Whaaa? Who? What friend? To that Little Caesars on Lawrence? You walked there?"

Suck-suck. Suck. Shlooorp. (YYeah! BOOOO! BOOOO!) "My friend from my class."

"Jamal. Who? I . . . don't know. I think you should stay in the schoolyard. I was looking for you."

Suck. Shlooorp. (Boooo. Boooo) "He didn't have no lunch."

Jamal tells me his friend sits next to him and doesn't like to do schoolwork. He does like tic-tac-toe. But when he's losing he reaches across the aisle to erase Jamal's x's, makes a fuss so the teacher notices and scowls.

The boy says he collects baseball cards. "What's your best card?" Jamal had asked.

"Topps. Bo Jackson. 1991," he answered.

"What's it worth?"

"$300."

Jamal snorted. "No 1991 Topps is worth $300."

Jamal's gonna be okay. But they are doing baby arithmetic in fourth grade. Jamal was accelerated at the magnet school. Now he's decelerating. But he can walk home in 5 minutes. Go out for recess. Play, a lot. He's okay. He leaves me with his collapsed juice box and runs to get in on a basketball game. I ride through the schoolyard. Mr. S rings the bell. BOOO! YEAH! The biff-men are now throwing a baseball bat at the hornet nest. Chunks of paper-hive room additions litter the yard.

Next night Jamal tells his mom what his friend had told him: He'd had a dream. In the dream he and Jamal were brothers. They went home together. They saw their mom.

"Who's mom was it?" Jamal asked. "Yours or mine?"

"Yours."

"Oh, yeah. What did she look like?"

"No. It was my ma." Jamal laughs at this lying boy.

"I knew he was lying when he told me he lives in an apartment, all by himself, right by the L tracks. Then I knew he was lying."

Jamal's gonna be all right. Won't he?

We pulled Jamal out of the magnet school, a school that scored at the top of the city in IGAP and IOWA scores. We enrolled him in our neighborhood public school, W Elementary. We were fed up with the magnet school, an intensive, accelerated traditional school—with the long, slow, smelly bus trip every day; with the months of practicing for IGAPS; with the dilemma of having friends scattered over the crowded breadth of the city.

I made this promise to Jamal: As long as he is at W, I would involve myself in the LSC and try to make the school better. I didn't really believe in or understand Chicago's school reform. I thought it was another sneaky Reagan-era decentralization scheme to isolate people from one another; another way to avoid putting the necessary money into the schools and social services in our collapsing cities; and finally, a way for yuppies to take over their local school, pour in the grant resources and achieve top-quality education without the expense of private school. I saw a lot of bad motives!

But just as we were getting fed up with the magnet school, we were also figuring out our family's life in the city, in what passes for a community. We wanted our kids to go to school with children of different backgrounds. Our local school is integrated and multicultural; a large majority of students are from Spanish-speaking homes. It was close to home. The friends he made would live close by, helping him and us to spin the webs of friendship and neighborliness that might make our community feel more whole. They had recess and open campus, 1-hour lunch—time to run home for real food, or splurge on a slice of Little Caesars pizza.

Earlier in the year Jamal and I had stopped by for an exploratory visit. The principal was polite, but seemed suspicious. We visited Jamal's potential room and teacher. Jamal leafed through the math and reading books and snickered at their remedial level. I spoke to two teachers about our intention to transfer Jamal and they exhaled in a hushed duet: "Don't send him here. Oh, God, don't send him to this school." But we did.

I knew nothing about reform except that there were councils. That people were elected: six parents, two teachers, two community, and the principal. I put my name in and won a seat. I remember our first meeting. Of the six parents, only four showed up to claim their title. Of the two absent parent winners—no one had ever heard of one. The other, Mr. S said, had moved out of the attendance area the week after the election.

We had to elect a president, and, by law, it had to be a parent. It seemed everyone on council was so unassuming and nonaggressive. Nobody wanted to be president. I didn't want to be president. But I did.

We set our regular meeting schedule and one parent, on hearing that we would meet every month, until 9 PM—resigned! "I didn't realize council would involve so much. I got kids! I gotta be home." Three parent vacancies within the first day.

Gary, our Community Rep, and a lawyer by profession, said that part of school reform law required us to receive training by . . . November 1st or something like that. And I thought, "Oh yeah, what'll they do if we don't?" I mean, there was no way to get people off work. There was no stipend or incentive. I didn't know of any resources. I, myself, was working shift work, rotating shifts every week. The whole thing seemed improbable.

We were supposed to learn about the SIP, whatever the hell that was. I found out that the SIP was the school improvement plan, the guide for making things better. I got a copy of the existing document from Mr. S. It was page after page of goals—basic instruction, parent involvement, career training, and so on, written in an awful format and language impossible to understand. And almost each goal had been responded to with the same three words—continue current program.

I really didn't have a clue what to do. But, because I was president, I started to get piles of mail. Dozens and hundreds of fliers and journals and sales pitches and political appeals. Our other community rep, Jerry, did have an idea what was going on. He'd been involved in all sorts of community issues and political struggles. I'd first met him during the first Harold Washington election campaign. We worked our neighborhood together.

We were rudderless, but I remember thinking that everyone was really very kind and interesting and unique. The council's new secretary, a teacher, called me on the phone one night to tell me that she'd been "to the library researching the secretary's job." She wanted to know whether she should sit to my right or left side. Her research revealed that this was a preference deferred to the chair. Hah! what a kick.

Another parent member, Anna, caught my attention right away. She had a wandering eye, a strange eye, following things from behind slightly shaded glasses. This eye was emblematic of Anna's role in the group—perceptive, sharp, all-seeing. A psychic, a teacher, and a reader of cards—Anna reminded us when we were skipping over uncomfortable issues. She was an immigrant from Romania, had been a teacher in Colorado, and had two girls, kids at the school. We fumbled around and got some training and some experience, and time went on and in the spring of that first year through Jerry's energy we brought in a consultant, Keith Packard from the Institute for Cultural Affairs (ICA), to help us produce our first real, inclusive, process-written SIP. We had a couple of open meetings with a dozen and a half parents, a sprinkling of teachers, some neighbors—and we brainstormed and filled out idea cards, and collaborated, and posted the cards on the boards. All the sessions were bilingual, in Spanish and English. Finally, through this elaborate process, we arrived at some kind of live document that at least reflected the hopes and thinking of the people in that room. And we all felt good about it.

A month later our principal told us that he would retire at midcontract, at the end of the spring semester. This was really unwelcome news. Although Mr. S was an assigned principal from pre-reform days, he seemed to me to be enthusiastic about the possibilities opening up. Maybe he saw the work, too. The council has the power to select a new principal, an enormous task for which we were hardly prepared. Our budget was zero. Our staff was zero. Just us.

A sudden fury of teacher interest erupted in the choosing of a "boss." Like someone had pressed the button on a blender, the council got sucked into this business. The assistant principal let me know right away that he was interested in the job. He said something like, "I don't know how you intend to go about it. You can do it the hard way. Or you can do it the easy way." He advised me to simply select him. A vigorous campaign got under way to promote his candidacy and almost as quickly another to stop it. We decided to do it the hard way—a full-fledged national search, through the summer, performed by a LSC subcommittee of six bolstered by an additional teacher representative.

One thing we decided right away was that we had to know more in order to make a decent selection. So we organized a number of learning sessions at the beginning of summer. I invited Anna Bensinger, a Golden Apple teacher from Inter-American Magnet School (a Spanish bilingual school) to my house to tell us about multiculturalism, and abolishing traditional grading, and cooperative learning. . . . She told us so many wonderful things that they were doing, so fine and ennobling. But somehow she ended up in a debate with one of our teachers, the chair of the Professional Personnel Advisory Committee (PPAC), about multiculturalism in general and bilingualism in particular. The PPAC chair saw bilingualism as a threat. The majority of our staff had been at the school for many, many years. They'd watched the ethnicity switch from European to Hispanic. Rumors floated around at school the next week that we were going to turn W into a bilingual school and get rid of all the monolingual teachers.

Ms. Bensinger also offered us parting advice that we ought to investigate something called "whole-language learning," a concept that I hadn't heard before, and our teachers weren't very familiar with. Ms. Bensinger gave me the name of someone from the Center for City Schools at National-Louis University. She said to call them. And we did.

Marilyn Bizar, Professor of Education at National-Louis University, came out to my house and told us the most wonderful story about the way children learn. She told us how quickly and competently kids construct language, its symbols and meaning, from life, from their every experience. And how schools had traditionally interrupted that child-centered, exploratory, self- and community-constructed knowledge, with a compartmentalized memorization of discrete skills rules and phonics and drills—and then were confronted with children who would lag, lose interest, become disorderly and disruptive. Researchers in education had formulated, tested, and proved out a whole revitalized approach to teaching that empowered a child, harnessed their latent need to learn, to integrate, and to apply their knowledge to their life and world.

I was so surprised! What a revelation! Prior to that summer, my vision of "improving" the school mostly involved getting toilet paper and soap in the bathrooms, putting a stop to the yelling at and hitting of kids, a campaign to turn off the TV sets and do some family reading. After talking with Anna and Marilyn, the vision burst with a cascade of new possibilities in reading and writing, math and science and art. What good luck! And it must have impacted on others on the selection committee because from that day on, each prospective principal's attitudes toward whole-language learning became a criteria for evaluating them.

"No Jewish," the teacher told me, standing on my back porch. "You don't want any more Jewish," the husband agreed. "Already too many Jewish . . ."

"The parents don't want a Latino. The Spanish parent [sic]," the teacher told me. "The Spanish parent [sic] want an American."

"Just don't pick a woman," the teacher told me. "No, really," she said. "I've worked for women and for one week outta four they're useless. You just stay outta their way."

The teacher said, "I hope you understand that it is not necessary to hire a Hispanic simply because the population is Hispanic. Do you understand?"

The teacher said, "Let me say this very clearly: The teachers do not want a Hispanic principal."

Maybe 120 resumes were received. We made copies for each member. We looked at them and kept notes. Finally we got together and agreed on this method: Each of us would select and nominate three candidates. Our top three. Each would be discussed and voted on, majority rule. I don't think any of my candidates made it through, although some of my top 10 were accepted when nominated by others. The teachers formed a block sometimes and I mentioned that it would probably be unwise to select any candidate who the teachers were uniformly against. Someone suggested that we ought to interview the assistant principal (AP) as a courtesy. Others disagreed. We decided that anyone who felt strongly about this could use one of their picks to nominate the AP. No one did. We were really getting caught up in all the possibilities offered by the torrent of candidates.

I was proud of our interviews. We would set the dining-room table at my house. Put out buns and jam and coffee. Light from the gangway would flicker through the lace curtains. Leaves of grape ivy glowing green. Even the videotaping was less obnoxious in a home, tucked away in a corner of the room. Our council members arrived fresh, easing into this new role. A little proudly even.

T gave a great interview, I thought. He seemed full of energy, and concern. He handled each council member well, complimenting their contributions and skills and commitment. He lavished praise on our council and SIP, holding it up as the only bilingual SIP he'd ever seen. At his second interview, he told us how moved and excited he was by his first meeting with us: "I got home and my wife was watching the Democratic convention on the TV (we're political junkies, he laughed), and I told her, 'Turn off the set. I have just had the most amazing experience with the W LSC.'" And he went on about how focused we were on teaching and curricular issues, rather than petty squabbles. . . .

I remember thinking, "Oh, listen to him—ingratiating himself with us. Hah!" But it also felt good. It did! We had worked for a hundred hours over the summer, maybe more, on this selection. We had learned about new things in education. We did care. We were focused. We asked him, as we had all candidates, to share with us one self-criticism about his past work. And he said that he needed to listen better to other people, to colleagues, to kids. . . . That he had been told this by his last supervisor and had agreed and had "spent the next year, just listening."

And I thought, "Well, that is one damning, tough self-criticism. Yet kind of a courageous one to share."

He knew everybody, it seemed. Knew all the ropes and connections at the board to win for our school the resources we lacked. He said he was a proponent of essential schools, which included much of the theory of whole language. Finally, we asked him about first steps, the pace of change. "The first thing to do is secure the school, physically. To make sure it is safe for the kids and the staff. That's first. You will see dramatic change within 1 week."

Our eyes met across the table, dancing, like we'd just won some prize that we didn't expect or . . . maybe even deserve. This is the guy we've been waiting for. Dramatic change in a week!

"He's a power freak," Anna told me. We were walking toward a small park in the neighborhood. I had Eli in a baby buggy and we were heading for some swings. Anna said she read T as power hungry and ambitious. "And I say 'right on.' If he sees this as one step for him on his trip up to the top, more power to him. We can all be successful. But it's dangerous, too. Anyway, I read his cards," she said. "He came up riding a horse. He's got it. We'll see what he does."

We signed the contract at my house on a Sunday morning, everyone dressed nice and fresh. Rolando filling the house with the antiseptic musk of his Aqua Velva aftershave. We breathed deeply and were relieved to be finished. We sat around my dining-room table with platters of pan dulce, jams, fruit, and pots of steaming coffee.

Anna spoke. She said she looked forward to visiting classrooms during the school year.

"I will not allow that," T barked. Our eyes collided all around the table.

"I don't get you." Anna stared at him like a crow.

"I will not permit anyone into those classrooms. I am the principal and that is my responsibility." He paused and we all held our breath, wondering what was happening. "I say this very sincerely," T continued. "I will not have council members evaluating my teachers."

Anna says, "I am not talking about evaluating anyone. I am friends with many of our teachers. I have kids in this school. I am interested. . . ."

"No. We have to make this very clear. I will not have . . ."

"This is bullshit . . ." someone muttered. Cups clattered.

"It is very important that teachers not be interrupted or interfered with in their work. Whatever went on in the past is over with. I am the principal and I evaluate our teachers."

Aqua Velva silence held the group and someone suggested that we take a break. In the kitchen Nancy says, "Uh-oh, did we screw up hiring this guy, or what?" I explained the exchange to my wife. And she could see his point, that teachers need to be respected in their work, and perhaps T was talking about uninvited, unannounced interruptions.

Back at the table T relented. Of course, if arrangements were made, parents and volunteers would be welcomed. But the group felt like we'd been whopped by a mallet blow to the head. Reeling. What was that?

I hosted a reception for T at my home a few evenings later. He brought his son and his wife. We toasted champagne to our future hopes, and talked and laughed and tried to relax.

I introduced T to staff, the day before school opened. He told them that he had been hired to make change, to renew and improve W School:

> I invite each and every one of you to be part of this process. Many of you have been at W for a long time. The thought of change might make you a little nervous, but I want you to know that there is a place for you in this process. And what's more, you are important. Our kids need a sense of continuity. They need to see familiar faces, stability.

> You know, I left my last school in a rush to get here. I didn't even have time to say goodbye to my colleagues. But I did take time to call each and every one of my stu-

dents to let them know that I wouldn't be there, and why. To let them know what was happening. Because I think that is important. Kids count on us. How they feel matters.

What a great story, I thought.
T continued:

I also want to tell you that starting today this school will no longer practice homogenous, ability-based grouping of children. All your students have been mixed heterogeneously. And starting tomorrow, boys and girls will enter together, not at separate entrances. You will meet your classes at . . .

Hey, hey. That's how easy it is to change. Important change on the first day!

At our first council meeting with T, we had a good turnout. Maybe 50 people in our library. We had always run these meetings as community councils. Everyone spoke and participated as they saw fit. I don't remember what it was about but T took this opportunity to lay into one of the teachers who said something he didn't like. It really set the tone. To speak up at these meetings was going to be a high-risk thing.

At the next monthly meeting, a parent brought in a complaint about the way some issue was handled at the school. The molesting janitor issue. This parent got up with quavering voice to make her point. T, barely able to wait his turn, informed her that in fact everything had been handled perfectly (by him). Everything was done exactly right. And further that he deeply resented her coming to council with such input when his door is always open.

T told me and maybe others that, in his opinion, LSCs should be run like boards of directors. That allowing non-LSC members equal participation diminished the authority of official LSC members. That because time was always a big constraint, we should allow only LSC members to speak, except during specially allotted times during each meeting.

He had got me again. In a way what he had said made sense. We did have people showing up to council who gabbed noisily on every issue while less aggressive council members sat silent. There was something to the idea of upgrading the seriousness and authority of the LSC position by favoring LSC members' participation. But there was also a nagging feeling that we were closing out unwelcome voices.

The LSC rejected the idea of codifying member-only participation. But T's outbursts affected the change anyway. Soon few persons outside the council attended meetings. We had it all to ourselves. I didn't know what to do when T blew up, when he hounded or harassed someone. I watched dumbly, too slow to act. I thought too slowly to judge whether he really had a point, even if it was badly made. I'd mull it over for 2 days at my work. And then it was too late to make a difference, to intercede. In this way we slowly poisoned the spirit of our council. Anna and Jerry wilted under the dosage. Others slowly peeled away. I gave myself the private name "Slo."

T was talking to me about those few staff members who weren't on his side. "We have achieved excellence in teaching in 95% of our staff. It's just a couple of teachers who aren't making it." He asked one guy, a reading resource person who had been at the school for 30 years, to return to a classroom to help reduce class size at the fourth grade.

T tells me this teacher warned him that if he has to teach a full class again, he's gone, outta there. He would retire. T said, "I'll help plan your retirement party." Hah. And I'll be there too, I told T. One more obstacle overcome!

After the holidays we were finally ready to "begin" staff development. We had a whole free day, marking day, to work on it. T brought in a team from the Chicago Teachers Center (NEIU), including Heather Pathe and Noreen Moran. The whole staff assembled in the library. I don't know how they felt about it, but I was very excited.

Heather began. I sat at a back table, irritated at several teachers who jabbered on under breath, behind their hands, at the table in front of mine, chuckling and paying no attention. Heather went on about her background in social psychology and education. Then she told about the teacher's center on Halsted Street and how it was full of resource materials and equipment. She invited teachers to visit. Then she asked staff to think about the kind of professional development help that they might need. The teacher next to me, Mr. Z, was an old-timer. He kept muttering quips and gripes. Finally Heather paused and said: "I'm sensing some discomfort in the room. Like we're not all focused on this task, on what I'm saying. Is there something going on that needs to be talked about?"

Mr. Z spoke up, "Frankly, I'm thinking about report cards. I'm wondering how I'm going to get my report cards finished . . ." There was some tittering and mumbling of agreement.

"Are other people feeling a real . . . pressure to work on report cards . . ."

"Yes, yes," the chorus grew as people sensed an escape route opening.

"Maybe what we ought to do is spend the morning working on report cards or whatever else you have to do in your rooms, and get back together after lunch? How does that sound?"

Before the group bolted, T jumped up and said:

Just a minute. Wait a minute. Who is feeling pressure about getting report cards done? Who? Who are you feeling this pressure from? Because it's not from me. You gotta realize that this is important. We are paying for these consultants to come here because we need their help. Folks, we are gonna have to admit that we have failed as teachers. That we're not succeeding with our kids, and not keeping up with our profession. I say this in all sincerity. We have to admit these things if we're ever gonna change.

If you feel pressure to get report cards done, then let's forget the report cards. I'll tell you right now as principal. If you feel pressure about getting your report cards done today, forget them. This is school reform. We decide what has to be done. We don't have to have report cards ready for Friday. We can wait till next week, or next quarter. That's not nearly as important as what we're doing here. So, anyone feeling pressure, just forget report cards.

"Wow," Heather said. "Let me tell you, you won't often find a principal willing to take that position."

T continued, "This is school reform, folks. This is serious. We can decide what we want to do." Heather divided us into groups to meet and brainstorm about what kinds of help we needed in the different grade levels. I tagged along with the upper grades on the third floor. I sat very quietly, intending to observe, only. Mr. Z, who'd sat next to me in the library, unofficially chaired the meeting. He started off by saying, "I hope we all . . . duuuu-ly noted . . . allll the [quoting gesture] buzzzz-words." He chuckled.

"Oh yeah," someone else joined in, "you gottta have the buzz words."

"Thirty years. They always have new ones. I thought I heard them all." And on and on for some minutes.

So what are we gonna do?

What do they want us to do?

Eat lunch!

I brought mine.

Where are you going?

I thought we were gonna go to that Greek place on Lincoln.

I'll go. I didn't bring anything.

Where is Angela? She wanted to go.

She must be with the primary group.

Where are they?

Buzz words.

112, I think. I think that lady is in there.

Cooperative learning!

I need to get something to drink.

Tracking!

I brought my lunch but I wouldn't mind going out for a drink.

What did she want us to do?

Yeah. We're supposed to say something when we get back.

What about that Mexican place, on Western. Has anyone gone there?

Do they serve drinks?

They want us to visit that "teacher's center."

I heard they had a laminating machine.

When are we supposed to go there? We don't have another in-service day until June. I can't eat Mexican. Not at lunch.

So, next in-service let them set up a field trip, a bus to visit this place.

She said they had a laminating machine.

So we can see the laminating machine.

I'm gonna see if Judie wants to go for Mexican foods, she loves . . .

This is what is so silly. If they want us to go there they should give us lunch.

Okay, that's what we'll say. Next in-service we'll visit this place in the morning, see this laminating machine, and then go out for lunch.

I think there's a lunchroom there.

It's just a vending room, I went there last year one time.

The AP entered the room, sagging, clipboard in hand, taking attendance, sour. "He wants to know who's in each group."

Someone whispered, "Somebody should go get Carol or she's gonna get marked absent." She spoke loud to the AP, "Mr. S . . . Carol just stepped out for a minute. Make sure you mark her down."

"So are you getting anything done in here?"

"Oh yes," Mr. Z, chipped in, in his usual good humor. "We're gonna take a field trip to this place they have . . .

"Fluff," S spit out. "All this is fluff, waste of time." He walked out. Everybody looked at each other. Then giggled and relaxed.

So what did we decide?

Mexican or Greek?

I can't eat Mexican at lunch.

New school year. September 1993. I was talking to T about Jamal. About how dismal his school day was. I mentioned to him how Jamal hated rote work, like copying of spelling words 20 times each, and copying the exact definition from a dictionary. T called to his assistant, Ms. R, from his desk, "Ms. R! Ms. R!" No answer. "H. H!" He bellowed like a cow.

Someone peeks in. "Yes?"

"Find Ms. R and have her see me."

A moment later Ms. R arrived. "Ms. R, prepare a memo that teachers are not to have their students copying spelling words or definitions. Spelling should be done in context."

Another improvement. Just like that!?

T told me, "I can say that at this point that 95% of the teachers are with me, are superior. Only two, three, maybe four who are still a problem."

I was never comfortable as chairperson of council in my dealings with the principal. I was always astounded, dumbfounded by things he would say and do. And usually, lacking a better response, I sat stunned. Like something was wrong with my head. At best I would tell T, "I have to think about these things."

I tried to prepare myself for our private meetings—with lists of issues, things I for sure wanted answers on. But T baffled me with his flooding words, his indignation, his side stories, distractions. I just didn't enjoy it. And I was so slow to respond. So retarded. This was not a satisfying way for me to interact with the school.

I was interested in science, the land, the river, the neighborhood. I'd learned that real-life explorations of these things made for good educational practice. I thought I could put our school in contact with neighborhood folk, environmental advocacy groups, agencies. I suggested this to T and he said, "Yes. Yes."

I organized an environmental education resource fair at the school. I brought in the Sierra Club, Friends of the Chicago River, the principal of the local, ecologically focused high school, and the Nature Conservancy. It was a 3-day, after-school offering up of resources for study of our local ecosystems, prairies, savannas, river, water and sewers, recycling, camping. It didn't go very well. Four teachers signed up for the Nature Conservancy's Mighty Acorn program. But no one bit on river studies, camping, the rest. I hoped that it would take hold over time.

I had just been accepted into a program at Northeastern Illinois University to finish up (after a 20-year pause) a bachelor's degree based on an independent course of study of ecology, education, and neighborhood. As part of that, I offered to lead a writing project for seventh-graders at W based on their experiences on our local Chicago River, or rivers of their homelands.

I worked with the language arts teacher, M, of our newly founded middle school. It was an attempt to try out and model process-writing techniques, things that I'd read about in Nancy Atwell's *In the Middle,* and from my sister Ilona and my wife Debbie, both English teachers.

We brainstormed our prior knowledge of and experiences on the river. I had students fill out little index cards to suggest some initial approaches to the topic. I met and conferenced with each student over a number of weeks. We visited the river. We interviewed parents and relatives about river experiences and

---

Haybanda, A Furious River
(Batangue Lobo, Phillipines)

by Beu Love L. Batayola

Haybanga River, the people call it, because it descends from a high place. It is located between high mountains. This mountain river reaches to our wavy sea. This connection makes it rich, a source of income to the people because of the multitude of fishes. It is, however, dangerous also. If somebody is being drifted by its strong current from the mountain and was brought to the sea the percentage of survival is very slim. Sharks and fishes are already waiting for their sure prey whether they are humans or animals.

FIG. 1. Excerpt from student work included in the Sipi book.

memories. Finally we published a volume of river stories titled "Sipi," after the Algonkian word for river (see Fig. 4.1). I got help from the Chicago Teacher's Center (they have more than just laminating machines!) in publishing a book. They provided a computer desk-top publishing expert, Bill Campillo, and duplicating facilities for a 200-copy run.

It was a beautiful book and really helped to draw attention to our school, bring in partners and resources. The Chicago Academy of Science invited me to be part of a leadership group on watershed studies. The owners of the Chicago River Channel, the Metropolitan Water Reclamation District, expressed interest in partnering with our school, and republished a thousand copies of "Sipi." The Ravenswood Historical Archives made itself accessible to our students. It involved me with a whole network of environmental educators on the edge of a movement for hands-on, land- (place) based science and social studies.

Blown-up copies of "Sipi" were displayed at the CPS superintendent's office at Pershing Road as a sample of the things going on at W.

But inside the school I felt a strange vacuum of disinterest, ambivalence toward environmental education. Maybe I feel too much, count too much on impressions during my frequent short visits.

During that summer the Chicago Academy of Science ran a 3-day seminar for teachers on river studies. I had a hard time to find any interested teacher at W. Finally Ms. Q, a young, 1st-year teacher volunteered. The next spring Ms. Q and I teamed up, with a grant from the Chicago Community Trust and Friends of the Chicago River, to do a unit on the Chicago River and riverbank ecology with her sixth-grade class.

The students learned to key-out plants, analyze habitat, select appropriate native plants, and participate in the restoration of a section of riverbank in our neighborhood. They also helped create a savanna garden in the schoolyard to serve as a seed bank for future projects. The kids visited flood plain slopes in the local forest preserve and toured the river on a boat, courtesy of our partners at the Metropolitan Water Reclamation District. Neighbors and school kids worked shoulder to shoulder. It became a great source of pride in the neighborhood. We received a national award for river education from the American Rivers Association for our work.

These projects were so delightful for me—to work closely with students and teachers and neighbors, to create, restore—to leave things better than they were. It was a relief from the school governance agenda. But I think that maybe the whole environmental program, like the whole-language, best-practice approach to education that the council had committed to, was hobbled at the start by the fact that they were parent and administration initiated, rather than originating with our teachers—the main day-to-day practitioners. Only a few of the most open-minded or young novice teachers were willing to open their doors to this educational vision.

Maybe a different principal, or council, or set of teachers could have avoided the hurts and distrusts and realized all the potentials available. But I felt that we had really picked a special and peculiar individual in T, someone who was allergic to process—he squirmed away from and bucked off all the consensus strategies and participatory processes that we as a council craved—all the techniques that have become popular for inviting all constituencies into a process.

T wanted support from the council and loyalty from staff. He said we owed him our trust. He needed it to do his job. But for me it was very unsatisfying.

As chair I thought it was my job to stay accessible to everyone. So I found myself unwilling to build a challenge to T's autocracy. The burden of demanding real dialogue and accountability fell on Anna and Jerry, and later, on new members.

Many more interesting things happened over the next few years. But so much is personal or confidential, it doesn't seem right to put it down here. In short, Jamal graduated. T was rehired for another term as principal with strong teacher and parent support. After Jamal enrolled in the Best Practice High School, I resigned from the council and worked as a volunteer in the garden ecology program. I organize parents to help in classrooms and on field trips. Our school looks more and more beautiful. It is covered with student-made murals, full of computers, and small-group work is the normal thing. The bathrooms are clean. The garden is planted in abundance and diversity, an oasis in the center of the city. Kids, whose little hands I held in the woods on the Mighty Acorn field trips, wave to me—young women and men making their way in the world.

Epilogue.   T is still the principal at W School. Things are going very well, and most of the teachers who have remained and those that have been newly hired share a vision for student-centered instruction. Since 1995, the reading, writing, and math IGAP test scores in Grades 3, 6, and 8 have increased and are well above the CPS average.

Analysis of Leadership

This case takes the reader through the 1st year of reform as a very committed council organizes, and is forced into exercising their most important power, that of finding and hiring a new principal. When the principal announces that he is going to leave, the school community is thrown into a chaotic situation just at a time when they are figuring out and defining their new roles. In reading this case, it is obvious that the council was attempting to do the best job that they could, and they were bombarded with pressures from many different factions. It sometimes seems that many of the participants lose the focus on the children in their effort to satisfy all factions of the community.

The new principal of W School was very adept at talking the language of reform, but he felt more comfortable operating in an authoritarian style. He was hired by the council to be the leader of the reform effort at W School, and on the day that he was offered the position, he issued an edict that parents and visitors were not welcome in classrooms. His work with the council was of a top-down nature, not trusting the council to contribute to the running of the school. Instead, he seemed to feel threatened when he was not completely in charge. He was a school manager with the personal charisma to be a leader. The culture of the school was in dire need of focus on the central importance of students and the establishment of norms that placed high value on teaching and learning. T came to W with an ambitious plan that has taken a great deal of time to implement.

It was interesting that teacher and community support for him and his programs increased at the time that he went up for reelection. Pete speculates that perhaps he campaigned for his job or that people were uncomfortable with starting over with someone new and unknown. Nevertheless, as Pete noted, "I think that there is something inherent in the nature of the Principal's position in the Chicago Public Schools in Daley's Chicago—something that causes them to act so crazily. It is a very, very hard job. We ought to say this."

In the area of curriculum and instruction, Pete worked vigorously with children and with teachers to create an integrated science curriculum that was infused with hands-on experiences and opportunities for real reading and writing. The experience was an excellent one, but it is only now being taken over by the teachers. This attempt at curriculum reform was hampered by the fact that it was driven by a parent and administrator, and that the teachers were not the originators of the plan.

EXTENDING THINKING

Questions

1. The LSC at W took their leadership roles very seriously. How did they handle the important task of choosing a new principal? What were some of the characteristics they were looking for in a new principal? What were some of the challenges they encountered?
2. The legislation places the job of hiring and firing the school principal in the hands of the LSCs. Consider the implications of this power from the perspectives of the council, the teachers, the parents, and the principal applicants.
3. Reflect upon the professional development event described in this case. What was happening? Who was in control? What about shared decision making?
4. The author of this case, Pete Leki, who was the chair of the council at the time of the principal selection, reflects upon his role and what he could have done to improve the process. Can a parent assume a leadership role without the sanction of the principal? What are your impressions of his role and how he handled it?

Activity

1. A site-based management school operates very differently than one where the principal operates in a strictly top-down manner and where roles distinctions are very specific. Make a list of all of the skills and personality characteristics a leader willing to share power should have. Think about your own style, as a teacher or as an administrator, in terms of management versus leadership.

Reflection on Cases 3 and 4

The story of Field School reveals the power of a committed principal to change the way business is done in a school in fairly substantial ways. With enormous energy and missionary zeal, the new principal sets about to ensure the safety of the students at Field School and to develop a challenging and engaging instructional program. With the support of the Local School Council (LSC) and the faculty, she oversaw a massive internal reorganization in which small schools within the school were created.

In the process, she empowered teachers, based on their knowledge and interests, to create new programs for students. The first group to form, classical, were also the most successful in transforming their instruction. Journalism and environmental science came next. Apparently the least successful were the eighth-grade teachers forming the high school prep who were later divided among the other three schools. The foundations school, which initially included teachers from Headstart and kindergarten to third grade, later became reorganized based on classroom location, with the third-grade teachers in the main building splitting off from the others in the annex. As part of the plan, teachers within the same small schools had special time to plan.

The different ways in which teachers responded to this radical change gives some insight in to the difficulties inherent in tapping the energy and imagination of teachers. The reflections of the principal describe the teaching force as changing from a highly stable and cohesive group before the neighborhood changed in composition, to a less cohesive one during the principal's tenure because it included many who were unable to move as well as many new teachers. She notes that given the small schools and their new curricula, the achievement of students stayed at a low level. Still, she remarks that there was variation among teachers that covaried with the quality of their instruction. That the small schools proved to be a viable structure is suggested by their continuation after the principal's departure.

Both the principal and the librarian-teacher paint a picture of the principal as having won the respect and trust of parents in the community. It is suggested that some parents on the LSC were diverted from pursuing topics of interest because of the control that the chair of the LSC exercised. The constant tensions from working with the LSC and the likelihood that her contract would not be renewed by the LSC led to the principal's resignation and early retirement. In a sense, this is an incomplete story because she avoided the tensions inherent in seeking contract renewal. Perhaps the school community, sensing positive changes in the school, may have brought pressure on the LSC. Nevertheless, the picture painted of the chair of the LSC is not one of a person enlightened and informed about education. To the contrary, there is suggestion of self-interest and corruption through the misuse of funds.

In her case study, the principal pursues the question of whether people without citizenship, and with limited education and understanding of the complex issues facing schools should have decision-making rather than advisory influence in the running of schools. She is most concerned about groups of community members who seem to be unresponsive to the goal of improving the learning of children. Should the LSC have the power to hire and fire the principal, or should the contribution of parents and community members be advisory in form?

The case of W School offers a contrasting situation in which parents and other LSC members from the community were committed to improving the instruction and learning of their children. The LSC, taking their responsibility of hiring a qualified principal seriously, became informed about what constitutes good instructional practice. Given a thorough and time-consuming process, the LSC made its choice. But the new principal's leadership in the school ran counter to what some on the LSC had hoped for. Though giving lip service to democratic forms of leadership, he assumed an authoritarian role in relation to the LSC and the teachers. All candid conversations, particularly those involving criticism of how the school was being run, were silenced by him. Though he seemed to support the use of constructive instructional procedures and teacher involvement in in-service activities, teachers got the message that business would be done as usual, as long as they acknowledged that the principal was in charge.

The LSC chair's heavy investment in reforming science instruction raises another set of issues. Teachers, probably with the support of the principal, did not respond to the opportunities that the LSC chair made available though his network of environmental educators. Indeed, only a 1st-year teacher responded to his invitation to undertake a collaborative project. Highly informed parents may pose special threats to teachers, both in terms of challenging teacher competence and in providing competing sources of leadership. This may explain why the principal, through such actions as keeping parents from going into classrooms, maintained his own control and won the support of teachers in W School.

Reflecting back on earlier cases, similar sets of dynamics are shown in the cases of Jackson and Field Schools. Considerable skepticism was expressed by the teachers and principals about the contributions that parents with limited education could make. The views seemed to range from parents having no expertise that would be relevant to parents having an advisory role. In contrast, the parents in Saucedo Academy, with the support of the principal, seem to have developed open communication with school personnel that helped in solving problems and in enhancing the programs of the schools.

As discussed in the first section, the initial reform legislation gave new powers particularly to principals and the LSC. The way in which leadership would evolve in particular schools could not be predicted. Among possibilities, we suggested that principals might continue to exercise control as they had prior to reform. This turned out to be what occurred in Jackson School. A more complex and acrimonious set of relations developed in the cases just presented. The LSC, through its power to hire and fire principals, seemed to gain an upper hand in Field School. Unexpectedly, given the preparation of the LSC in W School, the new principal once hired was able to gain control, develop a coalition with teachers, and to defuse the power of the LSC.

The reformers also believed that the structural changes of reform would alter the culture of schools, their instructional environments, and ultimately the learning of students. The lesson of these two cases, as well as the two preceding ones, seems to be that if changes are to be made in instruction, they need to be initiated and supported by the principal. Moreover, they take a long time to become adopted by teachers and even longer to effect student achievement.

SECTION 4

Reform as an Opportunity for Creating Responsive Instruction

We have paired the fifth and sixth cases because they provide good examples of schools where teachers and administrators viewed reform as an opportunity for implementing instructional change that could impact the lives of students. In the fifth case, Madeleine Maraldi, the principal of Washington Irving School, oversaw a move to a new school and was the driving force in transforming a low-achieving school into one with a quality educational program for all children. Discussions about the instructional program, including how and what students should learn, permeated the texture of daily life. The reform was seen as a means of creating opportunities, such as the hiring of new teachers and making discretionary money available.

The sixth case focuses on Anzaldúa School, an overcrowded school located in a predominantly Latino neighborhood in Chicago. Here, teachers and parents used the power they gained from the reform legislation to bring about change in the leadership of the school and its instructional program. Anzaldúa had been the site of constant internal struggle between a more traditional group of monolingual teachers and a small group of predominantly bilingual teachers who felt silenced in discussions of how and what to teach an increasingly Latino student body. Reform provided the opportunity for teachers, with the support of parents, to question the status quo and challenge it. In this case, the struggle over issues of leadership and authority in this school is closely linked to a struggle over ideas about education.

In both of these cases, the culture of the schools was changed. At Irving, Maraldi made a concerted effort to build a professional community among teachers—teachers who had not been part of one in the past. This change in norms and expectations was crucial in opening the school to ideas about responsive instruction. At Anzaldúa, a chain of events occurred, leading to radical change in the organization and culture of the school. Teachers gained the power to develop instruction that was responsive to the needs of children from a changing community.

CASE 5

Washington Irving School:
Its Development
and Change

Madeleine Maraldi
Washington Irving School

Background

Washington Irving School is located on the near west side of Chicago in the shadow of the Cook County Hospital and the Juvenile Detention Center. Madeleine Maraldi has been the principal for 11 years since the reform legislation was passed and since the school was moved from its old school into a new building. Although the student body remains a 50/50 balance of African and Latino Americans, this is a neighborhood that is slowly gentrifying, leading to a new set of issues including the loss of some discretionary funds, as the poverty level decreases from 90% to 86% over the last few years.

Over the past 11 years, the test scores at Irving have steadily risen, although Madeleine has never focused on test scores. What she did focus on was teacher growth and development. At Irving, the teachers have experienced many ongoing opportunities for professional growth, and have worked together to develop and implement a challenging curriculum for all students. The perspective revealed in this interview is that of Madeleine Maraldi, principal of Washington Irving School, as told to Rebecca Barr from National-Louis University.

THE CASE

RB: Madeleine, how would you describe your experiences over the past few years in the context of the Chicago school reform? Talk about the opportunities it made available, as well as the problems it created.

MM: The reform bill, the legislation, was signed by the governor at Irving School on the day we opened the new building on December 12, 1988. I had been assigned as interim principal in September 1988, 3 months before the signing of the bill. Since the principal of Irving was on sick leave, they needed someone to move everything from the old building to the new building, and I got the job. About a month before the time when everything had to be in order, someone said, "Oh, the day you open, the governor is going to sign the reform bill at Irving School. The mayor is going to be there and the superintendent of schools as well!"

RB: Sounds really overwhelming! Had you been an administrator before?

MM: I started teaching in 1961. I went out on maternity leave in 1974, and I stayed out for 3½ years. I chose to return in September 1978, the year that they integrated teachers in order to racially balance the faculties in each school. Previously I had been teaching in my own neighborhood, but my new school was on the south side near the Robert Taylor homes. I spent a year there and interviewed for a job that was two blocks away in a brand-new school called Beasley Academic Center. During that year before going to Beasley, I watched the opening of Beasley. I was able to observe what the principal was doing, how he was selecting staff, how he was ordering materials, and so on.

Five years later, a district superintendent asked for my help in converting Harrison High School to an elementary school. I got in on the ground floor, again observing and this time helping a new school to open.

I then went to the district office and worked there for a year. Next there was a job opening in a west-side district where I interviewed for a math coordinator position; I worked there for 3 years when the opportunity at Irving School opened up. The district superintendent asked me to be interviewed by the chairperson of the Local School Improvement Council (LSIC). The LSIC signed off on accepting me as the interim principal with the task of opening up the new building.

RB: You were well prepared, but you had more than knowledge about what to do, you had a vision for the school. Would you talk about that?

MM: The district superintendent encouraged me to take the principal's examination. The exam was about how you deal with the public, how you work with the board of education, the policies and procedures, the state law, the school code, and the legalities of supervision. But there wasn't much on curriculum and the teaching/learning process and how you improve a school that's not doing well. If your goal is to change what happens inside each classroom and to improve student achievement, the exam does not reflect those goals. Many principals come to the job pretty well prepared to be administrators, but many are not prepared to be educational leaders.

I think you get that preparation as a teacher. You need to know the curriculum, you need to know how children learn, and you need to have an extensive repertoire of teaching strategies that address how to provide opportunities for children to learn in different ways. Most teachers fall back on their own experiences as students. They go on as if nothing has ever changed, and they teach exactly the way they were taught when they were in elementary school. If you don't have the will and desire to read the current research, to actually study on your own, then you kind of teach in that one way that doesn't reflect all that we have learned about best practice in teaching.

When you become an administrator, what ideas will you have? What visions will enable you to look at your school critically to see what is needed. If children are not learning, you, along with your teachers, need to construct a vision for how to make things better

RB: Take me back to that first year at Irving. You were really busy thinking about the transition; what else was going on?

MM: Before the move I talked with teachers about their vision for the new building. The former principal had a year to work on these things. She gave faculty opportunities to order materials with the money that was provided for the opening of the new building. There was a science lab, and those materials were ordered. There was also a room that had outlets in the floor, and the board was going to give us an opportunity to order 30 computers for that room. So I sat down with people who just volunteered to sit down with me—we called ourselves the Wednesday Morning Group. I asked that the group be representative of the different sections of the school—primary, middle school, junior high school, special education people, and career service staff. We met and we talked and I said, "We've got this science lab and we've got this computer lab. Maybe we should think about how to use this computer lab." I asked, "In what subject are students doing badly?" Most responses were, "Well, everything is pretty bad because the scores are low in all the areas." I said, "Well, we can't work on everything at once." The teachers said, "I guess it's writing. They don't know how to write. They don't like to write. Writing is hard to grade. There's a lot to keep up with so we don't do a lot of writing."

So I asked, "How about using this computer lab as a writing lab. Let's not call it computer, let's call it writing. And let's send kids in there with you, so you can learn, and you can become computer literate. It'll take some time, but we can all learn how to be computer literate people." So it was kind of a consensus.

I'm a math person, and I was glad they chose language arts because I believe that first children have to know how to read and write. Reading and writing involve thinking and listening and speaking and all of those essential skills that many middle- and upper- class students come to school with, and that our children do not. They come with limited skills in those areas, so the language arts program had better be solid before you begin to do anything else because everything else flows from language arts.

I told the teachers that we were going to receive 30 computers for our new writing lab, and I asked if anyone would like to entertain taking that job.

One person applied, Pat Mark. She gave me her resume and asked to be interviewed for the job. She told me that her background was in literature and she loved to write and loved to read. She said she was a lover of the written word and thought she could do this even though she didn't know a thing about computers.

I was pleased because I wasn't hiring a computer person. I was hiring a writing teacher. I didn't advertise outside or interview anyone else. I just said I'm going with Pat Mark. And so we decided on that before we moved to the new building.

And then I asked them, "What is your worst subject to teach?" The consensus was science. They did not like to teach science. They were two pages in the textbook ahead of the children. Their repertoires of experiments were limited for that grade level, and they did their one or two best shots at giving this good lab period to their students and that was it for the year. So, I said, "Well, this is fortuitous because we've got this new science lab, so what if we use the same procedure? We have a master teacher, you accompany your students to the lab, and you begin to understand science as it's taught by a master teacher."

So we had a plan to begin to work on writing, computer literacy, and science that we began to implement. It took us a while to open those labs. We moved in December, and Christmas break was the next week. When we returned in January we really got started, and the materials and equipment began to come in for the labs. Once we got everything set up, it was March before we really started sending teachers and their students to the labs. These three changes actually emerged naturally from my talks with teachers.

RB: Did you have a science teacher then too?

MM: No. I interviewed and was very lucky to get Dennis Dandeles, who is such a hard-working gentleman, and has earned the most wonderful credibility with the staff. It's a very ticklish situation in schools to hire what teachers call "resource teachers," because teachers who have full classes of children and are responsible for their academic achievement resent resource teachers who they feel get away without bottom line accountability. You know, "The kids go to the special class and they come back but who's really responsible? I am. I'm the homeroom teacher." These resource teachers need to be outstanding people who not only can perform as master teachers in their laboratories, but also can help teachers with the transition work in their classrooms, preparing materials for them, getting supplies for them. They need to work 150% of the time to actually earn credibility. Otherwise there's a high level of resentment that this person has really got a cushy job. If resource people don't have credibility, then most teachers don't learn from them. They dismiss them.

RB: Really a tricky balance. So the first year was really a busy one.

MM: Yes, the move, setting up the labs, hiring some new teachers, and trying to figure out how to approach working on being better teachers in the classrooms. I think it was near the end of that year that we had to write a school improvement plan. We selected three very simple goals; all had to do with people. Our whole school improvement plan was people development. So we called it staff development, student development, and parent development. Our three goals focused us, as a parent or a student or a teacher, on being the very best that we could be. And we were going to use whatever resources were out there to read, to discuss, to debate, to monitor what we were doing, to evaluate what we were doing, and always with the goal of becoming better at what we were doing.

RB: And were parents and students involved in this, or was this mainly a teacher thing?

MM: At first parents really weren't, but students were involved because we were watching their reaction to these new laboratories. I remember one anecdote. Along with the writing lab and the science lab, we developed a reading program that involved sustained silent reading. Because we had some discretionary money, I said to teachers, "I would like to offer, on a voluntary basis, a free bus and field trips to a bookstore of your choice so that you can ask your children to browse the shelves and select a book. I want you to begin building some classroom libraries and give your children a 30- to 40-minute period each day where they can simply sit and read books of choice."

The junior high teachers were very enthusiastic and they started the sustained silent reading program. We were trying to watch student reactions to these different new programs, and one day this student came into Pat Mark's writing lab and said, "Why are you doing this to me?"

And she said, "What's the matter?"

"Oh! This is terrible! It's painful!"

And she said, "Oh! Are you sick?"

He said, "No, I'm not sick. You're making me read for 50 minutes a day. I can't take this."

She says, "Come on, you're an eighth-grader. Get real."

He says, "No, you don't understand. I've been at Irving for 8 years. Reading is: you sit in your reading group, the teacher calls on you, you read your sentence or your paragraph and you are finished with reading for the day."

When Pat Mark told us that at our meeting, I said, "This student is telling us that this is his concept of what reading is. We need to listen to him."

And they all said, "Yeah, well, they don't read at home. Most don't read at home. They don't have any books at home. They don't have any reading materials at home."

From this conversation, we agreed that this child was expressing a very typical feeling among students. But we needed to do something. We needed to look at the culture in our school. What did our students believe about education? And with that, a lot of people started talking. The student culture was, "I don't see a future, no hope." The culture was, "I'm just going to bear this until I can reach a certain age and get out of school." Little investment—that was the real problem.

There was this one view of what the culture was, but from other members of the staff, a large number, there was the view that everything was OK: "These kids are not disorderly kids. We are good people. We are intelligent people. We've been teaching for years. We're doing our very best job. And sure the scores are low, but that's not us. That's not our fault."

From these conversations, the differences among people in the way they viewed the culture emerged. I decided that we would explore this issue, and I said I was going to show them our history of scores. I got everything together that I could find, made graphs and charts and slapped them up on the overhead. And I said, "You know, these kids are graduating from our school. This is the median, the middle score. The middle score is way down in the low seventh, high sixth for eighth-graders, who should be at nine."

So they all looked at it and said, "Yeah, yeah. That's not our fault."

I said, "Well, who's fault is it? What are the reasons for this?" So I invited them to get into self-selected groups and take a couple of weeks and talk about this. Sit down over coffee and talk about this. What are the reasons? List the reasons you think these children are not achieving. And so they did, and they gave me their lists.

I took the lists and there were about 60 items. There were duplications, but I didn't care because the duplications showed frequency. Then I called everyone together and I slapped them up on the overhead and I said, "OK, here's your list. This is yours. I haven't done a thing to it. I haven't removed any; I haven't added any. This is your list. Now, we're going to discuss each item and we're going to decide, is this something over which we have control or not? And if it's something over which we have no control, we will cross it out. No control. It's not our fault."

We crossed them all out! I got down to the bottom of the list and said, "OK. I hear you. It's crime, it's drugs, it's gangs, it's simple fear of families, or it's wards of the state, or it's foster children, or it's abuse, sexual abuse. It's everything out in society and in the families. Lack of families."

I said, "Are you telling me that there is no hope here? That we don't have control over anything? That's a terrible feeling. The reason students aren't achieving is everything out there, things over which we have no control? We may as well hang up our keys and go home because whether we're here or not is not going to make any difference. You've got to find something over which we have control. Isn't there anything inside this building we control?"

And there were a few people who sat with me and decided to open the dialogue and find out if there was anything over which we had control. We realized it's the curriculum and the way we teach. It's the way we set up the teaching/learning situation. So maybe we need to look at what we're doing and study what we're doing and read about what other people are doing and what research says other places are attempting to do, what results other schools are having, and talk about what it is we can do—one step at a time to broaden the teaching/learning repertoire.

RB: And that discussion was with the small group?

MM: Yes. Because everything is voluntary. Anything I have tried to do has been voluntary. Remember that bookstore thing I told you about? The first year, six people took me up on it. The money was there for all of them, but I didn't want to force anyone to do anything. I believe that change comes from within. Yes, things from the outside impinge upon you. There'll be stresses and there'll be opportunities. But it's the way we react to them in one way or the other that would be able to orchestrate change. People can't be forced. You can do a lot of staff development, you can bring in people and you can send them out. You can do anything you want, but when those teachers go in their classrooms and shut the doors, they do what they want. That's one thing over which I had no control. I can only control what I do.

RB: Then it was this small group who were really uncomfortable with the kind of conclusion that could be drawn from the list that you put together. Were these from your Wednesday Morning group?

MM: It was the junior high team. One of the things that I found when I became a principal that was very disconcerting to me was the fact that I lost my colleagues. First of all, these people were all strangers to me. It wasn't as if I was a teacher selected from the very school to become the principal. I've heard people who talk about that, say it's really hard because one day they're your buddy and the next day you're the principal and it's very strange how the roles diverge. It was very difficult for me because I've always been a very collaborative person. I want to discuss. I want to debate. I want to be part of the group that's in on the hard work and try to figure something out and try to problem solve. I don't want to direct. I want to be in there as part of the group. I want feedback, and I want to give them feedback and have a real discussion, a good dialogue and a good debate.

Pat Cantarelli was the first person to tell me, "You know what? You're full of baloney. You're never going to get anyone around here to change. You're just going to spin your wheels until you finally burn out. So take my advice and don't even bother." But he was saying it to my face. The others might have been thinking it, but they weren't saying it.

Pat Cantarelli and I had some time to dialogue during the school day. After we got to know one another I said, "You're such a pessimist!"

He said, "Yeah, well, you're an optimist. We're opposites. We really get along, don't we? I'm going to tell you the worst scenario and you're going to tell me the brightest scenario. What are you trying to convince me of? I don't know why you're trying to convince me, you're not going to change me."

RB: So that was your first real glimmer of a more collegial relationship with the staff?

MM: He was the first person to say, "I am your equal, and I can talk with you in an open way because there has never been another principal who has ever intimidated me and you're not going to be one either, and I will tell you like it is and if you don't like it . . ."

And then I was able to say, "Hey, you know, if we're going to talk this way, then I'm going to tell you what I dream and what my visions are. I think people can change. You think people can't change." It was fresh air. I really craved that. I wanted to open the dialogue. I wanted to have whatever it was. One on one, if it had to be. But I wanted to talk to people.

RB: So this dialogue began in the spring?

MM: Yes, I think so. And we continued for years. Our program evolved from the conversations, things we would try to do. We started with the sustained silent reading, and the bookstore visits were offered to everyone because we had this money. We got a bus. It was a shuttle. You know, some people took me up on it, and some people didn't. The following year, a few people came to me and said, "Are we going to have money again for the bus and for the bookstore?"

I said, "Oh, we had it last year. In fact, I told you there was an allocation for you. Someone else spent it though because you didn't take me up on it."

They said, "What? Someone? You had money?"

I said, "You weren't listening. It was there. I said it several times. I wrote it out. You weren't a buyer or a taker so what can I say?" It was in connection with this innovation that people became willing to come out and tell me what they really thought.

I would listen to their objections to the bookstore field trips: "Uh, a lot of the kids in my room will pick something they can't read."

I said, "So what?"

"Well, that's a waste of money."

"No it isn't. It's in your library. One year you may have kids coming up who can read those books."

"Well, they might pick something too easy."

"So what?" I said.

"Well, they're not going to get to be better readers if they are picking easy stuff."

I said, "Oh yes they will. They have to learn to love to read first." I said, "Let them read easy stuff if they want to. It's their choice. This is a program of choice. You've got to stay out of it except for pornography." At the register you can say, "No, that's from the wrong department. Put it back and find another one."

"They don't know what they like to read."

I said, "You're right."

"So how are they going to know what to pick?"

I said, "I don't know, they'll guess." I said, "But I think what they will do, if they do read something, and they like it, they will recommend it to others. And the strongest incentive to read is recommendation from your peer, not from a teacher." So there were all these objections.

"It's a waste of money."

I said, "It's not a waste of money. It'll be in your library. It's your classroom library."

So you have to know what objections teachers have. What are the impediments? Why do people hold back?

There's the writing program. They go in with Pat Mark. They go into the classroom with the children. They started in March of the first year and Pat Mark says to me, "They're not doing what you want them to do. Come in and take a look. Do something about this. They're reading their papers or their marking their papers or they're writing in their lesson plan books or they're writing in their grade books, but they're not helping me and they're not learning how to use the computer."

And I said, "So what?" I always say, "So what?"

She said, "But it's not happening."

I said, "There are reasons why they're not doing this. Talk with them." After the end of a year, I called the teachers in small groups into the writing labs, and I said, "I want to let you know that next year when you come in September, you will have had a year and a half with Pat. And I'm going to move this lab out of here. I'm moving it down to the library and you're going to be going in by yourself with your children." They were shocked. I also told them that they had April, May, and June to learn anything else that they needed to learn because, in September, they would be in charge.

The next day Pat Mark said, "Madeleine, how did you turn this around?" They came in, "What do I do? How do you get this? What is this? Return? Tab over here? How do you move that? How do you use the mouse? I mean, it was incredible."

RB: In a sense, you were giving them the responsibility and that changed everything. How did you know up front that was the right thing to do?

MM: I didn't know. It was kind of instinctive I guess. I think I really have faith in all these people. I knew that they were absorbing something and that they were very responsible people. If they were given a task, they would take on the responsibility. It's just that in the team-teaching situation, there are impediments to working together. Teachers are not used to working in teams. Their classrooms are their private domains. I could see there was movement toward trying to work with Pat, and they were really listening in the background. She was role modeling. And I felt that they could do it, but they needed something to move them off the dime. That did it. It was an incentive to really get going and really zero in now in a conscious way so they could learn. And I also think, they were absolutely amazed at the writing that was coming out of that lab: "These kids can think! They really have something to say." I think that they began to see that this was something that was very productive. And they actually could do it on their own. I had the confidence that this would work.

RB: So this experience went some distance in changing your culture.

MM: If we want to create a culture of literacy in this building, we need to create this culture among ourselves first, and we need to do it in the open where students and parents can see that we are learners. We began to buy teacher resource books and put them out on the shelves in the classrooms. I shared everything that I thought was wonderful.

There were some people who said they saved all the reading matter up and read it over the summer. We used it to argue about ideas. Some people said, "You just pick up everything new out there, just because it's new. That doesn't necessarily mean it's good. That doesn't necessarily mean I want to do it."

I said, "I'm not giving this to you as a mandate. I'm giving it out as ideas to read and to consider, and then get rid of it if it's not useful or if it doesn't fit, or if it doesn't expand and enrich the way you teach." I maintained an open attitude and considered the implementation to be voluntary.

I brought in a staff development workshop in writing during the second year, every Wednesday from 3:00 to 6:30. It was voluntary. There were 12 people who took it with me.

In the second year, 12 other teachers took it. And the third year some people took the course a second time.

I would talk about these opportunities at faculty meetings and some would say, "Do we have to do this?"

I would say every time, "Look, everything we do is voluntary. I'm sure going to argue my position. I'm sure going to try to persuade you to do this, to try this, but if you say, 'No I'm not doing this,' then I'll back off." I have been really strong in presenting rationale and arguments and backing ideas up with research and data, but if I can't convince teachers to try it, they don't have to do it.

RB: What about those people who didn't move at all, who don't make an iota of change?

MM: I don't think there was anyone who didn't change. There were people who changed very, very slowly. Several things happened to motivate people to take me seriously and to believe that I wasn't going to punish them. In April 1989 I was formally assigned to the school. The following October, Local School Councils (LSCs) were elected. In January 1990, the council offered me a 4-year contract, and again in 1994, I was offered a second 4-year contract. The reason I'm telling you this is because in the first year I was interim. That was a major impediment: "Why should I dialogue with this person if I don't even know if she's going to be here?" In April when I was selected by the committee, dialogue began to roll a little bit because, "Well, she's here at least until the new LSC is formed and selects a principal."

In that spring after I was selected, I wanted to remove what I thought was another impediment. And that is teacher evaluation. At the end of every year, the principal evaluates the teachers: superior, excellent, satisfactory, and unsatisfactory.

Essentially the system is that the principal goes into each classroom and observes a minimum of twice a year. You could go in and observe for 10 minutes. And you sit and have a postobservation conference and then at the end of the year you write out an evaluation; strengths/weaknesses, and you give this summative grade.

Then you call the teacher in to receive a copy so that the union contract is fulfilled. After I was officially made the principal, I said to them, "I've been working with you since September and I want you to know that I do not want to give you the summative evaluation because I don't really know you. If you'd like to discuss this we'll take a vote later."

They talked about it. The scuttlebutt was that I didn't want to do my job. And so I called them to the next meeting and said I heard the rumors. I looked every single person in the face and said, "I don't think you want me to evaluate you." They all looked at each other and voted, "No, we don't want her to evaluate us." We submitted a waiver to the union, and they gave us one.

The next year I went in and said at the beginning of the year, "I don't want to evaluate you."

They said, "What do you mean? You didn't evaluate us last year."

I said, "I don't ever want to give an end-of-the-year evaluation. I want to be a person who can look at things in an objective manner and give you some formative evaluation. I'd like to give you some feedback on what I see, and if you want it, you take it, and if you don't want it, you leave it. But I don't feel that any administrator will ever know what you really do. They'll never know how much you prepare. They will never really know what you put into your lessons. They'll never know the variables as well as you do. They may not know your children as well as you do. I believe the best evaluation is self-evaluation. There's no doubt about it in my mind. And you can give yourself your own evaluation of who you are as a teacher and what you can do and how you are progressing."

So someone called for a vote and it was unanimous. I have never rated my teachers.

Six years went by and someone said to me, "Well, you know, it's 6 years, we'd better get something down in our record at the board."

I agreed, and I asked my teachers to evaluate themselves. This asks teachers to look at themselves critically. But the one thing I did not waive on the union contract was my right to give "unsatisfactory." I was unwilling to do that because, as an administrator, I must protect children from unsatisfactory teachers.

There are other ways to "get" teachers, to give them a bad deal. One way has to do with the classes assigned to teachers. I removed that impediment and I asked my teachers to design the classes for the set of students going on to the next grade. I gave them guidelines. They had to balance for boys and girls, and for race, because I want my classrooms to reflect the diversity of the school. When I came to Irving, there were classrooms that had all Latinos or almost all African Americans.

So gender and race, and behavior problems were to be balanced. It was also important that the classrooms be heterogeneously grouped as far as academic achievement. So they were asked to stay within those guidelines to make the class rosters for the next term's classes. If everything is balanced, then teachers won't care that I am the one deciding which group goes to which teacher. They agreed that this was fair.

A principal can get teachers on duties. I said, "There will be no duties. No teacher will have a duty." I use my Career Service staff to supervise during lunch and in the morning.

Another thing that I felt that was really important to establish right at the very beginning was that teachers are people who have basic needs that must be met before they can free up their minds to teach. It's just like kids who are always thinking in certain schools—I'm afraid to go around the corner because I might get beat up and if I go into the washroom someone might accost me, someone might strong-arm me, someone might try to sell me drugs. If kids are fearful in a school, they're thinking about their fears rather than freeing up their minds to think about new learning.

And so, teachers have basic needs. According to the union contract, in Chicago teachers get a 10-minute break in the morning and a 10-minute break in the afternoon. That's it for the day. Now that is crazy. In some schools, they combine it and give teachers 20 minutes. By the time they get their kids to where they're going, drop them off, run to the washroom, and maybe get a cup of coffee, they have to go back and pick up their kids. They also get three to four prep periods a week. Now that is inhumane. So I devised a schedule where my teachers get a 1-hour break every day. And I did that up front and told them, "You deserve this. You are a person. You are a hard-working person. You are working with 30 children. That is an intensive 5 hours with children. You are always on. You cannot let down. You cannot walk out of the room. You cannot sit down and relax. You are responsible not only for safety and security, but for their learning, and you need a break."

The two teachers at each grade level have the same hour available each day for planning. In addition, two other teachers with classrooms on the hallway also have planning periods that overlap that of the first set of teachers, for a half-hour period, in case they wish to plan activities together. So I work hard to design a schedule that gives teachers time to plan together.

RB: What about the LSC? In many ways, your story really revolves much more around you and teachers.

MM: You're right. It does. And it still does. My parents on the LSC made it clear to me when I first came to Irving School, there were some things they wanted for the school. They wanted a full-day kindergarten. So we did that at the start of the third year. I also opened up a preschool that following September by writing a proposal. Then parents said that they really wanted a band. So we ordered instruments and supplies and I found a wonderful teacher. The LSC had some desires, and we accomplished their goals. And after that, the final desire was for their children to graduate from Irving and get into one of the best high schools. in other words, student achievement.

RB: Madeleine, how has your council been helpful to you?

MM: They are there to keep good people honest. They legitimate moves I make that I cannot make without them, such as the initiative to retain eighth-graders who were not learning. I spent hours and hours with them talking about student growth, uneven learning progress. They hired me to lead, but I'm always learning, asking for debate. In the end, it is the teachers that must make the changes in their classrooms. And it is the principal who must help the teachers. I try to educate the council. One LSC member recently asked why there was no "direct instruction" at Irving. This led to a discussion about achievement test scores, and that they are going up, so that a formalized version of direct instruction is unnecessary.

RB: What is your relationship with your council?

MM: I was secretary for many years because no one wanted to be the secretary. My LSC is made up of nice people, and they generally support me. I invite them to visit classrooms. How can we give each other educated advice if you don't see what the teachers are doing?

RB: How have you forged a productive relationship with the LSC?

MM: I think that from the beginning, they trusted me. In the first year I knew about their hopes and dreams already as a small parent group, and then they became these official board members who had to hire the principal. It was the fact that they felt confident that they had hired a person who was going to be able to get the job done. They wanted a full-day kindergarten. We got it. They wanted a band. We got it. We wanted our kids to graduate from this school and get into the best high schools, so they trust that we are going to work on student achievement, which is the major goal. And the way we work on student achievement, is to get the teachers to be better teachers. They realize that I'm the only one who can do that. So they trusted that they had hired the right person to get this job done. For everything that I proposed, I gave a rationale, and I tried to talk to as many people as I could. I hold a meeting with parents once a month where we get together and talk about what's going on in the school.

RB: How does this fit in with your goal of parent development?

MM: I asked for funding for a parent coordinator, and we hired this woman who is fantastic. When I first started at Irving, there were five parents active in the school at the old building; now we have 55 registered volunteers. They don't all come every day, and they don't all spend the whole day. Some of them do come every day and spend all day. But they're involved with working for one special teacher. They found their perfect match.

We have a bookstore outside our lunchroom. I go to suburban libraries that have their book sales and for a quarter or fifty cents I buy all these used books. They're children's books, and I put them out. I bought a showcase, and we put them all on the glass shelves in there. So parents and I played Bingo, and the winners picked five books for their kids and took them home to read to their children. Once I took them to the library, and got them library cards. We had a session at the library where we talked about the importance of reading to their children. We gave them a lesson on good books for primary children because most of those who came with us were primary parents.

I heard them saying that they don't get out of their neighborhood and that going to the library required crossing gang territories. So we opened up a library, a parent library, at our own school. I also started a program where I came on Saturdays and picked parents up. I rented a bus and took parents and their kids to the Harold Washington Library, and they could use their library cards.

But I was trying to get parents involved at another level. They're people who can help with cutting things out and helping a teacher put up a bulletin board, go on a field trip. But then there's another level. That is, if you want your children to be readers you have to be role models, you have to be readers. So parents got involved that way. So these programs are educating them in a way, giving them all kinds of information about the school and about the programs

In the same way, the members of the LSC have their own mailboxes right in the same room that the teachers have their mailboxes. Their names are on the label of the pigeonholes, and anything I give to my teachers I give to my LSC members: policies, procedures, new ideas, meeting dates.

The LSC also supported extended conference time during the report card pick-up. Our school improvement plan calls for students to be present and to take an active role in the conferences, which last at least 20 minutes. We allocate 10 hours to conferences each of the first three quarters of the school year. Parents sign up for all three conferences when they come to the school for orientation night in September. I think we're the only Chicago Public School (CPS) that conducts report card pick-up three times a year and by appointment only. This initiative has contributed to the creation of a culture of academic press.

RB: Tell me about your relationship with the board of education.

MM: I'm very much interested in what the board of education is doing, and I participate on many of their committees. I speak at those committee meetings if there's something on policy and procedure that I think needs to be changed. I speak up. I ask questions. They know me. When I come to committee meetings they know Mrs. Maraldi from Irving. And I attend board meetings—the full board meetings. I've spoken at full board meetings. I've been on committees this year, to help change the way staff development is done and I helped to develop a new school improvement plan format. I'm an active person who wants to give some of my time and my effort to helping change things in the whole system. I think that the board has had a very hard time giving up their top-down approach. However, I certainly think this present administration has made the best changes of any other since 1961. They have spirit, and they are good listeners.

RB: Is it mainly in the area of budget that you have to negotiate with the board, or what are some of the other areas?

MM: You don't negotiate budget at all. Budget isn't negotiated; it's given to you through formulas, formula driven. So the state says if you have free- and reduced-lunch-eligible kids, you multiply the number of children by the per pupil allocation and that's your discretionary money from the state.

The law says that the principal proposes the school improvement plan, and the principal proposes the budget. The council disposes it. They vote to approve or disapprove. If they disapprove, the principal has to go back to the drawing board. If you're a smart principal, you're involving everyone along the way, because you want to go to that meeting and have them say, "Oh yes, we know about this, we're in on this, and we approve of this. This is the direction we should be going." My LSC has always had a large contingency of teachers in the audience, and whenever they're questioning the principal, they turn to the teachers, and say, "Well, what do you think?"

RB: Do you think you could have done all this without the LSC?

MM: All I can say is I would have attempted to do it. I didn't need an LSC to do some of these things because I was basically trying to change teachers' perceptions of what my role would be in that school. And I can do that without the LSC. But then there are some things that could not have been done without the LSC.

In 1992, the LSC backed a move to retain eighth-graders if they do not meet the minimum requirements of the eighth-grade curriculum. This initiative was born from the wise observation of Pat Cantarelli who said at a meeting, "You guys don't get it, do you? Can't you understand that these kids have us figured out. They know if you work, you graduate and if you don't work, you graduate." That was a powerful dose of reality. The LSC agreed to tackle this problem. After several months of discussion, the LSC voted to retain those eighth-graders who got failing grades on their report cards. Since this was already a board of education promotion policy, we placed this statement in our school improvement plan.

We called sixth- and seventh- grade parents to an evening meeting to apprise them of our plan and how it would affect their children. Of course, the LSC asked me to introduce the plan and to answer questions. Before we got started, two parents got up, began to shout at me, accusing me of being a racist. They brought Channel 32 Live!! After what seemed like an eternity of yelling, while I quickly developed dry mouth, our LSC chair jumped up and yelled, "Shut up, give Mrs. Maraldi a chance to speak." Things settled down and I was able to review the scores and show parents the high schools our present graduating class would be attending. The audience murmured, "Not that school. My kid's not going there."

As they left, many parents approached me, held my hands, expressed outrage at the attacks, and said, "Not to worry. We support what we were about to do." The next day a kindergarten child ran up to me in the hall, threw her arms around my legs, and cried, "They said on TV that you're fired." I reassured her I'd still be her principal and not to worry. It's so hard to stand firm in the face of fire. It was great to have the strong and universal support of the LSC.

Before reform, the principal could not hire teachers. There was a seniority system that just moved the next person in, and you had to select from the group that was presented to you. You could not select from the wide world. I think one of the most basic essentials that reform gave to principals is the power to hire teachers. Because I need to hire people who have a like philosophy of education. When I'm hiring people and I am with a good person, we're connecting already. I do my interviews as we walk and talk through the school because they see things, and it triggers something, and they say something, and I can tell if they are genuine. If I can get to the stage with them where I'm grabbing onto ideas that they have, things that they are saying, then I know I have a potentially good teacher who would work into the kind of culture that we are creating at Irving School. I am very lucky to be able to hire. In addition to hiring, reform provided each school with the discretionary money to design programs that support the school's academic vision. Those are the two most important changes that were brought in by reform. Those two changes most helped me to work with everyone to change Irving School.

Analysis of Leadership

At Irving, Madeleine Maraldi worked with teachers to focus on changing the culture of the school. This entailed building a professional community that could work together to bring about change in classroom programs. Her emphasis was always on teaching and learning for the students, and she understood that in order for teachers to make

changes, they had to become a discourse community where ideas were shared. It repre-
sented a dramatic shift away from the way business had been done in the past with
mandates handed down from above. Madeleine was a principal for the era of reform
because she understood that a new form of collegial interaction involving shared power
was necessary to get things done. She enabled teachers to contribute ideas more freely
and to debate issues with her and other teachers.

Probably the most important gesture was that of giving up her role as teacher evalu-
ator. In this way, she communicated to her teachers that she was not there to judge their
worthiness in the usual too short observation method that does not consider the com-
plexity of the teaching situation. Instead, she was there to help them to grow and change
by talking with them and providing them with the necessary supports. Teachers were
treated as professionals, and they rose to the occasion.

The children of Irving have benefited from this evolutionary process. In 1989,
Irving ranked in the bottom 100 low-achieving schools in Chicago. Now, standardized
test scores validate the improvements made in the classrooms by teachers and students.
From 1990 to 1999, the percentage of students who score at or above national norms
on the IOWA rose from 16.6% to 46.8% in reading and from 15.3% to 49.2% in
math. During this period, student demographics have not changed. What has changed
is the actual day-to-day teaching and learning in the classrooms—the untimate chal-
lenge of school reform.

EXTENDING THINKING

Questions

1. What are some of the steps that Madeleine Maraldi took in order to create community among her staff?
2. Ms. Maraldi decided to discontinue her role as evaluator of the teachers. Reflect on this event. How did this impact the culture of the school. Do you agree or disagree with her decision? Why?
3. In what ways was the instructional program for students impacted? How was professional development used?
4. In considering management and leadership functions, how would you characterize the roles of T at W School and Madeleine Maraldi at Irving? What are the similarities and differences?

Activity

1. In this case, the principal makes many efforts to support teachers in doing what is good for kids, (bus trips to bookstores, providing volunteer professional development opportunities, giving teachers permission to fail). In your school, how does your principal support teacher growth, and how are these efforts accepted by teachers?

CASE 6

La Lucha Continua: Teachers Engaged in the Struggle Over Ideas and Authority

Peggy Mueller
The Chicago Community Trust

Background

Anzaldúa Elementary School is an old neighborhood Chicago public school that has in the last two decades become surrounded by a new community.[1] Nestled deep inside the side streets of a Mexican barrio in Chicago, Anzaldúa's fortresslike red brick structure dominates a dense neighborhood of humble single-family frame houses, two- and three-flat dwellings, and small family-run storefronts. As has been the case for many schools in the predominantly Latino communities in Chicago, yearly enrollments have far outstripped the capacity of the building. Mobile "temporary" units have existed alongside the main building for years, and even though the Chicago school district in 1995 began to open new buildings in the community, the school was still overcrowded. Classes that could not fit inside the main school, mostly bilingual classes, were moved to a vacant Catholic school building within walking distance.

Also like many schools in the city, Anzaldúa has been the site of ongoing internal struggles about the institutional culture of the school and its curriculum. As the community grew increasingly Latino over the last decades, some teachers disagreed with the way the school was administered. Until the Chicago reform broke the struggle into the open, however, the dissenting teachers were either silent or not heard.

The case of Gloria Anzaldúa Elementary School illustrates how some teachers have responded to the opportunity for leadership that is inherent in the decentralization of governance in the Chicago public school (CPS) system. The struggle over issues of

---

[1]The exact name and location of the school, names of individuals, and other defining details have been altered to preserve anonymity.

leadership and authority in this school is closely linked to a struggle over ideas about education. Anzaldúa's story portrays a dramatic chain of events in which teachers exercised leadership in the micropolitical world of their school to initiate radical change in the curriculum and climate of that school.

The author of this case spent the 1995–1996 school year talking with teachers and other members of the Anzaldúa community and participating in their activities. She engaged in this study at Anzaldúa as part of a larger inquiry focused on teachers' authority and influence in Chicago school reform.[2]

THE CASE

Even though recognized for steady improvement in attendance and performance since the reform began in 1989, Gloria Anzaldúa Elementary School has been the site of a pitched battle over competing views about education. The struggle has been mainly among teachers who represent varying ideas about what education should mean in this community.

As is often the case in Chicago public schools, Anzaldúa teachers' involvement in local school governance structures such as the Local School Council (LSC), Professional Personnel Advisory Committee (PPAC), and school improvement planning process (SIP) is better understood in the light of the school's local history, climate of decision making, and internal power dynamics. This chapter begins with a portrait of that broader climate. The second section describes defining moments in which teachers exercised notable influence among their peers, with parents, and with principals at this "typical" Chicago neighborhood school. The third section explores the extent to which the governance structures have served (or not served) as a vehicle for Anzaldúa teachers' influence. The fourth part considers how teachers have related to others with local authority, and the fifth summarizes the domains in which teachers have or have not influenced decisions. The chapter closes with an epilogue and a summary.

A History and Climate of Struggle

When the Chicago reform was implemented in 1989, Anzaldúa teachers took advantage of the opportunity to question what was happening in the school.

---

[2]The larger study from which this chapter is drawn was an investigation of two large Chicago elementary neighborhood schools widely recognized by researchers as improving since the beginning years of the reform. The goal of the study was to learn how teachers in these schools used or did not use their authority and influence in the new public forums of the LSC and the PPAC, how teachers have interacted with other local authorities, and in what schoolwide decisions they have exercised influence.

The story, now quite familiar to many, was retold by a teacher who came to teach at Anzaldúa only a few years ago: "There was a recognition that things weren't appropriate . . . that things needed to change," and people began to challenge "all of those institutional practices and cultural ideas" that constituted what they believed to be the reason for the dismal failure of education in this school. The "things that weren't appropriate" according to some teachers were numerous:

1. Unspent funds that belonged to the school for materials and staff development were returned to the central office yearly.
2. Students were being accepted from outside the school boundaries in order to increase numbers in the school, while the school suffered from overcrowding and high mobility rates.
3. A few teachers, designated by the principal to control decisions about resources, mandated curriculum that other teachers felt was educationally inappropriate and ineffective for the children in this school.
4. Cultural insensitivity to the community prevailed in the administration and the school as a whole.
5. Little effort was made to work with the community to provide safety for children in the gang-infested areas surrounding the school.

During the first several years of the reform at Anzaldúa, a core group of teachers tried to precipitate changes to these conditions, another group fought ferociously against the changes, and still others straddled the fence. The core of the struggle centered initially on deeply rooted differences about education for this community. These differences about curriculum, pedagogy, and cultural sensitivity led to serious conflicts about who owns the power to decide and about how much diversity in philosophy the local school could tolerate at one time. Ultimately, by 1995–1996 (the year of this study), the teachers' struggle had led to the creation and implementation of two new and distinct curriculum programs (some would say small schools) that were functioning along with the long-standing traditional program, which includes about half of the teachers and students.[3]

All three programs serve children of all age groups, but the classrooms do not interact across programs. There are bilingual children in all three programs; and all three cover all the basic subjects, but the curriculum content and teaching approaches are strikingly different.

---

[3] For purposes of clarification, in this chapter the two programs are called BETA and THETA. The traditional curriculum that remains is called ALPHA.

During the 7 years from the beginning of the reform until the time of this study, Anzaldúa also had three principals. These three administrators affected the climate and administration of the school in drastically different ways, but when asked who was responsible for the actual changes that had taken place in the school, many veteran parents and teachers agreed that teachers constituted the creative force that was "putting the school on the map."

Nonetheless, teachers reflecting on the reform climate at Anzaldúa commented frequently on the conflicts they still experienced across the three groups of teachers. Teachers who had created the new programs talked about their ongoing struggles as the "battle of the week" syndrome. One such recent battle, one that actually lasted longer than a week, concerned assessment. The Chicago Board of Education had directed each school in the district to develop assessments aligned with the district's curriculum standards. Some teachers in ALPHA, the traditional preexisting program, felt that everyone in the school should use exactly the same standards and assessments, whereas the BETA program teachers strenuously asserted that the ALPHA approach to standards and assessments was totally inconsistent with their program philosophy, goals, and teaching approaches.

Despite the struggles among teachers, or perhaps because of them, a surprising conviction prevailed among teachers that the school was moving forward. Teachers in all three programs agreed that teachers and parents could voice opinions and did feel a sense of ownership of the school. Individuals from the traditional and the two newer programs explained that the struggle, although painful and difficult, strengthened them and the school.

Although it is often assumed that changes in Chicago schools have been driven primarily by strong principals or active LSCs, the intense reform activity at Anzaldúa, from the vantage point of most who work inside the school, had its source elsewhere. Reforms in this school resulted from initiatives taken by teachers whose thinking extended beyond their own classrooms and who considered how the larger school affected the children they were teaching. Their perspective brought these teachers into direct conflict with other school personnel whose own positions and work were threatened by the changes the activist teachers proposed. The Chicago reform of local governance provided the opportunity for such differences among teachers to emerge.

Defining Moments: Teachers Taking Hold

Teachers at Anzaldúa often referred to three "moments" in the history of the school that have significantly improved the school. These events help to convey to the outside observer the historical context in which the present group of teachers found themselves during the year of this study. What is common in each of these events is that teachers played key, proactive roles; moreover, each event affected in some way the distribution of power in the school. Teachers cited these three defining moments as not only challenging but also strengthening. These events, briefly recounted here, are (a) the first time Anzaldúa's LSC replaced a sitting principal, (b) the year teachers participated in the CANAL (Creating a New Approach to Learning) program, and (c) the decision to initiate separate programs in the school.

Replacing the Principal.   A key event for many Chicago schools in the early years of the reform was the decision whether or not to retain their current principal. Chicago principals prior to the reform had been appointed by the superintendent and enjoyed virtual lifetime tenure. Every Chicago LSC within the first 2 years of the reform was required to go through the process of hiring a new principal or rehiring the current principal on a 4-year contract.

Anzaldúa teachers played a key role in their LSC's decision, even though by law they had only 2 of 10 votes on the council. Not only did a core group of teachers make known their interest in changing the administrative leadership of the building, but also they shared with the parents and community representatives on the council critical information about the administration of the school, information to which the parents would not otherwise have had access. That information, for example, about the school's funds that had gone unspent and returned to the central office, strongly influenced the parents' votes. Parents respected and listened to the teachers who had long-standing relationships with the community, even though, according to many teachers, it was extremely uncharacteristic for parents in this community to stand up against the principal. As one teacher explained, this initial task of the LSC was a challenge "especially with this population who has teachers up on a pedestal, and the principal is even higher. The principal must be adored and respected. [There is] no questioning of authority."

The two teacher-representatives on the LSC at the time described the experience of that decision as a watershed moment in their professional careers, because it was a chance to change conditions in the school. It required soul-searching decisions for both of them. A serious dilemma they faced was deciding whether to represent the views of the majority of more traditional teachers (to keep the principal) or to vote their own consciences (to remove him). For one of the two who had never really considered the extent of differences among her colleagues, it was a "political eye-opener" to learn that she and her colleagues could disagree over fundamental issues. She also learned that representing a faculty of 75 was not so simple a matter, because of the wide variance of viewpoints. For the other teacher on the LSC, the experience "changed [her] completely." It involved tremendous personal and professional risk but gave her confidence in herself as well as in the new system of local community authority, a system whose strength had not yet been tested.

Many teachers remember the drama of that first election vividly. They recall the extreme tension in the room when one of the two teacher representatives on the council stood before the entire faculty, declaring that she would vote against the principal, against the majority will of the teachers and in the face of personal threats because, although she was representing the teachers, she had to think first of the children. Many teachers told her that, although they supported her personally, they could not "outwardly divulge" their agreement with her stand against the principal. After weeks of mounting conflict and pressure from the principal and the majority of the other teachers, the LSC voted to dismiss their long-tenured principal.

According to most teachers, the new principal brought a complete change in the tone of the school. The new administration was more welcoming to parents, and there emerged a new kind of conversation about the importance of developing a curriculum that was sensitive to and inclusive of the community's culture. Veteran teachers attributed this change to this new community-minded principal, but even they quickly acknowledged that the groundwork for that change had been laid by teachers:

> [The new principal] was hired who was very political, very PR oriented, and very community oriented, very progressive, but she couldn't have come in on her own. She couldn't have just walked in and made those changes. But because that spark and because that grass roots kind of organizing . . . had already happened, she walked into a situation where people were starting to evaluate what had been happening and [she] really just took it from there.

Thus, although teachers cast only 2 votes of 10 on the LSC, they were the central influence in the crucial decision to replace Anzaldúa's long-tenured principal. This was a monumental action for teachers in the first years of the reform. As one teacher explained, "It sounds real easy . . . but I'm going to tell you it was the hardest thing, because one small group of people that recognized the need for change had to suffer dearly, because to effect that change meant going against all the current tides." Some Anzaldúa teachers, particularly in the innovative programs, today believe that such critical questioning of the institution remains their function and responsibility in the school: "The momentum for change now just doesn't compare to the kind of grand upheaval of change that was in the school in the beginning of the reform, but [we] still need to work at challenging . . . institutional practices and cultural ideas."

Participating in CANAL.   A second critical "moment" actually lasted for about 3 years. In the first years of the reform, some Anzaldúa teachers had learned about a training program available through the district called CANAL. An acronym for "Creating a New Approach to Learning," CANAL used desegregation funds to train entire faculties of schools how to work together to improve their schools. Anzaldúa teachers initiated the application for these funds, and the new (second) principal agreed to support their participation.

The project enabled half the faculty at a time to be released from school to attend training. At these sessions, Anzaldúa teachers worked together in teams, sometimes learning about new approaches to curriculum, new models for schools, teamwork and conflict resolution, and building a shared mission for the school. Teachers were paid for their involvement in these sessions. Although, as a teacher explained, they did not all agree about the value of the training, many teachers reported that their participation helped them to develop an "attitude" of ownership of the school, to articulate ideas and "start things," and to break through their long history of isolation from one another.

Some teachers began systematically talking to one another through this in-service training program that took place outside of the school during the first years of the reform. CANAL became a regular opportunity for people to work on projects such as the school improvement plan, which was now required of every school. But it also became the venue through which people began to realize that it would be virtually impossible to reach agreement about their school's mission.

After 3 years, funds were no longer available for Anzaldúa's participation in CANAL. By then, however, it had become clear that teachers had fundamentally different visions of what the school should be. Some teachers began to think of alternative ways they might develop and support completely distinct programs within the larger school, patterned after the schools-within-schools model. The decision to create the first such separate program was the third defining event in Anzaldúa's history.

Starting Separate and Distinct Programs.   The decision to start separate curriculum programs seemed a logical outcome of teachers' taking charge of the curriculum, thinking about new options that would be more responsive to the community, working in smaller groups, and dealing with the radically different opinions about education and the school's mission. Several teachers together wrote a federal grant proposal to fund separate programs within the school that could operate somewhat independently of one another. When the funds didn't come through, a few of these same teachers pursued other avenues and found funding to get one program (BETA) started.

As might be expected, instituting the first separate program—with its own arts- and culture-based curriculum, its own faculty, and its own outside resources—precipitated hard feelings and much debate. Not everyone was pleased about this option because, as one teacher noted, this process meant a "diffusion of the power" in the school. Another teacher confirmed this reaction: "When we voted to start a new program, there were all-out fights. Very heated. Very much clashing over what was happening." Nonetheless, because the principal at the time was in favor of the development of innovations and because the parents were supportive of these teachers, the project was easily approved by the LSC.

During the following year, another group of about 20 teachers came together to develop another distinct program (THETA), based on a thematic values-oriented curriculum. Although some teachers contend that this effort was an attempt to access the type of resources that had been available to the first program innovation (BETA), others contend that the development of these alternatives was actually a sensible solution, an extension of a good model, a "way out of the chaos of disagreement."

Thus, by 1995, the school had three distinct programs and faculties all under one roof: the two new programs (BETA and THETA) and the original traditional program (ALPHA). Teachers led the new programs and functioned as discrete faculty teams within the school. In effect, these teams relied on continued conversation among teachers as they developed separate programs with distinct curricula. Teachers in those two new programs reported that it was through these teams that they became involved in collegial decision making and that it was in these groups that they felt valued and heard. Prior to this, teachers reported, in the "big school," it was hard to get involved with everybody, to "talk to other teachers," to have time to share ideas. Prior to this new team experience, many felt their "word didn't count, and now it [did]. The faculty in the small new programs [was] more like a family."

In spite of these changes in programming, Anzaldúa as a governance unit remained a large school. There was still one principal, one LSC, one PPAC, and one budgetary unit from the vantage point of the Chicago Public Schools central office.

The removal of the first principal, the CANAL schoolwide staff development experience, and the initiation of separate programs within Anzaldúa thus constituted three defining events as teachers established their influence during the first 6 years under the 1988 Chicago reform legislation. By the 7th year, a majority of Anzaldúa's teachers had turned a corner in expressing their viewpoints more publicly, forming working coalitions with other teachers, influencing parents, and entering into struggles with their peers to define and implement a more effective education for this particular school community. This historical reality of competing visions provides an important framework for understanding teachers' ongoing involvements as leaders, both within and outside of the structures of local governance.

Teachers' Authority and Influence Under the Reform

Anzaldúa teachers in all three of the programs asserted in 1995–1996, that they now have a voice and that this represents a significant change from the past. One might assume that teachers would be expressing their views through the mechanisms of reformed local governance, that is, the LSC and the PPAC. In reality, however, neither of these structures has been the central forum in which the core ideas for improving teaching and learning in the school have been born, debated, or planned.

Local School Council (LSC).   Teachers' influence and participation in governance through the LSC during 1995–1996, the year of this study, was minimal. Even though the LSC had been a critical means through which teachers exercised authority and influenced parents in the first years of the reform, in subsequent years teachers' roles through the LSC became less visible and instrumental in school change.

An exception occurred when the second principal decided to leave and there was another opportunity to select a new principal. Teachers who were not members of the LSC but who had links to parents in the community spoke with parent representatives on the council about which candidate would be the best choice in their opinion. Teachers who were not themselves members of the council thereby influenced parents and the selection of the principal in an informal and indirect way.

The more activist teachers in the school have not had positions on the LSC. The teachers elected to the LSC after the initial 2 years of the reform have represented the views of the more traditional faculty, who have remained in the majority. The two teacher-representatives on the LSC have supported the administration and seldom raised alternative viewpoints at meetings or engaged proactively in critical examination of the curriculum or culture of the school.

During the year of this study, few teachers attended LSC meetings regularly, and communications on the part of the teacher-representatives to the faculty were erratic. There were seldom open discussions across the three programs in the school, except when decisions of one group directly affected one or both of the other groups, for example, with respect to the schedule for faculty meetings. Discussions of a substantive nature about the school, teaching, and learning were more likely to occur among teachers working within the same program, for the most part in the two innovative programs (BETA and THETA). Teachers in these new programs reported that they were able to talk more freely among themselves, that they trusted one another more within these groups than in the larger faculty.

Many teachers observed that the council itself had become a rubber stamp for the principal and that true dialogue on the council was rare. Activist teachers who represented viewpoints contrary to the majority of the teachers, to the administration of the school, or to the district typically did not regard the council as a vital arena for critical discourse and decision making about the school. The teacher representatives on the LSC spoke seldom or not at all at most meetings during the year of this study. Monthly council meetings consisted mainly of reports and the distribution of awards to students.

Most teachers who are among those most actively engaged in innovations at Anzaldúa thus did not think of the LSC as a conduit for influencing the school, even though several individuals believed that, done in a different way, the council format could become a powerful arena in which to dialogue with parents about important issues of curriculum and school climate. At every election held every 2 years since the reform, teachers who represent ideas that challenge the status quo have run for the council and lost. Nonetheless, they proceed, in the words of one teacher, to "push" and "keep pushing" for what they need in their own programs by increasing their knowledge of the system, engaging with resource agencies outside the school, informing and including parents, and negotiating whenever necessary with the appropriate authorities (the principal, the LSC, the PPAC, the teachers' union, and the board). Although two teachers have formal authority on the council, in reality the informal authority of individual teachers and groups of teachers that derives from their knowledge, alliances, and commitment appears far more influential in improving the school than the formal authority of those with positions on the LSC.

Professional Personnel Advisory Committee.   Conceptions of the PPAC, what authority it has, what its functions are, how it is organized, and how it is related to other committees and organizational entities in the school have been blurry and changing at Anzaldúa over the course of these first years of the Chicago reform. As a result, the use of the PPAC by teachers for advising the principal and the LSC has been less than effective or systematic.

During the CANAL project, in the first years of the reform, for example, a coordinating committee for site-based management was set up. This committee of about 15 people, which came to be known as the "Central Planning Board," functioned like a PPAC, alongside the PPAC. A veteran teacher recounted the annual changes that occurred subsequently:

When CANAL money ran out, the Central Planning Board was gradually re-placed by the PPAC. The PPAC then controlled the budget and the school im-provement plan. One year the PPAC was organized by curriculum teams, you know, social studies, fine arts, math, and science. And there were two representa-tives from each of those on the PPAC. Then, last year the format was changed, al-lowing every grade level to have representation, one monolingual, one bilingual, and then having one from auxiliary staff, one from the Union, one from the people on the LSC. . . . So this year [the question] was again, how do we organize it?

To decide, the faculty held several meetings in which a number of different models for the PPAC were proposed and heatedly debated. The end result was a compromise that consisted of a combination of all the models. The PPAC dur-ing 1995–1996 would have two representatives from both new programs, two from each grade level, two auxiliary teachers, and two nonteaching staff. The PPAC ended up having more than 20 members, a compromised size some teachers thought was unwieldy and inefficient. Leadership of the PPAC went to one of the nonteaching staff, a common phenomenon in this school because classroom teachers lacked the time and schedule flexibility to do the commit-tee's work.

Ambiguity About Lines of Authority.   Many teachers could not say whether the meetings to decide the structure of the PPAC were union meetings or faculty meetings or PPAC meetings, indicating ambiguity about who had the authority in the first place to assemble teachers to organize the PPAC. Meetings to determine the PPAC were run by the union delegate, an individual with con-siderable authority in the school prior to the reform and generally resistant to changes in the school.

During the year of this study, furthermore, the principal became directly in-volved in the work of the PPAC, providing in-service training to members of the PPAC as they worked on the school improvement plan and the budget. Ulti-mately this action drew a warning from the union. It was assumed that the PPAC was the central clearinghouse for the development of the school im-provement plan (SIP) and the budget, but the relationship of the principal to the work of this committee of teachers was not clear. As the principal noted, tensions among people in the school often derived from the lack of clarity about these new structures: "A lot of the issues that come into play are because this is cutting edge and it's new and . . . there's no set or firm policy . . . established, no union guidelines on it."

The relationship between the PPAC and the LSC has also been unclear in teachers' minds, even though the LSC teacher representative was for some years an ex officio member of the PPAC at Anzaldúa. Typically, teachers said that the work of the PPAC was to develop the SIP and the budget, and the principal would take it from there. Most people assumed that whatever the principal took to the LSC would be approved.

Knowledge as Power. Several teachers talked about the importance of their gaining information and knowledge of the school system in order to have more influence. In particular, they noted, it was important to know how resources are allocated, how to write proposals, how to deal with central office policies and reporting demands. They equated lack of this kind of knowledge with their lack of voice and power in the school and the PPAC in the past.

One teacher who has been behind many of the initiatives in the school claimed that one source of teachers' ability to take action is knowledge of the system at large, in particular, the way budgets are derived. She explained that this is how teachers originally gained authority, that is, by learning the system:

> Once you get information . . . once you know something about budgeting, programs, how things work, that empowers you. Because you know how things work then. . . . The more we started going to meetings [for federal projects], the more we started finding out that we were supposed to be helping to write the proposals every year; we were supposed to be looking at the budgets. 'Cause we never knew how much money we could use for ordering. We never knew. And we never knew how it was placed, who was doing this. Once we read the proposals, we realized that in the proposals the money was delineated and it had to be distributed under each one of our programs.

> [Knowing these things] allows you to readjust and redefine what it is you are using your resources for. That's not the only thing, because then it takes getting different people on board, having an agenda, setting an agenda and priorities about what it is you want to do. But you need to align all these things . . . and before that I was sick. I was literally sick. I just came home and cried . . . because of what others were ordering for us that . . . made no sense at all.

An ALPHA program PPAC representative noted that her program lost out this year, because she didn't know as much as other teachers who had participated in the process before. She concluded that it would be important in the negotiations process to gain extended experience as a member of the PPAC in order to hold her own against those who know more:

> I've learned that if I'm on this group next year, I'm going to become much more knowledgeable. . . . So if I stay on the committee next year, we're trying to get people on there for two years, I'm going to try to know more about what's going on. . . . Little by little you learn. . . Some people are on this PPAC for years, so they know what the ropes are. This was my first year.

Function of the PPAC.   The most powerful function of the PPAC at Anzaldúa in past years appears to have been making budget recommendations to the principal. This practice was a natural outgrowth of the power that a few teachers had been given by the original principal prior to the reform period. After that first principal was replaced, this group retained control of budgets through the PPAC. During the year of this study, when available funds were severely cut back by a redistribution of poverty funds by the district, the PPAC's internal negotiations about money became even more critical, even though the principal retained ultimate authority over the final budget. One teacher leader expressed frustration about the fact that the PPAC's preoccupation with the distribution of resources kept them from considering more important issues:

> There's potential to change things and shift the way things are done there . . . it's just not happening. . . . There's no real attempt to look at curriculum and what's being taught and how it's being taught or how things are organized. There's none of those kinds of discussions.

Nevertheless, through the PPAC, Anzaldúa teachers have had more direct influence on the governance and operation of the school than they seem to have had through their formal positions on the LSC. The PPAC has been the main meeting place and battleground on which the struggles to effect change or stay the old course in the school are being waged by teachers, primarily because of the budgeting function that has taken place there. In the eyes of the more innovative teachers, however, it is not the place where teachers are engaged in the exchange of critical ideas about teaching and learning. Those ideas are typically discussed inside the separate BETA and THETA programs.

Relating to Other Local Authorities

In large schools, establishing relationships in which people can work together on issues in which there are often seriously conflicting viewpoints is a complex and difficult task. Anzaldúa's staff of more than 100 persons serving more than 1,000 families confronted this reality head-on in the first year of the reform when the community of the school had to meet for the first time to make a critical decision about the leadership of the school. Since those first years, a complex web of alliances has been established between teachers and each of the three principals, between various groups of teachers, and between teachers and parents. These networks have enabled teachers to initiate—or resist—change.

Personal relationships and interactions are valued in this local Mexican community. Teachers who grew up here or who have lived here for any length of time are painfully aware of how the school has treated parents in the past. They are intimately familiar with the negative messages school personnel often conveyed to parents about their children, their culture, and their language. These teachers talked about the new challenge they face of establishing contact with, listening to, and conveying respect to, a huge number of parents. One teacher who lived in the community described the nearly impossible task of establishing a strong working relationship with so many parents in a large school, even with parent representatives on the LSC:

> One thing about the LSC . . . is weird. . . . They're representing, what, a thousand parents or something? Who do you talk to? How do you really know these people? It's really hard. . . . Once you make [a school] smaller, the idea of sharing that power becomes more reasonable. You can really do it, because you can all sit down around the table and look at each other and try . . . and say, "Is that OK with you?" or "I don't understand." And you can know people more intimately.

Teachers also discussed the challenge of having an inclusive and productive dialogue among teachers in a professional community in which there are different cultural norms for acceptable styles of discourse. Anzaldúa staff is comprised of Anglo-American, African-American, and Latin-American individuals. Interactions inside the school among teachers who are just beginning to work together and engage in public conversation seem to have been even more challenging than teachers' public dialogues with parents and the community.

Human interactions that lead to productive working relationships within this local school context have been rife with challenges. The next section of this chapter explores the complex dynamics between teachers and other partners with whom teachers share authority in Anzaldúa, the ways in which teachers think about their relationships to each, and some of the ways they have interacted with others on governance issues.

Teachers and the Principal.   Many teachers described how, even before the reform, some teachers had a considerable amount of power that was derived from and was "in league with" the power of the principal. A few veteran teachers in the school had been designated by the principal to manage certain functions, like purchase orders. In the words of one veteran teacher, "these people kind of ran the school. . . . No one really thought of going to the principal, you know. You would go to these other people who had been kind of put in semiadministrative positions." Although other teachers knew they could make requests, they did not feel that they were privy to critical information about resources. This kind of teacher power, some teachers explained, was the antithesis of teachers' sharing authority with the principal. Rather, it reinforced the power of the principal's office and kept most teachers from participating equally and intelligently in critical aspects of their work in the school.

The power vested in that group of teachers and others who supported them was threatened by the dismissal of the principal in the first year of the reform. The privileged authority that this principal–teacher alliance represented and the educational philosophy behind it has been at the center of the struggle at Anzaldúa since those beginning months of decentralized governance. As one teacher explained, "We have been fighting against control by a few."

The three principals who headed the school during the first 6 years of the reform responded differently to teachers who have wanted to initiate improvements at the school, and thus directly affected what teachers could achieve. The first principal represented the old guard and the authority of the central office of the district. A small cadre of teachers functioned as a second tier of his authority, managing funds and controlling the school from the central office. Teachers who wanted to initiate change had little support from this administrator. Some, for example, wanted to apply for the CANAL opportunity while he was in office, but he did not approve their request.

The second principal, Angelina Perez, opened the door to the community and to innovations from teachers. She also delegated responsibilities to teachers but went far beyond her predecessor in including bilingual teachers and members of the community in the decision-making process. It was during her tenure that teachers began the CANAL training program, and more started to view themselves as responsible for the school. Some teachers expressed total surprise that there could be such a principal in the system who was, as one said, "willing to allow teachers to pursue what they thought and would totally back them up." Nonetheless, during this administration, the privileged power that a few teachers had been given by the past principal was not completely displaced, so the tension among teachers grew across groups.

When the second principal decided to move to a higher administrative post, a new principal was hired from within the ranks of the school. This third and current principal falls somewhere between the first two in his conception of his role. He supports teachers' innovations and involvements, but he also feels accountable to the central office of the district and to what he calls the "outside world." In principle, he supports the development of innovations and the separate programs teachers have created, but he expresses anxiety about his own responsibility to be in control and to "make things happen":

> You know, you come in and want everything to be better overnight and you want everything to be fixed. And one thing that I've learned since I've taken this job is that you see things from a totally different perspective—because all of a sudden the weight of all the responsibility is on your shoulders and you know that many people from the outside world are looking in at you—and that it's a very slow process. It's not anything that's going to happen overnight. . . . It's a mind-set, not

only with teachers, but with parents and with students and things that just kind of perpetuate. And just because a new leader comes in and wants to change things, and just because the new leader has ideas . . . It takes a long time for that to filter out.

One of the teachers in the group who has pressed for the most change in the school described the BETA teachers' new relationship to the principalship that began when Angelina Perez, the second principal during the reform, came into office:

We thought of Angelina as a colleague, not a boss. In the past, it was always us against the board, us against the principal, us against others. What we represented was something different, a shift in that mentality. We looked upon the central office and the principal as allies who could help us get what we needed for the school.

This understanding on the part of some teachers represented a shift in *their* expectation of more collaborative relationships between teachers and the chief administrator of the school. Teachers even began to perceive the central office as more of a resource and less of an adversary. These shifts furthermore led teachers to begin to perceive themselves as key agents in the system. They became allied with other authorities in the system, working together as advocates for the good of the school. Even the current principal, who tends toward greater administrative control, admitted that reinventing the school requires teachers' leadership:

You have to have a group of teachers who want to do it, and you have to have an administrator that wants to let it happen, because they see the greater good. . . . My personal feeling with the [new small programs movement] is that if it is not teacher centered, if it is not created and sustained by the teachers, that if it is something that is perceived as being imposed from above, it will fail.

Even though some Anzaldúa teachers exhibited phenomenal courage by speaking out against the first principal in the early years of the reform, and even though subsequent administrators have encouraged people to become involved, some teachers still expressed fear about the fact that the principal is still their boss and evaluator. One primary-grade teacher, for example, admitted that she was not willing to engage the principal in a discussion about their differing philosophies of education: "He's still my boss and I'm not going to get into debates with him."

An Anzaldúa veteran teacher who had been involved in many innovations agreed that the power of the principalship does inhibit teachers' participation in governance roles:

> I think that there needs to be more participation coming from teachers, but there's always that hierarchy of power. You know, you have . . . the teachers saying, "I have to be careful because he evaluates me." That's a major factor in how teachers behave. When the principal evaluates the teachers. . . when that hangs over them, it impedes them from being active, really active.

Teachers know that if they do not have a constructive, working relationship with the principal, they may achieve fewer of their own purposes in the school. Although teachers have been the driving force behind reform, the principals of Anzaldúa have been powerful actors in the reform of the school for better or for worse. Even if teachers assume new leadership roles in their school, the principal, under the Chicago reform law, has primary responsibility and accountability for the school and still hires and evaluates teachers. Power relationships between teachers and the principal require skilled negotiation and good faith—a lesson that is quite familiar to the reform-minded teachers at Anzaldúa.

Teachers and Their Peers.   Since teachers at Anzaldúa have assumed greater responsibility in the governance of the school, their relationships with their peers have been at one and the same time the primary source of their struggles and of their sustenance. Teachers have established influential relationships within their separate programs and across the faculty, though the dynamics of these two professional contexts are dramatically different.

In the 1994 citywide survey of teachers' assessment of the progress of reform in their schools (Sebring, Bryk, & Easton, 1995), Anzaldúa teachers rated their own professional community negatively. Teachers' reports showed little evidence of staff collegiality, reflective dialogue, and open classroom practice, ranking the school in the lowest quartile on this factor by comparison with other schools across the city. This contrasted sharply with their views about school leadership (LSC, SIP, principal leadership, teacher influence) and parent and community partnerships (parents' involvement with the school and the school's outreach to parents). In comparison with other schools in the city, Anzaldúa teachers were extremely positive about those aspects of the reform.

In discussing the contradictions in this profile 2 years later, teachers explained that the survey occurred at a time when the faculty was deeply divided about the introduction of the new programs and changes in the school. They also suggested, however, that although the faculty as a whole was dealing with wide rifts, some teachers were also forming affinity groups around curriculum issues. Within these small groups, they were establishing strong professional communities.

While the faculty's union meetings and whole-school faculty meetings were often contentious, teachers' relationships within the separate programs during the year of this study had characteristics of an emerging professional community. Teachers in these programs were doing "joint work." Little (1984) observed that when this occurs, individual's conceptions of their teaching are replaced by a kind of community authority, thus strengthening their potential and influence.

During the year of the study, teachers in the small programs (BETA and THETA) met systematically for several hours weekly to plan curriculum activities together, to discuss individual students' learning and how they might improve strategies with children who were not succeeding, and to coordinate their program's events. Within their program teams, teachers worked on a common mission and values, strategized about how to reach individual children, had conversations about curriculum and pedagogy, opened their classrooms to their colleagues, and disagreed with one another within the safe confines of the group.

Several BETA teachers talked about the way the group's conversations now influence them. An upper-grade teacher in BETA, for example, described the way talking together has enabled people to work toward common goals:

> Communication is [why things happen in this group]. Just the fact that it's people, a group of people coming together who have, I can't say the same way of thinking, but do have that wanting, that desire to say . . . "OK, we're here. This is our goal. So we're going to work towards this goal." And whatever I could do [to] share it, you know, that particular thing, that we're all working towards a common goal. And anywhere else [in the school], everybody's doing their own thing, and they close the door and say, "Well, this is how I'm going to do it. I know these are the state objectives that I have to do. How I teach it is my business and nobody else's." And that's what they say [in the rest of the school].

Another upper-grade BETA teacher discussed how this group has helped some teachers who have been silent in public conversation in the past to assert their opinions. This teacher also recognized how she has been influenced by observing another teacher work with students in the same age group with which she was working:

> We can voice our opinions a lot more. There's this more open forum, and I think we've moved a lot from last year when some people never talked and they're speaking more. Those kinds of things will push us to push each other, expose each other to new things. I observe Cecilia [team partner], the way she interacts with kids, and I've learned a lot about how to interact with kids and have strong rela-

tionships with them that don't just have to be teacher–student relationships. And that's just because now I've seen that.

Finally, an auxiliary teacher in BETA, who has led much of the program development, noted that teachers in these smaller teams have been able to discuss sensitive issues that have been prohibitive in the larger faculty:

> As long as you stay smaller, discussions [about language, culture, racism] can be had at a more intimate level where everyone is truly included. Once you get to a faculty size like eighty, it just automatically goes underground. . . . There are people hiding there, people who don't care, people who, you know, are just hanging out, waiting to see what's happening.

One teacher in BETA discussed the ways in which the small programs also influence the whole faculty. "We have influenced the whole school, because we are obliging them to continually consider us." By this, she explained, she meant that the new programs challenge people's beliefs, assumptions, and practices, just by providing new models of education for this community. She went on to describe the somewhat alienating side of this effort, that of being marked as a person who's promoting change, that you're not about business as usual. . . . "You know, you're pushing the school in another direction, changing the way things have always been done here. . . . The trick is to be audacious and congenial at the same time." Collaborative work and collegial relations within the smaller programs have provided numerous opportunities for teachers to influence one another's goals, teaching, relationships with students, and orientation toward change and at the same time to challenge the entire staff to rethink what they are doing.

Each of the separate programs has its own culture and individual teachers who are considered by those both inside and outside the program as spokespersons, leaders, or liaisons to the administration of the school. In the case of THETA, the teacher-leader was designated by the principal, and in BETA, that role evolved out of a teacher's long-term leadership in the project. These individual teachers have taken on coordinating and administrative tasks, but many other teachers also grant them a special place of authority in the program.

Some teachers in BETA have resisted vigorously the creation of a new hierarchy among teachers that might, as one said, suggest that "classroom teachers [are] the lowest you can be within a school and administrative positions [are] the highest." They constantly raise the issue that BETA teachers need to challenge themselves to figure out how teacher-led groups can truly share authority across their ranks, use the expertise of individuals on the team to the best advantage of the school, keep good teachers teaching, and maintain efficient operations. The challenge is compounded by the reticence of some teachers and parents who feel safer with the familiar hierarchical structures of leadership and who are often not that eager themselves to take on leadership roles.

New understandings of authority are evolving inside Anzaldúa. Across programs, teachers talk about the respect that is due teachers who have demonstrated commitment to this community. Within programs, teachers identify authoritative persons in their group as those on whom they can depend for help, not only because of their knowledge, but even more because of their approachability. One novice teacher in BETA explained why she considered someone in her program to have authority:

> It's her knowledge. Her way of being. In Spanish, you would say, "la persona que se presta," which is a person who is willing to help. That definitely is one thing that matters above all. Because one can have the knowledge, but if one doesn't say, "Sure, I'll be there to help you out," or [if one] doesn't have that charisma or that character of being, you know, a helping person, nobody's going to go to you no matter how much knowledge you possess. . . . It's her wisdom . . . the knowledge that she has, not only as a teacher, but also as a leader.

A veteran teacher in BETA described the fundamental differences between the kind of power that teachers are attempting to exercise now in the school and the kind of power teachers had in the past. This description also suggests that the fundamental shift has been toward greater individual commitment, not in their own interest but in the interest of the school and community:

> There's a world of difference between the power some teachers had before in the school and what we are about. [First}, they had a gatekeeper mentality. We don't operate like that. We try to share as much information as possible with everyone. Secondly, they were not responsive to the community. There were undertones of racism there. Third, there was no real attempt to educate and include everyone. Finally, there was tons of dead weight. No spirit of real change. Their work was characterized by a maintaining of the status quo. No real sense of work. At 2:00 the day was over, there was a mass exodus at the end of the day. There was a "marking time" mentality. A victim mentality. No desire. They were very cynical, even about the board. They focused on the bad things, instead of figuring out how to get something going to change things.

Anzaldúa teachers thus identified a myriad of ways in which changes have occurred in the extent and nature of their influence within their own ranks in the school. Teachers had power over other teachers in the past, and it reinforced the system of hierarchy that kept teachers silenced and uninvolved. Since the reform, many teachers in this school have grown more interdependent, and that interdependence has strengthened their ability to take on the project of transforming the school.

Studies of school reform in which teachers have been the primary force for change have often found that reformers become an isolated group, the faculty becomes "balkanized," and the reform becomes a kind of alternative fringe (Fullan & Hargreaves, 1991). In the case of Anzaldúa, the faculty is clearly not in agreement about the mission of the school, and they did begin programs with distinct curricula. However, in many ways they are not completely cut off from one another; teachers continue to influence one another across programs. Since the beginning of the reform at Anzaldúa, teachers have mobilized one another to action—or resistance, negotiated compromises, and influenced one another to rethink the curriculum. Beyond a doubt, not only have teachers emerged from the classroom, but also they have become interdependent and influential among their peers in the task of reculturing and redefining this school.

Teachers and Parents.   Teachers' relationships with parents at Anzaldúa are central to the story of teachers' roles in school change. In fact, the core issue that teachers have been debating is the priority of community concerns in the development of the school. The debate began during the first years of the reform when teachers who were intimately familiar with the community encouraged parents to run for the council in order to have a voice in the school. These same teachers were the ones who then gave parents the information they needed to make an informed decision about the retention or dismissal of the principal. As recounted by a veteran teacher in the ALPHA program, it was teachers whom the community trusted that influenced parents in that first election:

> Two teachers on the council were the major reason why the principal was taken out. It was with the support, obviously, of the parents and the community, but if the teachers on the council were not strong enough to stay strong and with the belief that [the school] has to be better, it has to be better than what we have now, it wouldn't have occurred. I don't feel that that time, being the first council, that parents were trained or had the knowledge where they would be able to do something like we did. They didn't have the background and information to use . . . to make change happen. But they had enough confidence in the two teachers to go with [them].

Teachers now exert less direct influence on the council's deliberations. A few parent leaders have been strong, and the teachers who are serious about making radical improvements in the instructional program rely on the parents to support their efforts to develop innovations in the school. The chair of the council, for example, attended meetings about small schools and accompanied the principal and several teachers to a small schools workshop and site visits in New York City. These activist teachers express confidence in the parents on the council and feel supported by them. A BETA teacher asserted that conflicts regarding the separate programs arose between groups of teachers, not between teachers and parents. As a result, her group now goes to the parents if they need anything: "The LSC isn't anti-us. The parents aren't, even though the teachers are. So we just go to the parents. . . . that's my technique."

Some teachers refer to this community as the primary authority that directs their work. The community is the focal point of their energy and the source of their sense of purpose. One BETA teacher in particular who has been instrumental in the change explained what has influenced her:

> I think [what has influenced me was] just living in the community, talking to parents, seeing their reality, [my student teaching experience working in Chicago schools], my own parents. All those [experiences], you know, and I just come from a family of fighters. There's that piece of me, and then combined with the fact of living in the community and working there hopefully raised my sensitivity level . . . so that I have been able at least thus far to combine those, that kind of fighting spirit, that kind of confrontive spirit, and trying to do things in different ways, see things differently. And then just not being willing to settle for something . . . given what kids are confronted with and the lives that they are leading and the options that they have or don't have.

Although several of the reformist teachers expressed these concerns and purposes, not all teachers are that focused on the community's involvement or the development of a culturally sensitive curriculum. Many still believe in assimilating children from all cultures and language groups into a standard curriculum, hence, the debate about the curriculum. Parents, nonetheless, have a presence in the school and participate in school events. A core group of about 30 parents is very active, and some of these parents are present nearly every day. Many say that they feel far more welcome in the school now than they did before the reform.

The second principal at Anzaldúa hired several new bilingual teachers, and this has begun to close the communication gap between the school and parents. Since then, too, more teachers have advanced the philosophy that the community is important.

Several of the reform-oriented teachers expressed concern about the fact that there is still a power imbalance in the school. Cultural norms of the community and the traditional culture of the school make it difficult for parents to put themselves on a par with teachers. Some teachers are attempting to break that barrier by including parents as resource teachers and participants in school events as often as possible. The desire to establish better partnerships between parents over critical issues is a goal of several teachers.

One veteran teacher concluded that the balance of power at Anzaldúa is ultimately weighted on the side of the professionals, in spite of the fact that parents have the majority of votes on the council. The principal and teachers have power merely because of their positions from the vantage point of parents, he asserted, but he also recognized that teachers and the principal have exercised persuasive power:

> I guess each is as strong as they want to make their role. The teachers obviously only have two votes, but they have a lot of influence. The parents obviously have the numbers, so if they want it, they got it. And the principal as the school leader can really direct the whole course of action. He or she holds the ultimate cards as far as I'm concerned. BUT I'd say the teachers and the principal here basically hold the power . . . basically persuade more.

Anzaldúa teachers' new relationships to parents and the principal have engendered complex shifts in their understanding and exercising of their own authority. Sharing authority, eliminating privilege, and breaking down hierarchies are intense struggles that teachers have engaged in with their peers and, to a lesser extent, with administrators and parents who have certain expectations of the system. Participation in school wide reform and governance activity has altered the isolation of Anzaldúa teachers from one another and enabled them to influence changes among their colleagues. The webs of relationships teachers are threading with others who have interests in and responsibility for the school is a complex and delicate weave.

Domains of Decision Making

The domains in which LSCs are designated by the Chicago reform law to have influence are threefold: the School Improvement Plan (SIP), the budget, and personnel. Through their generation of the two small programs in the school, Anzaldúa teachers have exercised considerable influence on the school improvements plan. Nonetheless, teachers' authority in the plan has been limited. Although Anzaldúa teachers, like those in many Chicago schools, have assumed responsibility annually for assembling the parts of the SIP, ultimately the plan is considered the responsibility of the principal, who submits it to the district. Teachers are considered advisors. Similarly, with respect to budgets, teachers can make recommendations for the expenditure of discretionary funds; but even this amounts to less than 20% of the entire school budget for most schools.

Personnel issues have remained very much the domain of administrators' authority in Anzaldúa, as in most Chicago schools, with the exception of the small programs. Lead teachers in the separate programs have been consulted when there were vacancies in their programs. This has remained purely discretionary, however, on the part of Anzaldúa administrators and has not been considered a function of the PPAC or teachers. Some Anzaldúa teachers, however, have sought to become involved in teacher selection, and the subject remains a delicate issue. One teacher spoke about how she knew "[teachers participated in teacher selection] in the suburbs," but that it was not even considered here.

Even though teachers were central players in the first process of evaluating and selecting the principal early in the reform, Anzaldúa teachers have on the whole been minimally involved in principal evaluation and selection. Teachers do not formally evaluate administrators, nor is this easy to discuss in the school. As a veteran teacher in ALPHA remarked:

> You're not going to bring up principal evaluation at the PPAC because someone will know you just said [something] about the principal. So there are certain things you just don't say. In fact, some of the areas that should be dealt with probably aren't, like race, the principal selection, and perhaps the school day. Some people will not touch them, because they don't want others to say that they said anything about anyone.

Areas of decision making that are not included in the reform law but that have come up on occasion involve altering particular work rules. For example, the entire faculty decided to waive the work rules to change the daily schedule in order to provide time for teachers to meet weekly. There are limitations to the waivers that faculties can make, and at Anzaldúa, like many schools, the waiver votes have been the center of intense debates.

Thus, teachers through the structures of the reform have become involved in domains of decision making that extend beyond their classrooms. However, from the perspective of the teachers who have been engaging the most actively in reforms, these rightful domains of teachers' authority have not begun to be fully enacted or exploited by the school at large.

Epilogue

During the year after this study, the BETA program teachers applied to the Chicago Board of Education to become an autonomous unit. They found that contentious interactions with the dominant group of teachers in the school interfered with their work. They sought autonomy for the same reasons as they had sought to remove the first principal, namely, to be able to continue the work of transforming the curriculum and the community of the new school. They were successful, the program doubled in size, and they moved to another location in the same community. The faculty of this new school continued to work on developing a creative and culturally inclusive curriculum as well as to include parents and the community in a central place in the curriculum and programming.

Teachers developed a new structure for the LSC in this new school that includes an equal number of teachers and parents. Unlike the reform legislation that does not provide representation for elementary students on councils, this school's LSC has two student representatives elected by students. The PPAC is not a separate entity, but the faculty as a whole. Guided by a vision of current practice, the district insisted that the new school have a principal. This role was filled the first year by a part-time nominal principal assigned by the district. When this principal retired, a second principal was assigned, again by the district. This second principal imposed ways of doing things administratively that ran counter to the goals of the BETA teachers. Finally, during the third year, a teacher-leader from their ranks became certified as a principal. In an action not unlike the removal of the first principal, the traditional principal was removed by the LSC because the LSC had not voted for her in the first place, and they insisted that this was their right.

The events that have transpired among the Anzaldúa faculty and this school community since the beginning of the reform have deeply engaged teachers in public spheres, in collaboration with parents, and in serious rethinking of the curriculum. New models of authority, of teaching, and of learning are evolving, but not without intense struggles. As Katz et al. (1997) observed, "Reform that is more than cosmetic rearranges local hierarchies. . . . The extent to which it shakes hierarchies, in fact, may be a measure of whether reform penetrates below the level of superficial change" (p. 153).

Analysis of Leadership

In the first year of the reform, when Anzaldúa teachers publicly criticized the quality of their school and the principal who had been in charge for several years, they began an interrogation that has not stopped. As some teachers observed during the course of this study, the process of replacing the first principal was a revolutionary act, but not an end in itself. The replacement of the principal opened the door for teachers to continue to question and begin to transform the prevailing power arrangements that had (a) silenced parents, the community, and teachers, (b) kept these same participants isolated and devoid of access to resources and knowledge about the school, and (c) reinforced a monolithic curriculum and instructional program. Teachers moved to alter these arrangements not because of their interest in possessing power for its own sake, but because of the failure of the school to educate the children in this community.

The questioning of authority by Anzaldúa teachers thus led to the creation of new curricula and instructional arrangements, the constant struggle to reorder the PPAC so as to ensure representation of varied ideas and equal access to resources, and an effort to bring parents into the heart of the school. Out of these activities, largely spearheaded by teachers, emerged two new programs and collegial communities within the larger school. The system of local governance reform thus created opportunities—opportunities for the expression of diverse views and opportunities for the constant questioning of the meaning and processes of education, of the source of curriculum, and of the role of the community in the production of knowledge in this school. The work of these teachers thus began to change from its former private, isolated, and fragmented character to approximate more what Giroux (1988) described as the work of teachers as intellectuals:

> [Teachers] will need to re-imagine teaching as part of a project of critique and possibility. But there is more at stake here than simply a change in who controls the conditions under which teachers work. This is important, but what is also needed is a new language, a new way of naming, ordering, and representing how power works in schools. It is precisely through a more critical language that teachers might be able to recognize the power of their own agency in order to raise and act upon such questions as: What range of purposes should schools serve? What knowledge is of most worth? What does it mean for teachers and students to know something? In what direction should teachers and students desire? What notions of authority should structure teaching and learning? These questions are important because they force educators to engage in a process of self-critique while simultaneously highlighting the central role that teachers might play in any viable attempt to reform the public schools. (p. 39)

EXTENDING THINKING

Questions

1. This case presents three "defining moments" that significantly affected change in the school. How did these three events cause the school to improve and why? How did teachers make sure that their voices were heard in the council vote to replace the existing principal? How did the second two "defining moments" directly affect teaching and learning in the classrooms?

2. One teacher who was interviewed talks about knowledge as power? How is this exemplified in this case?

3. How do teachers at Anzaldúa take on new leadership roles? Consider the way that power has been dispersed in the school. How did that happen? How does this compare with Irving School?
4. Consider all of the implications of breaking the school into three programs, Alpha, Beta and Theta? Small schools can provide opportunities that are unavailable in larger settings. Compare the school that you work in with the small programs at Anzaldúa . What are the advantages and disadvantages of small size?

Activity

1. Consider the cultural issues that are dealt with among the teachers, between the teachers and the parents and the students, and between the principal and the rest of the school community. Observe the interactions at your own school; how do cultural norms and expectations affect them? What steps are taken, if any, to make the necessary cultural connections?

Reflection on Cases 5 and 6

As described in section 1, an important hope of those designing the reform legislation was that a shift in leadership would lead to changes in classroom instruction and learning. The two cases in this section show how in quite different ways school leadership can lead to differences in teaching and how teachers think about their teaching. In Irving School, the principal came with a vision of how she and her teachers would work as colleagues to create challenging instruction for their students. The process was a slow one that occurred over a number of years in which teachers were nudged and rewarded into accepting new responsibilities.

Writing, for example, was identified as an area of major weakness. Through the creation of a writing lab, the guidance of respected teachers, and a sharing of responsibility, the teachers became actively engaged in learning how to teach their students to write through the "process writing" system with the support of computers. Sustained silent reading was initiated through an incentive program in which students selected books from well-stocked, commercial bookstores.

Perhaps most critically in terms of the more democratic dialogue that she worked to establish, the principal refused to fulfill the traditional role of evaluating her teachers. Instead, with time, teachers took the responsibility for their own self-evaluation. The ongoing struggle the principal faced was getting the teachers to assume a collaborative role in instructional decision making and to accept responsibility for the learning of their students.

The role of the Local School Council (LSC) seemed to be a minor concern. The principal accepted and followed through on their suggestions to develop several new programs. She accepted their authority to determine whether she should continue in her leadership role. The LSC seemed to have confidence in her ability to make future opportunities available to their children through the development and realization of high achievement.

This system of shared leadership is not unlike that shown by the principal of Saucedo Academy (Case 2). In that situation, the principal was responsive to the concerns of the community and the goals of the LSC. Moreover, she respected the knowledge and dedication of her teachers, got them the resources they needed, gave them time for planning, and worked with them to develop effective instruction.

Anzaldúa School would, on the surface, seem to represent a quite different case. It is unusual for a group of teachers, particularly those in the minority, to wield sufficient power to make a change in school leadership. This would not have occurred without the reform legislation's empowerment of the LSC to hire and fire principals. But it also would not have occurred had there not been a group of teachers, respected for their knowledge and philosophy of education by parents and other teachers, who were willing to act. Through the cooperation between this minority group of teachers and parents on the LSC, it was possible to rid the school of a leader who silenced the comments of many teachers and parents, who was partial to a traditional group of teachers, and who did not seem to have the interests of children at the center of his agenda.

After that initial action, Anzaldúa teachers experienced continuing struggles around issues of leadership and authority in their efforts to improve the school. The second and third principals, in differing degrees, allowed these teacher to work as teams on reforms in programming. Nonetheless, traditional understandings of leadership roles and responsibilities endured and often created obstacles. The teachers in this school were beginning to envision roles and modes of operating that the traditional bureaucratic system could not easily accommodate, such as peer evaluation and alternative scheduling of teachers' work. Their persistence seems closely linked to the leadership capacity of a core group within their ranks, as well as to their increasing ability to function as a professional community.

It is interesting to speculate how this story might have appeared if it had been written by the second principal. The BETA teacher, might have been seen as working collaboratively with her to fulfill their joint vision for children in the community. Indeed, the report might be similar to those written by the principals of Saucedo Academy and Irving School. It is perhaps not surprising that public perception during the term of the second principal was that the school's progress was due to her strong leadership and community sensitivity.

The epilogue reveals the courage and the drive of this group of teachers to be guided by their evolving vision for children to continue their work of transforming the curriculum and the community by creating a separate new school.

These cases suggest that the curriculum and the school community can be transformed. It can be changed in ways that lead to greater involvement and higher achievement for students. Such transformation depends on someone with authority having the vision of shared leadership and the desire to create the conditions for conversation and debate about instruction among teachers. Through discussion of their respective ideas, the basis for instructional programs and decisions becomes clear.

SECTION 5

New Beginnings: Making Changes in High School Instruction and Learning

During the years 1990 to 1997 of the Chicago school reform, test scores were rising in about half of the elementary schools (Designs for Change, 1998). In contrast, before 1997 little improvement had been shown by Chicago high schools. Indeed, the failure of large urban high schools to adequately educate students for the important transition to mainstream society has been recognized as a problem across the nation. The final two cases focus on the issue of improving the high school education of urban youth.

Amundsen High School was distinguished during the second wave of reform, as were many other large high schools, by being placed on the "watch list" in 1995 and on "probation" in 1996, with 1 year to raise scores or be "reconstituted." Assistant Principal, Ken Hunter, and his university partner, Donna Ogle, tell the story of the pressures experienced and the positive steps taken during the probation year to make changes in curriculum and learning.

The second case, written by a university partner, Steve Zemelman, recounts the challenges and successes that occurred in the development of a small high school, the Best Practice High School. The new teacher-led, student-centered school opened its doors in September 1996 after 3 years of planning by veteran Chicago high school teachers and three faculty members from National-Louis University (NLU). Its creation tested the shared belief of its founders that an innovative, progressive curriculum could succeed with students from diverse backgrounds and a range of achievement levels.

The stories for both these cases begin in 1996 when the reform legislation was 8 years old. They illustrate two different strategies for bringing change to a segment of public education that is most resistant to change, the urban high school. At Amundsen, the case describes an important effort to work within the

177

existing structure of the large urban high school. The Best Practice High School is an example of a school that starts out from scratch and still experiences many of the problems of working within the bureaucratic system.

CASE 7

Developing Leadership in Literacy at Amundsen High School: A Case Study of Change

Donna M. Ogle
National-Louis University

Ken Hunter
Amundsen High School

Background

Amundsen High School is a large school of 110 faculty and 1,750 students situated on the far north side of Chicago. The students attending the school have changed in composition over the last few decades. At the time of the case study, the student population represents a mix of ethnic, racial, and national origins (49% Latin; 16% African American; 10% Asian; 28% White ethnic). Over 70% of the student body were born outside the United States, and about half of these are designated as low in English proficiency (LEP). Ninety-five percent of the students come from low-income families and participate in the free- and reduced-lunch program. Amundsen's students enter with fairly low scores on the Iowa Test of Basic Skills (ITBS). For example, in 1996 only 12% of the entering class were reading at or above grade level.

Although a variety of efforts had been made by the school during the early years of reform, a program of academic accountability based on test scores during the second wave of reform in 1995 served as a precipitating event. Shortly after Mayor Daley charged Paul Vallas with the oversight of the CPS (Chicago Public Schools), Amundsen was put on a state watch list, and a year later received notice that it was on "probation." This external pressure, in combination with the commitment of the school professionals, provided the energy to begin the serious initiative. The effort to improve the academic achievement of Amundsen's students and to rethink instructional priorities was informed by a variety of sources. In particular, the Goals 2000 project professionals provided a specific staff development initiative focused on reading and learning across the curriculum that matched the school needs.

In this chapter we, an administrator at Amundsen and a University Goals 2000 project director, look more closely at the way these forces converged to help create a whole-school reading program with faculty taking ownership and leadership of the effort. We describe the various threads that combined so that Amundsen was the first high school to be removed from the probation status—in just 1 year. We look specifically at the way Goals 2000 and Amundsen administration and faculty combined their efforts in an ongoing staff development program that has resulted in a continuing rise in scores. We conclude with some reflections on what we are learning through this process. We especially chafe under the increasing standardized testing mandates and address the problems posed by this too-narrow evaluation framework. At the same time,we recognize that the testing focus has also provided some "fuel" to fire the efforts of reforms that were badly needed.

THE CASE

The Early Years of Reform

Stories of reform are the stories of people with vision, people who are willing to lead and respond to challenges and concerns. Dr. Ed Klunk, a major "thread" in this story of change, has been instrumental from the beginning in accepting the challenges posed by changing demographics and testing declines. He had been part of the Amundsen community for many years, first as a science teacher, then as assistant principal. When he became principal in May 1990, he knew the school community well and was himself well respected. In fact, his selection as principal was one of the first decisions made by the newly formed Local School Council (LSC).

During his first years as principal, Dr. Klunk had little time to focus on curriculum and instruction. The school had become unsafe, had a bad reputation in the neighborhood, and both safety and order needed to be restored. Only after the school was put in order and had a better identity as a place where students *could* learn, could he and the faculty turn their attention to the issues of instruction and learning. For these changes to occur, the whole school had to work together. As he explains, "This was not an easy time. As in most changes, there was much initial opposition within the school." What made the turnaround possible was Dr. Klunk's choice of leadership style typified by a commitment to support and encourage teachers and his strategy of trying to anticipate trends.

Through the efforts of Dr. Klunk and the LSC, in 1992 Amundsen became an "Options for Knowledge" school and chose an environmental theme. This status made it a quasi-magnet school; as a result, students from outside the school's geographical boundaries could be enrolled at the school to help it maintain its racial balance. This special focus meant that environmental issues and concerns were to be part of each class taught at the school, part of all course syllabi, and used as a criterion in the teacher evaluation process. Because CPS specialty schools and private/religiously affiliated schools had taken a disproportionate number of students from Amundsen's attendance area, this "options" designation was an enhancement to Amundsen, making it more attractive to such students, many of whom were academically most able.

As the school gradually came to greater order, Dr. Klunk was able to attend to issues of curriculum and instruction. Based on the school's improving climate, he knew that he had a professional faculty that was not satisfied with their results and that he could count on their willingness to take the steps necessary to improve student achievement. He also knew from the start of Vallas' administration that testing was going to be a major factor in the upcoming years. Therefore, he decided to hire Ken Hunter as an assistant principal with responsibilities for testing. He believed that this appointment would provide the depth of support to help faculty think seriously about the possibilities they had before them.

The Beginning of the Journey

The journey of school reform at Amundsen High School began in 1995, with new accountability from the Illinois State Board of Education (ISBE) and demands from the new Chicago school superintendent Paul Vallas. It was clear from the first of his administration that Vallas' agenda would focus on academic accountability. Schools needed to change and they were going to change. The messages from the ISBE and the city were becoming more focused: School success would be monitored in relation to student test results. Improvement on test scores was required!

These messages came through clearly. Amundsen in 1995, like many other urban high schools, had been experiencing a change in the composition of the student body and a corresponding decline in test scores. When faced with the mandate to improve test scores, Dr. Klunk determined that the whole school needed to work together if they were to be effective.

Almost before he had begun his new job as assistant principal in 1995, Ken Hunter had his challenge defined. The ISBE decided to make the Illinois Goals Assessment Program (IGAP) a high-stakes exam for student achievement. As was true throughout the entire Chicago system, faculty at Amundsen knew very little about the nature of this exam, what was assessed, or how it was scored. Beginning in September 1995, the ISBE and the CPS began a partnership to provide Chicago with necessary information concerning the IGAP process.

Also at that time Amundsen was designated as part of the new ISBE project called "Project Jump Start." This program was designed to provide schools on the state watch list with technical and financial support. In one of their first major efforts, Ed and Ken put together a team to work on Project Jump Start. Amundsen's team was asked to identify areas of curricular need. At a meeting in November 1995, the team identified two areas—reading and writing. The ISBE consultants who came to the school and met with the team suggested that Amundsen might wish to target writing as its first step and move to reading later, because based on their experience they felt that writing is amenable to direct instruction and the results of the effort would be more visible. With little experience to guide them, the team decided to take this advice and target their efforts on writing and participate in the activities provided by the ISBE.

This was the beginning of a journey toward a more focused schoolwide effort to improve students' achievement in writing and reading. By participating in writing workshops provided by the ISBE, Amundsen faculty and administrators met leaders from other Chicago high schools who were responding to the need to improve student performance. Among key people, Phyllis Henry from the CPS and a writer of IGAP social studies items became a presenter at a winter in-service for Amundsen. She suggested that one of the teachers at Morgan Park High School, Sue Heminger, might be a useful advisor because they had already successfully improved their writing performance. Morgan Park scores on the IGAP writing test had increased by 25%. Ms. Heminger had developed a professional development strategy, which was essentially a collegial training model. Teachers at the school were trained to understand the Illinois rubric contained in "Write On. Illinois," a guidebook provided to help schools understand the writing evaluation model. From that training, Ms. Heminger and her team developed writing prompts and set a schedule for student writing in each of the content areas. Teachers also participated in the process of rating samples of student writing. She reported that for the first time teachers became part of the process and developed some understanding of what was considered "good writing" according to the state assessment guidelines.

When they heard of the Morgan Park process, Amundsen team members responded positively. Ken Hunter invited Ms. Heminger to share the model at Amundsen in early February 1996. At the close of her presentation, Dr. Klunk asked for volunteers to replicate this process and a small group of 12 faculty came together with Ken to form the Amundsen High School's writing task force. This new writing task force followed the Morgan Park plan. They learned the rubric and then taught that rubric to the Amundsen faculty. The task force set up a schedule for writing practice across the content areas and provided teachers with IGAP-style writing prompts. During the last 2 weeks of February, each department was given a writing day and students in every class in the building did IGAP-style writing daily. As a result of this effort, teachers were much more aware of what the IGAP process entailed and why it was being given. Most important, they knew that they could do something to help students improve their writing scores.

Although Amundsen faculty would not see the IGAP results until summer, writing scores rose from 28% at or above grade level in 1995 to 41% in 1996. Equally important, the all-school nature of the process was positively experienced, and staff felt energized by their corporate effort. In reflecting on this first-year experience of raising the writing scores, it was clear that this experience provided a positive basis for other collegial projects and helped the school maintain its direction and momentum during the next, difficult year. Because of the success on the IGAP, faculty became willing to try to do different things in the classroom, once they were given the opportunity and the knowledge needed to help the students.

At the close of the IGAP testing cycle in March, CPS policy called for another set of exams, the ITBS-TAP (Test of Achievement and Proficiency). These exams had been de-emphasized throughout the system and, after intense preparation for IGAP, the school leadership (Ed and Ken) decided that the TAP would be used simply as a local assessment indicator. After that additional set of testing was completed, Dr. Klunk suggested that a reading task force be developed, modeled on the writing task force. With the positive experience of working together on this "easier" area of writing, it was time to turn attention to reading.

GOALS 2000—Reading Across the Curriculum

At this same time, the Goals 2000 grant was funded for Chicago high schools. This project had been designed by a team of CPS central office administrators and area university faculty with the explicit purpose of assisting secondary schools to improve reading achievement by working with teachers across the curriculum. Rather than focus on instruction in reading classes, the project is built on the premise that if secondary students are going to improve in reading, all content areas need to be involved. Teachers need to use reading materials and ask their students to engage in reading on a regular basis. Students need strategies with which they can approach content texts and be successful in gaining meaning from them. These habits of good readers will become automatic if students are encouraged to be strategic readers in all their courses.

A professional development component was designed around the idea of developing a leadership team in each participating high school, with faculty representation from the major content areas. These faculty members would form the Goals 2000 Team and would become a staff development resource in their building. The leadership and knowledge of strategic reading would be developed with the support of university faculty. The grant was designed as collaboration between area universities and the CPS Teachers Academy for Professional Development. Each university would partner with five high schools. They would provide an intensive summer institute for the leadership teams, followed by weekly seminars in the schools during the regular school year. University staff would serve as resources to the Goals 2000 team, meeting with faculty, participating and providing demonstration lessons in their classrooms, assisting in all-school staff development, and generally being a stimulus for increased attention to reading practices. An underlying goal was the development of an increased "team-oriented reading effort" in each school.

In order to meet this challenge, National-Louis University (NLU) engaged four doctoral students to work with the NLU project director, Professor Donna Ogle. Each university team member would collaborate with one school as their major partner. Amundsen applied to be part of the project. Due to similar locations on the north side of the city, Amundsen and NLU were partnered. The initial meeting between us (Ken Hunter and Donna Ogle) encouraged us to proceed. Our orientations were similar, we trusted teacher leadership, and as project coordinators (from the high school and university), we enjoyed working with each other. By late spring, a team of five teachers across the content areas had been selected at Amundsen representing ESL (English as a second language), science, social studies, English and library. They were introduced to the Goals 2000 project intent at a spring meeting at the CPS board building, before the major work began in the summer. They understood that they would serve as the central leadership team for the work that would be done at Amundsen the next year.

This group of faculty and the assistant principal participated in the first 3-week summer workshop at CPS headquarters in August 1996. That first workshop was not easy. Even though the faculty from the five high schools came as designated leaders and knew what the project intent was, some were defensive and not prepared to embrace a comprehension-focused model of reading. They were a hardened group of teachers, who had been in the field for many years; most had been quite successful in their classrooms. Because of this they had not been challenged to rethink their model of instruction and were hesitant to take on a major role in helping their students become better readers.

In recalling that first summer, the amount of energy needed to connect with the teachers stands out. Their years of frustration at trying to do well by students and having multiple roadblocks thrust in their way was never far from the surface and continually influenced our interactions. If there was one element that needed to be developed for this project to succeed, that element was mutual trust. For teachers to trust university types who do not share the same day-to-day struggles in urban high school seemed almost too daunting, especially when teachers in some schools did not trust each other. For the project to succeed, positive relationships were needed, as well as the belief that the reading across the curriculum effort could positively affect both teachers and students. Developing a sense of shared trust and respect was essential.

Both of us (Ken and Donna) were aware of the substantial risks that this joint effort entailed and worked together during the summer seminar to help establish the best context we could. At one point, for the sake of this fragile relationship between teachers and the Goals 2000 university team members, Ken asked the Amundsen team to decide whether one member, who had been particularly disruptive of the group process and antagonistic to other participants, should continue as a member. The group decided to allow the individual to continue as a member and helped him become a more positive participant in the project.

Each day the National-Louis team met after the sessions, debriefing, adjusting activities, and trying to find the best ways to reach the needs of each participant. Little by little, by experiencing strategic lessons together, teachers began to open themselves to thinking about how these experiences might be able to connect in their own teaching. Some shared activities they were doing in their classrooms—one science teacher brought books that his students had created illustrating and explaining the various body systems and how they function. Another teacher who was teaching summer school tried out ideas and brought back tales of how the strategies worked with her students.

The celebration at the end of the 3 weeks was very real. Two teachers (English and music) led us in singing "Starting All Over" and "I Believe I Can Fly," those wonderful Tracy Chapman and R. Kelly songs. We had come a long way both in building understanding of what can be done to engage students as readers and learners *and* in building human relations. This cross-school summer seminar also served to bring together teachers in the same disciplines from the five different high schools and served as the beginning of a network for some shared departmental exchanges.

Reading Task Force Formed

In the fall of 1996, Dr. Klunk invited members of Amundsen's Goals 2000 team and the seven certificated reading teachers on staff to form the reading task force. That task force came together for the first time in August 1996 during the CPS staff development days. That task force, representing major content areas, scheduled weekly meetings to address reading improvement at the school. Led by Ken, the group knew the important role it had to play, had seen the success of the writing task force, and wanted to make a difference. However, it soon became clear that these members had very different expectations of what their goals were and how they should address reading. Moreover, they were not ready to work as a team. The Goals 2000 team had been studying the reading–thinking process in August, and were eager to implement some of their new ideas. Other members did not share this same orientation to reading—some represented special education, some bilingual education, and some, a more traditional, skills-based perspective.

It was clear that the model for school improvement established by the principal was one that blended administrative leadership with faculty initiative. Both Ed's and Ken's styles encouraged "top-down and bottom-up" leadership. They want to give professionals in the school the opportunity to set and maintain their own agenda for school improvement, while the administration sets the general direction and provides the impetus for change. This orientation, geared toward action, made it necessary for the task force to operate on a consensual model of decision making. The reason was clear: In a collegial and consensual model, the task force should speak with one voice to give clear guidance to a faculty that was willing, but at the time, unable to teach reading.

High school teachers find it especially difficult to respond to demands placed on them to teach something other than their subject matter. High school faculty who see themselves as subject matter specialists do not readily embrace the old adage, "Every teacher a teacher of reading." In fact, the idea of teaching reading generally creates a tension that leads to an avoidance response because most teachers have no idea how to teach reading in their specialty area. Therefore, from the very start defining "reading" was a major item of business. In fact, the agenda for the first month was "What is reading?" These were not easy meetings. With strong, intelligent, and informed individuals voicing their opinions, most of the initial meetings were dedicated to letting members express their ideas. The Goals 2000 team members were critical in this discussion. They had spent 3 weeks considering reading as an active, strategic thinking process and had learned ways to help students engage with texts in all subject areas. Now they argued strongly for this newer understanding of reading and helped the group establish a focus on reading as constructing meaning in context and on strategies for "reading to learn." This was the new idea of reading and one Amundsen decided to adopt.

After making this decision, the task force then looked at curriculum concerns and asked what was being tested in those high-stakes exams that are given. They also asked what could be done in the individual content areas to support the kinds of thinking students need to do. With the help of the Goals 2000 teachers, Donna Ogle, and Karen Boran (the intern from NLU), the answers began to become clearer to the task force. Information was presented about the state test and how to take tests in general. The focus was not on "how to fake it" or "get the test" but on how students could become better readers and how faculty could become better teachers of reading in their particular content areas. As the task force gained knowledge and learned about teaching possibilities, they addressed the issue of how to present this information to the full faculty.

The task force decided they (we use this pronoun to indicate the teacher-led nature of the group even though Ken was an active facilitator) would need to provide in-service support for the full faculty, focusing on instructional strategies and further explanations of the testing programs. To realize these activities, they developed in-service days for the faculty where strategies were modeled and explained. The task force also decided that there should be a schedule for when particular skills and strategies would be used in classrooms across all content areas so these ideas would be translated into use. Finally, they established weekly meeting time for faculty to share their experiences with these strategies, their concerns and their successes. These meetings were both within departments and across departments. A basic thrust of the project was to develop some general across-content area strategies and then to adapt them to the specific courses being taught.

Monitoring was done by members of the administration who visited classrooms and followed a faculty-developed checklist, which focused on the implementation of the reading-to-learn strategies in the classroom. Throughout the time the task force worked, this monitoring was made easier as a monthly instructional calendar was developed that indicated which strategies were to be used by specific content area each day of the week. The calendar simplified communication about the focus and monitoring and provided strong incentive for teachers to plan to use the strategies.

A Year on Probation

Whereas the task force focused on teaching practice and application with students, other events happened in the school that gave focus to reading. One of those was being put on probation. In October, Amundsen was placed on academic probation by the CPS leadership because of low reading scores achieved on the formerly de-emphasized TAP tests. This sent a shock wave through the building and created a level of urgency that was initially unsettling. At this time the principal's leadership was critical; he treated probation as an opportunity to focus the school and direct it even more toward academic goals. As he explained, "The designation of probation was not all bad. It provided leverage for me with the faculty to intensify our work with instruction and with reading especially. Probation was the factor that made it happen!" The work of the reading task force was pivotal here as it provided the vehicle through which the professionals in the school could set and maintain their own agenda for school improvement.

With the increased urgency of improvement in reading, additional steps were also initiated that supported the effort. These included emphasis on test preparation, active proctoring of classes, and attention to student motivation. In the area of student motivation, students were informed immediately of what probation meant, how Amundsen was placed on probation, and what the school needed to do to remove that designation. The entire school community was brought in as partners in the process of school improvement. Site leadership in instruction moved from the principal through the reading task force. The urgency of probation made it essential that instructional improvement occur. We the leaders felt that we could not do enough quickly enough in response to the urgent need. The task force felt pressured. Steps were taken for the task force to be given more support administratively. The faculty decided to reconfigure how the time provided was used. "Flex time" was used to provide support in reading strategies. Lane-credit classes were developed and offered after the regular school day at the school. On Saturday staff development workshops were offered with reimbursement provided to those who attended.

Beginning on a snowy Saturday in January 1997 and continuing through June, an average of 20 faculty participated every Saturday morning. Saturday topics included constructivist strategies in the classroom, IGAP testing, writing and reading in social studies, math improvement, and teams adventure learning. Important to note, the continued presence of the NLU Goals team members extended the focus that had begun in the previous summer.

IGAP testing came at the end of March for all 10th-graders. TAP exams were given April 1–2; and the school geared up for these exams, especially because the school was aware that the TAP scores now were the most crucial. The week prior to the TAP administration, Dr. Klunk arranged for a student assembly to reinforce the importance of the process to the students. He gave a motivational state-of-the-school address. Students knew what was expected as did faculty. Two weeks after the exam, Amundsen was presented with its results. Scores in reading had doubled; scores in math had gone up over 95%, science scores increased over 60%, and social studies scores increased by nearly a third.

These scores led to Amundsen being removed from probation. However, although these test results have been exceptionally positive, more important is what has happened in the building. An entire school effort brought about total school gain. From the perspective of the reading task force, they became convinced that theory works in practice. Embedding instructional strategies within and across the content areas by over 90% of the faculty seems to have resulted in significant gains for the school and positive feelings in the building about what can be accomplished when faculty work together.

Sustaining the Effort

What happens after the initial challenge has been met? Would Amundsen stay the course and continue working to help students achieve more in reading? That was the question in 1997. The answer, again, reflects the solid school leadership at all levels and its commitment to students. The reading task force decided that its work was not completed and planned for its continued work with another year of Monday staff development sessions and departmental reading days. They knew that the work had just begun and that teachers who were learning and rethinking their instruction needed further support. Although the Monday sessions were not as good as they would have liked, the opportunity to learn together seemed important. The Saturday classes received good support and were continued. There was a sense of accomplishment among those who took part. Dr. Klunk and Ken made their support for these teacher efforts clear.

In addition, as shown in Table 1, Amundsen test scores continued to increase. On the IGAP, all measures improved. On the formerly de-emphasized TAP, reading again showed strong improvement as did mathematics. Most important on the TAP, the percentage of students in the bottom quartile had moved from 64% in 1996 to 28% in 1998. This was real evidence of improved instruction and the schoolwide nature of the effort.

As the word of Amundsen's success spread around the city, there were many opportunities for the administrators involved to speak to other groups. Both Ken and Ed used these opportunities to highlight the teachers' efforts and often asked teachers to speak with them about the Amundsen experience. As Ken described in one of his talks:

> I don't believe in luck. Credit for the tremendous success we experienced was due to a "we" not me effort. It's not about any one person, or one administrator. It is not about a magic strategy or magic bullet. It is not glamorous; it is hard work. Some people have used the word "miracle" to describe the work at Amundsen. But if miracle can refer to something wonderful guided by purpose, then we did create a miracle—it could be called miraculous.

Goals 2000, funded for a second year, also planned another summer seminar. The Amundsen team attended as active participants. One of the priorities of

TABLE 1
Amundsen High School Reading and Writing Test Scores
on the IGAP, 1995–1998

Percentage of Students	1995		1996		1997		1998	
	Reading	Writing	Reading	Writing	Reading	Writing	Reading	Writing
Not meeting goals	60	71	69	58	60	63	48	55
Meeting goals	35	25	29	34	37	31	46	36
Exceeding goals	4	5	3	8	3	6	6	9

the grant was to develop leadership. Accordingly, the summer model encouraged team members to develop short workshop-type presentations about what they had learned for their colleagues, especially those who were new. However, as the Amundsen and NLU team worked together, it was clear that few faculty felt comfortable in this role. Even with great encouragement and offers of time and support in preparing workshops, only a few were ever presented. Two of these were by Amundsen faculty, the first to step out among our five schools. Generally, though, more time and support would be needed before teachers would feel confident sharing what they were doing.

After the summer institute, the Amundsen and NLU team consulted together and decided that our intern, Karen Boran, would work closely with one team of teachers in a 10th-grade ecology class that had 10 inclusion students in it—a tough class. Together the three teachers worked to implement the orientation and strategies that were being used in Goals 2000. With this as grounding, other faculty saw what was being done, dialogued with the team, and worked together, at least within the science department to make further changes in instruction. Karen also continued to attend the task force meetings and provide counsel on critical questions. Regular communication among all of the participants at NLU and Amundsen nurtured and shaped our progress.

In this context of close collaboration, we savored shared achievements a year later. In July 1998, Amundsen faculty took the lead as daily presenters for the third 2-week Goals 2000 summer institute. The teachers had worked with Karen on making presentations, creating graphics using Microsoft's PowerPoint software program, and practiced speaking before groups. Each workshop designed around one of the strategies they had been using as a result of Goals 2000 was successful.

Listening to Frank, Colleen, and seven of their Amundsen colleagues present workshops on strategic learning to other area high school teachers in our Goals 2000 project, we realized that we were seeing the fruits of 3 years of effort. These teachers and their school have stayed focused on raising reading scores and developing the reading-to-learn strategies of their students. To achieve that goal, they have also stayed focused on their own instructional development. Now they are explaining to other teachers some of their new instructional strategies. They are also demonstrating newly found confidence in sharing what they do in their classrooms with other teachers like themselves, good urban secondary content specialists who really would prefer to teach their "content" in the more traditional ways they have been comfortable with for many years. Yet, they are doing something different for their students.

They know their students cannot demonstrate all they have learned on the high-stakes tests. The more they know about the tests and the factors that influence the school's scores, the more skeptical they are about these public "testing" ordeals. They also have much more confidence in what they can do to improve students' learning and in how important their joint efforts are in reaching the academic goals they hold high.

Conclusion

The relationship between NLU and Amundsen, though driven by the demand for improved test scores, was animated by the desire to improve instruction and serve students better. The narrowness of test improvement pales in consideration of the wider and richer aims of helping students become more effective and efficient learners. This was accomplished by teachers who saw what was needed in an increasingly low-achieving population of mostly immigrant and low-income students and took the steps necessary to alter their own instruction and priorities.

At the same time, we know that without some strong "mandate" to create a sense of urgency Amundsen faculty would have had a very difficult time turning attention to the issue of reading. High school teachers too often think of themselves as content specialists rather than as instructional strategists. Dr. Klunk is particularly aware of how even probation helped his goal of focusing on instruction. "Probation was the factor you made it. I knew we could take this and hit the ground running. We had to do it together." The public notice brought to low achievement only set the stage—the school then wrote the play. By bringing the faculty together, understanding the human dimensions that are central to school life, and finding a way to elicit the professional strengths of the faculty, Dr. Klunk has empowered the Amundsen faculty to be in charge of the changes being made. Rather than persist in the frustration and anger that dominated at the beginning of this era of testing, the school has turned this challenge into an opportunity to focus together on instruction that addresses students' needs in basic literacy. Goals 2000 has had a part in this, too, by taking on a collaborative role. As Dr. Klunk explained, "Karen Boran was willing to become one with the faculty—rather than stand apart as an 'expert' force, she 'walked in our shoes.'" Throughout the process, the focus has been on the central role of the faculty and the building of their competence in strategic learning.

Chicago public schools are now emphasizing character education. What took place at Amundsen was an object lesson in character education. Teachers acted with humility and courage in addressing the issues confronting Amundsen High School: humility in recognizing existing challenging conditions and courage in their willingness to do something about those conditions, even when it meant changing their regular and comfortable instructional priorities.

The story is not ended, but the script has been written, the director knows how to evoke the best from his "actors," and the outcome seems much clearer. In the fall of 1998, for the first time there were teacher volunteers to lead the Monday staff development sessions, in fact more teachers than Mondays. Dr. Klunk sees this as one of the clearest signs of the ownership of this process and the knowledge and confidence that have evolved over these past tough years.

Analysis of Leadership

This case exemplifies how difficult it is to make changes at a large urban high school. Due to the coming together of several forces, Amundsen was able to make curricular changes that seem to be sustainable. The new principal arrived and decided that his first task was to provide his teachers and students with a safe climate. Only after that important step was taken was he ready to address issues of teaching and learning. Because he knew that the board's focus would be on academic accountability through testing, he hired an assistant principal in charge of testing.

These two administrators understood that it was crucial to have the teachers become an integral part of the change process, and they made good decisions about ways to get the teachers to buy into the change process. This case provides a powerful example of the struggles that were faced each time a new constituency was involved. Because the school administrators and the university partner, Donna Ogle, understood the necessity for bottom-up support, and therefore took the time to involve teachers in the decision making, the change was able to take hold and to gain ground. The new instructional demands that were required of the content-area teachers were difficult because they were unfamiliar and there were many teachers who did not believe that helping students to become better readers in the content areas was part of their job.

In this case, the authors believe that probation became the "leverage for the faculty to intensify our work with instruction and reading especially." The urgency of the moment, along with the leadership styles of the school administrators and university consultants, helped to bring about change in a setting that would ordinarily be resistant to change.

EXTENDING THINKING

Questions

1. The state provides staff development to high schools who are on probation through the Goals 2000 project. What were some of the strengths and weaknesses of this initiative? Reflect upon the challenges of this type of externally driven change effort?

2. In this case, the authors take the position that the impetus for change was when the school was placed on probation. Do you agree? Reflect upon the concept of school probation from the different perspectives of teachers and principals.

3. Consider the role of the principal in this large urban high school. How did he conceive of his role in terms of management activities and leadership activities?

4. Writing was the focus of the first staff development effort. In what ways did this experience constitute useful staff development? What other factors in the school were altered through this schoolwide change effort?

Activity

1. Consider the use of standardized test results to determine whether a school would be place on academic probation.. How is standardized testing used in your school and in your district? Because it is well known that testing is a force in driving instruction, how does your testing program affect the instructional program at your school. What are the attitudes of the teachers, parents, students, and administration in regard to testing. Do you use less formal measures of evaluation? Why or why not?

CASE 8

The Best Practice High School: Creating a New Small School in a Big City

Steve Zemelman
National-Louis University

Background

The Best Practice High School, located on the near west side, across the street from Michael Jordan's United Center, is part of a multiplex of three innovative small schools sharing the same building. Each school is teacher led, with one multiplex principal. Students are picked by lottery from the Best Practice Network of 14 K–8 schools, including several in the west-side neighborhood that is served. All the feeder schools have been working with National-Louis University faculty for several years under professional development grants and are located all over the city. The student body is about 58% African American, 40% Hispanic, and 2% other ethnic groups. About 82% of the families are classified as low income.

The Best Practice High School opened its doors in September 1996 after 3 years of planning by a dedicated group of veteran Chicago teachers, faculty from National-Louis University's (NLU) Center for City Schools, parents, and community and school reform activists. At this writing, it has been running for 4 years, with 436 students, 33 staff members, and scores of partners all around the city. The school was created to demonstrate that effective, state-of-the-art curriculum can succeed with the full range of Chicago kids of all ethnic groups and achievement levels. Private or magnet schools often succeed in urban areas by accepting only the best kids, using extra funds to reduce class size, and other special conditions. But the aim of Best Practice High School is to show that public education can succeed with normal kids and a normal public school budget, when powerful curriculum, flexible schedules, and other educational improvements are allowed to grow within a small-school setting.

THE CASE

The sophomores were reporting to the class on their freshly drafted constitutions. After watching an animated version of *Animal Farm* and posing questions about the story, they'd worked in small groups to design new constitutions for the farm. These constitutions were intended to prevent the reintroduction of injustice and class domination by which the pigs had soured the animals' first revolution. Unlike the response to most student speeches in school, everyone listened intently, because after each presentation the rest of the class was expected to lob questions to the designers to test the integrity of their proposals. The teacher planned this unit as a way to prepare students to study for the required U.S. constitution test.

This was just one moment in an inner-city high school where such activities take place regularly in just about every classroom. Students thinking, participating, taking initiative. Teachers working intently to create settings where such engagement will blossom. Why can't this happen with ordinary kids like these in all the schools in this big city? What sorts of leadership does it take to create an innovative public school within a large, traditional, hierarchical urban bureaucracy? Can school reform enable people's initiative for such a project? How difficult is it to introduce change by creating new schools in an established system?

As a group of us worked over a 3-year period to conceive and launch the Best Practice High School in Chicago, we found that many different kinds of energy—more politely known as leadership—have been exerted by people in very different positions. Each has been necessary, each characteristic of a particular stage in the process: political energy to bring the Chicago Board of Education to endorse small schools and establish a program that would create a group of them; the work and thought to conceive what a model small high school ought to look like; detailed preoperational start-up efforts that included finding a site and getting it rehabbed, hiring teachers, designing and fighting for a start-up budget, obtaining furniture and equipment, recruiting our first freshman class.

Then, the moment the doors were opened on the first day of school began the intense first-year process of survival and self-creation, in which social and academic norms had to be determined and enacted among students and faculty, schedules and rules and procedures invented and adjusted, responsibilities and patterns of working together (and separately) negotiated, boundaries between the school and the rest of the world both defended and made permeable—all while everyone was teaching their classes every day. Now, after more than 3 years in operation, tasks and leadership have gradually shifted to deepen and refine some of the school's innovations, to take on issues that time and energy did not allow in the first year, even to bring to the surface problems and differences that would have been too threatening to face before.

School reform in Chicago was not particularly designed to encourage or support this complex process of change. But many visionary people took it as the occasion to make such efforts across the city. At a few crucial moments, district leaders and bureaucrats gave some needed support—though as people who work for any large organization can imagine, the bureaucracy creates new obstacles almost daily as it continues the hierarchical and self-preserving ways it has always followed. Leadership, as innovative schools will find, continues as a daily act of defense, re-creation, and survival. This chapter retells the story of starting the Best Practice High School, as it offers snapshots of these many kinds of leadership.

But we would be naive not to also go further and face a larger question. Will the kinds of leadership provided in our creation of one small high school be enough to sustain a new, innovative, even a successful program, as the larger bureaucracy continues to exert its always centralizing, conforming, testing-oriented power? And is there any possibility that our model could lead to more such schools or perhaps even a systemic level of change? The experience of gifted and determined leaders like Deborah Meier in New York is not encouraging. Reflecting on that system's resistance to the flourishing of the 140 new small schools there, Meier (1998) remarked:

> Except for small enclaves within the large institution, in which special constituencies carve out their own intimate sub-schools (the ones designed for the top students or for the most vulnerable), the school as a whole remains remarkably anonymous and unchangeable, the model of a non-learning institution. (p. 360)

Or, as Linda Darling-Hammond (1997) observed, "Big urban bureaucracies eat good schools for lunch and spit them out, over and over again.". What sorts of leadership are needed to help make real improvement more widespread and more permanent? Although we don't have all the answers to this question, we'd be remiss not to consider it.

Some Characteristics of the School

When a visitor comes to Best Practice to see what we're doing, what are the major characteristics he or she will particularly notice? Our visitor will see very quickly that our school features:

Small total size
Heterogeneous student body
Student-centered instruction such as reading–writing workshop
Thematic/integrated/negotiated curriculum units

Student choice during part of the weekly schedule
Inclusion of special education in regular classrooms
Daily advisory
Mix of block and traditional scheduling
Technology-rich instruction
Service learning
Authentic assessment
Parent involvement
University connections
Community and business partnerships
A caring environment

Our students represent a wide range of ethnic backgrounds and achievement levels, and come primarily from the Best Practice Network of 14 schools spread over the city, including 4 schools in the immediate neighborhood. The small size of the Best Practice High School ensures that no students fall between the cracks. The school started in September 1996 with a freshman class of 135 students, adding a new freshman group of 100 to 125 each year, until it has reached its total of 436 for the full school, Grades 9 through 12. Small size facilitates teacher planning and speedy, flexible decision making but does not need to engender high cost. Student-to-teacher ratios are actually based on the same formulas as those in other Chicago high schools.

At the Best Practice High School, students and teachers together plan in-depth study of significant issues and questions in students' lives. Two- to 3-week study projects scheduled regularly throughout the year integrate the various subject areas, rather than fragment learning into disconnected pieces. Students receive individual help with skills as needed in writing, reading, and math. For one half-day per week, all students travel to internships in social service agencies, museums, businesses, and other professional settings. The other half of that day, students participate in special activities of their choice, ranging from chess to dance to science lab make-up. Small advisories meet for half an hour every day to make sure each student has at least one teacher who knows him or her in a setting other than the regular academic classroom. A peer mediation program helps students deal with conflicts—and at this writing is one of the very few running in Chicago high schools.

Although the Best Practice High School is not a perfect place, it is a school filled with intense effort to make urban education work, enacting scenes of deep and engaged learning, and promoting gratifying growth as the students advance through each year. As we look at the story of how the school has come to be, we can contemplate some of the opportunities and obstacles to even rather limited change in a large bureaucratic school system, and what sorts of leadership have been required to make it happen.

Setting Wheels in Motion—The Role of Community Activists

The Best Practice High School could not have come into existence without the efforts of some determined activists in the Chicago community, and so it's a good idea to start this story with them. One is John Ayers, director of an organization called Leadership for Quality Education (LQE). LQE is a creation of a group called the Civic Committee, which is made up of representatives of Chicago's largest corporations. The Civic Committee addresses a number of social issues in the city, and when school reform began in Chicago in 1989, the Committee created LQE to join in that work. John's brother, Bill Ayers, heads the Small Schools Workshop at the University of Illinois at Chicago, and so it was not surprising for John to pick up on small schools himself.

Another activist Bill Ayers recruited for small schools was Alex Polikoff, director of Business and Professional People in the Public Interest (BPI). BPI's focus for many years had been (and continues to be) fair housing. Polikoff led the 20-year court battle called the Gatreaux case, which has resulted in demolition of a number of the segregated high-rise public housing projects in Chicago, to be replaced by scatter-site low-rise units and by vouchers for low-income tenants to obtain housing in other locations. As the buildings began to come down and focus shifted from the courtroom to creating viable mixed-income neighborhoods, Polikoff understood that without improvements in community services such as health, safety, and education, the project could never reach its real objective.

Together, John Ayers and Alex Polikoff created a Small Schools Policy Committee that set about defining what a Chicago small-schools initiative should look like, and then began lobbying the Board of Education to create a group of new small schools in Chicago, modeled after the New Visions effort in New York. When Chicago Mayor Richard Daley gained increased power over the schools in 1995 and appointed one of his chief advisors, Paul Vallas, as CEO, Ayers and Polikoff approached Vallas and board president Gery Chico immediately about their project. "I would have lobbied more incrementally," John Ayers commented, "but Alex went straight to the top, and it worked." Vallas moved a vote on small schools through the Board, but it took constant pushing to actually establish a procedure for creating new schools and an office within the board that would guide this procedure through to fruition. Ayers and Polikoff met with Vallas almost weekly, pressuring him to keep the steps moving within a bureaucracy that was preoccupied with numerous other programs and crises. And they and their assistant Robin Steans sat directly on the board committee organized to create and implement a plan. Ultimately, the Board issued an RFP (request for proposal) to choose 10 groups to start new small schools in Chicago. The Best Practice group was one of them.

It's important to recognize how essential the participation of BPI and LQE was in bringing the Best Practice High School and the other Chicago small schools into existence. Paul Vallas would never have taken time to meet every week with the Chicago teachers or university professors or other small activist groups trying to start new schools. We were small fry. But Ayers and Polikoff carried behind them the clout of large corporations, influential lawyers, and real estate developers. And they were sensitive to the issues of the school innovators besides. So they'd listen almost daily to the school planners' needs, their desperate howls every time a new obstacle would present itself, and they'd diplomatically carry the issues to Vallas' desk.

One example: When the Board approved the concept of small schools, and even after they established the RFP process, no funds were budgeted for start-up, except for tiny $10,000 planning grants. It's rather hard to imagine, but nothing was set aside for new (or even used) equipment, furniture, computers, libraries, textbooks, copiers, or telephones. It took a separate lobbying campaign to get funds committed, and even then the budget people couldn't come up with more than about a quarter of what the CEO finally promised.

Not surprisingly, the process of lobbying Paul Vallas couldn't last. Small schools offered a far too subtle, complex, and labor-intensive answer to improving Chicago's schools, for a politically minded CEO concerned with Chicago's brutal politics and media. Conservative critics whispered that small schools were a trojan horse for progressive education (true). Bureaucrats complained that they were being pestered with too many special requests for books, budgets, and furniture. Principals warned that teacher leadership would create chaos.

And so Vallas soon moved on to much larger, more publicly recognizable strategies like putting 139 schools on probation, with the threat to fire the principal and teachers if they didn't improve test scores enough. This, to the newspapers, looked much more like progress. Vallas' focus had shifted; but the door remained open just long enough for a group of small schools to be established, followed by a group of charter schools that were actually quite similar. "For eight months we were able to make things happen," John Ayers said. "Those were heady days. Instead of the usual school administrator's negativity, we approached each obstacle by asking, 'How can we get around this?'"

Ayers and Polikoff helped open the doors for grant money, as well. Aided by their testimony, we obtained planning grants from the Lloyd A. Fry Foundation, the McDougal Family Foundation, the Polk Bros. Foundation, and the Prince

Charitable Trust. John and Alex had done their job. Meanwhile, grant support has also come from the Chicago Annenberg Challenge, the Joyce Foundation (which funded the larger Best Practice Network of which the high school is a part), and the DeWitt Wallace–Readers Digest "Students at the Center" initiative in Chicago.

The Role of the External Partner—Conceptualizing

The Best Practice High School began as the dream of a group of university faculty and public school teachers who'd been focused for years on classroom curriculum, not governance or school restructuring. As the faculty leaders of the Center for City Schools at NLU, Harvey Daniels, Marilyn Bizar, and Steve Zemelman have worked with schools throughout northern Illinois on progressive approaches to teaching literacy, and have written extensively on the subject. And from well before the Center's existence, Daniels and Zemelman have directed the Illinois Writing Project.

Two of the long-time teacher-leaders associated with the Writing Project and the Center, Tom and Kathy Daniels, shared with the NLU folks the frustration that few high schools in Chicago took the kind of interest that many elementary schools had, in new approaches to teaching and learning. Though individual high school teachers attended workshops and developed exciting classrooms, it was difficult to find a whole school that embodied more progressive classroom practices. A few magnet schools could boast of success, but it was easy for observers to dismiss it as simply the result of creaming the city's best students and letting them blossom all in one place.

And so these teacher-dreamers began to consider that creating a new high school might be more effective than attempting to reform an existing one, at least for purposes of establishing a model of good high school education for regular students in an urban setting. An essential kind of leadership they first brought to the process, in other words, was their knowledge of, and commitment to, a particular kind of classroom.

Daniels and Zemelman, along with fellow faculty member Arthur Hyde, had written the book, *Best Practice: New Standards for Teaching and Learning in America's Schools*, gathering together the recommendations that came in the early 1990s from the many commissions and professional organizations writing standards for each educational field. These recommendations proved not only to be surprisingly progressive, but also to be in clear agreement about what makes education effective. Zemelman, Daniels, and Hyde summarized 13 principles they found embodied in the reports. Teaching and learning, the standards documents said, needs to be:

Student Centered: The best starting point for schooling is kids' real interests; all across the curriculum, investigating students' own questions should always take precedence over studying arbitrarily and distantly selected "content."

Experiential: Active, hands-on, concrete experience is the most powerful and natural form of learning. Students should be immersed in the direct experience of the content of every subject.

Holistic: Children learn best when they encounter whole, real ideas, events, and materials in purposeful contexts, not by studying subparts isolated from actual use.

Authentic: Real, rich, complex ideas and materials are at the heart of the curriculum. Lessons that water down, control, or oversimplify content ultimately disempower students.

Expressive: To fully engage ideas, construct meaning, and remember information, students must regularly employ the whole range of communicative media—speech, writing, drawing, poetry, dance, drama, music, movement, and the visual arts.

Reflective: Balancing the immersion in experience must be opportunities for learners to look back, to reflect, to abstract from their experiences what they have felt and thought and learned.

Social: Learning is socially constructed and often interactional; teachers must create interactions that "scaffold" learning with support not just from the adult but also from other students.

Collaborative: Cooperative learning activities tap the social power of learning better than competitive and individualistic approaches.

Democratic: The classroom is a model community; students learn what they live as citizens of the school.

Cognitive: The most powerful learning comes from developing true understanding of concepts, higher order thinking, and self-monitoring of thinking.

Developmental: Children grow through a series of definable but not rigid stages, and schooling should fit its activities to the developmental level of students, based on careful observation of individuals by the teacher.

Constructivist: Children do not just receive content; in a very real sense, they re-create and reinvent every cognitive system they encounter, including language, literacy, and mathematics.

Challenging: Students learn best when faced with genuine challenges, choices, and responsibility in their own learning. (Zemelman, Daniels, & Hyde, 1998)

These were the principles that the whole group hoped to enact in their school, and that provided a basis on which to build the project. This meant that the concept for the school wasn't just focused on size or organization or autonomy, as important as these might be. It was about what teaching and learning should look like in individual classrooms, where the real work of school takes place. Writing the book helped both to articulate these principles and to convince other people, including foundation officers and small-schools committee members, that creating the school was in fact a good idea.

The External Partner—Knocking on Doors

In addition to providing a conceptual framework, the other category of leadership the university partners could carry out was the pavement pounding, telephone dialing, and meeting sitting necessary to bring the school into existence. The teachers simply couldn't do this work because they were teaching classes every day in the schools where they worked, doing administrative tasks, and then grading papers every evening. Only university folks, with their sinfully flexible and open schedules, were in a position to pursue the quarry.

The most time-consuming task proved to be finding a location, though in truth the long effort we exerted was not what ultimately brought us our site. Real estate, it seems, is everything in Chicago. Without a location, no one took us seriously. Yet the more desirable the location, the more difficult it was to obtain. We were welcome to occupy empty and crumbling school buildings in the poorest areas, lodged between rival gang turfs; but unused or partially occupied schools in good neighborhoods were guarded by powerful forces. During one period as we negotiated to share part of a school in a gentrified north-side lake shore area, this writer spent many evenings attending neighborhood organization meetings, sitting in late-night strategy sessions in local eateries, bidding on items at fund-raiser auctions, and communicating with a skeptical alderman and his minions. In spite of extensive lobbying and explaining, a movement opposing the school sprang up in the neighborhood under the slogan, "Little kids, little problems; big kids, big problems." Did this represent simply a general fear of teenagers, or did it contain a racial overtone as well? In any event the ugliness was sobering. We withdrew from the fight when we realized that even the Local School Council in the building was ambivalent about our project and surprisingly negative toward teachers.

Ultimately, we obtained space through a series of quirky political twists of fortune. An old high school building, Cregier Vocational High School, just across the parking lot from the United Center, where the Chicago Bulls play, had been occupied by a poorly run program used as a dumping ground for troublesome kids. Its attendance rate was miserable. We'd already interviewed the principal and decided he'd be impossible to work with when he showed us the baseball bat he kept under his desk. The board CEO decided to close the school, and when Hispanic groups in the city complained about overcrowding in their neighborhood schools, he declared 2 weeks before the start of a new academic year that this building would take some of the overflow. The plan had nothing to recommend it, no time for it to gel, and parents didn't want to bus their kids to some unknown neighborhood, so no one came. Now the Democratic national convention was looming in the coming summer, with an empty, run-down eyesore uncomfortably close across the parking lot. Suddenly Paul Vallas recalled John Ayers' proposal to rehab Cregier and place several small schools there, and immediately called Ayers by cell phone from his car to discuss the matter. This was apparently one more part of the spruce-up that Mayor Daley was executing around the city for the convention. "We bailed him out," Ayers reflected.

The board of education's RFP for small schools was thus issued in September 1995. One major feature immediately caught our eye: the timetable. Proposals were due at the end of September, applicants would be notified some time thereafter, and the schools were to begin operation on February 5, 1996. Here was leadership to contemplate. The concept was that somehow a good new school could be brought into existence—space rehabbed, principal and teachers hired, students recruited, furniture and books ordered and delivered, scheduling and curriculum planned—in at most 3 months. This was breathtaking. We called it the "circus tent" approach to school creation. Roll into town, set up at night, and open the doors the next morning. We concluded that no one really wanted these schools to succeed, and that the request was in fact a trap.

This was the low point in our journey. The school would never come to be and we should now move on with our lives. There was one problem, however. Because we'd talked about the project so often, we'd lose credibility if we didn't at least apply for the opportunity. Not everyone understood that the board's timeline was suicidal. So we chose a solution that perhaps illustrates a principle sometimes useful in the leadership process. We'd go ahead and write a proposal, but preface it with a letter explaining the ill-conceived nature of the board's time requirement and listing a series of conditions we required. We'd offer them a school only if they promised to meet these conditions. This would either gain us the support we'd need or serve as a poison pill to protect us from an impossible situation. The night before Thanksgiving the call came. Our proposal was accepted, and we had until September 1996 to open the doors.

Putting the Pieces Together

In the following months, the tasks and obstacles came at us one on top of the last. The board would rehab the building. Plans had to be reviewed, computer wiring mapped out. The three schools to occupy the building had to negotiate how they'd share the space. The board's small-schools committee sought and interviewed principal candidates and we sat in on the final round of interviews (one of the aforementioned conditions). We advertised for teachers, held several large meetings to brief candidates and meet them en masse, and then interviewed the most promising individuals. We drew up lists of all the equipment and materials we'd need and a budget to chart their cost. We spent days at the board building and with our activist friends trying to convince the bureaucrats to give us a start-up budget and some furniture—bothersome requests that didn't win us friends in the administration, as we later learned.

One of the most pressing tasks was student recruitment. One widely misunderstood but key feature of Chicago high schools is that over 50% of students attend a school outside their own neighborhood—either a magnet school, a subject-focused school, or just a school with a better reputation. This means all the high schools begin recruiting students before Christmas. And because budgets depend on the numbers, the schools make it bureaucratically difficult for a student to transfer, once he or she has signed up. Wooing their signed-up students would guarantee lots of enemies around the system.

So we went to work designing and printing a brochure (with grant money), hosting a lunch for counselors from our Best Practice Network feeder schools, and visiting their eighth-grade classes to talk up our endeavor. We designed an application form that included teacher and counselor recommendations. We chose not to select students by test scores, because we didn't want to create another elite school; but we did want to ensure we'd have students who desired to attend a school like ours. Other new small high schools that have started on a less favorable timetable have been forced to begin with a population of disgruntled students who wished to leave—or were pressured to leave—the high schools they were already attending.

Typical obstacles were the board's decision to award Chapter I discretionary moneys based on enrollment the previous spring—which meant we'd get none—and endless delays in decisions on school-to-work funding. Without these funds, we'd be unable to place a teacher in our computer lab, or to establish the internship program that would involve our students in businesses and community agencies once a week. Each of these problems was resolved in our favor, but only after countless phone calls and visits to the board. The resultant delays prevented the internship coordinator from arranging student placements until late in the summer. Building principal Sylvia Gibson recalled, "I felt like it was a war. I had to plan for each of my battles—policies, union rules, money for books. I knew we wouldn't get everything we wanted. But sometimes I'd win a round."

There were so many concerns to address—Tom and Kathy Daniels, the lead teachers, kept a running list generally never fewer than 60 items—that talk about curriculum was nearly impossible. We'd schedule a retreat, make an agenda, and still find that decisions about basic structures and pressing practicalities kept us so busy we couldn't concentrate on the ultimate guts of the program—what would happen between students and teachers in the classroom. In the summer, the faculty attended the 5-day Walloon Institute, directed by Harvey Daniels, and spent each day planning for the coming year, only to run into the same blizzard. Special education teacher Sonja Kosanovic:

> We had so much to talk about before school started that we met for hours and hours and still weren't ready. One problem for me was discipline. We had few consistent rules or consequences. But there was no blame to be placed for this. It was just too far down on the agenda. What helped me through that time was the support of the other teachers.

Another development that made planning difficult was that the Mayor promised the Ameritech Corporation the use of our building as a base of communications in support of the Democratic National Convention. From midsummer until the weekend before classes were to begin, we learned, we'd have little or no access—though because the rehab work was behind schedule, it wouldn't have made much difference anyway. Furniture couldn't be delivered. Or computers. Or books. Or paper and pencils. Which also wouldn't have made much difference because the budgets for ordering these things weren't loaded until well into the summer anyway, and deliveries couldn't be scheduled until after school started. Our school opened on the day after Labor Day with nearly bare rooms, furnished with exactly one set of items: hundreds of blue plastic chairs. Students looking back on those first days recalled their disappointment:

> Edgar: "It was like an abandoned building."
> Itanzia: "You couldn't do labs. There was no equipment. We couldn't use the gym. The floor wasn't even waxed."
> Alex: "I thought—this is high school?"
> Elizabeth "It's new and you're expecting great things, and then this!"

Principal and Teachers as Leaders

The small-schools RFP recognized the role of teacher leadership in small schools, directing that in two cases schools would be grouped together under a single principal, with lead teachers handling many leadership responsibilities. In our case, three schools were placed in one building, called the Cregier Multiplex: Best Practice, a K–8 student-centered school called the Foundations School, and Nia School, which featured an Afro-centric program for Grades 4 through 8. Representatives of the three schools sat in on principal interviews and we chose Sylvia Gibson, who had worked previously as assistant principal in a north-side elementary school.

Sylvia proved to be a dream choice—a warm, confident African-American woman who'd had lots of practice at her previous job giving teachers broader roles and building consensus among them. Her position couldn't be trickier. Although the board above her regards her as a regular principal and considers her responsible for everything that happens in the building, the teachers vigorously guard their autonomy. Sylvia runs interference and fights battles for the school at the board, whereas back in the building, she calmly leaves much of the decision-making to the teachers, as long as things go well. In the area of budgeting, for example, the lead teachers have full access to the budget lines in the board's central computer and can therefore fully control the budgeting process, a privilege not accorded to teachers at most Chicago schools.

When serious difficulties arise, Sylvia doesn't hesitate to step in, but does so diplomatically and calls on the teachers to find solutions to their problems. Naturally, of course, the teachers perceive the reporting requests that are funneled through her from the board as impositions. As Sylvia explained the relationships in the school:

> The challenge was how to define my role and how to build trust with people who'd already been working together in each school. Theoretically, I have more power than they, and they were used to principals who threw their weight around. I met subtle resistance. The board says I'm the ultimate person in charge. The teachers prefer that I'd only be in charge of the physical plant. Yet, I'm held responsible. However, I do believe in teacher-led schools. I worked under a principal who delegated a lot of responsibility. We voted on curriculum, we voted on textbooks. He never forced new ideas on people, but sent me out into the classroom to sell new ideas.

Whatever the minor strains, the arrangement has worked, though it clearly depends on the individual personalities. It's easy to project that with a different person as principal, the school could have become a far more contentious place.

Seeking a Shape

The initial tasks of the first year of the school, beyond ruining our backs carrying furniture and equipment up two flights of stairs, were to survive as an entity while simultaneously defining ourselves, handling administrative paperwork, dealing with endless obstacles at the Board of Education office, keeping the day-to-day teaching going, and beginning to build a positive climate for learning and working together. Every detail of the school's operation had to be worked out, and there had been almost no time to do the planning in the months before school opened. What would the daily schedule look like? Exactly how would teaching address the knowledge and skills students needed while integrating the separate subjects? How would we build student voice and choice into the learning process? What would be the rules of student behavior and how would they be maintained? Would we have after-school sports and activities?

We'd decided to begin with just freshmen and add a class each year, to ease the complexities of getting started. This meant, however, that the first-year faculty was small, consisting of English teacher Kathy Daniels and computer teacher Tom Daniels (with these two serving as lead teachers and handling virtually all the administrative work), Peter Thomas in social studies, Mark Fertel in math, Arthur Griffin in physics, Aiko Boyce for art, Pat Gregory in physical education, Sonja Kosanovic in special education, Shelley Freeman heading the internship program, and Jackie Chappell the library. Our office staff consisted of two experienced clerks who found themselves handling a myriad of duties, including student discipline and responses to parent and public inquiries, along with all the usual school recordkeeping.

The tasks of the lead teachers, in addition to teaching their students, included drafting budgets, ordering equipment, books, and supplies (a many-stepped process in our highly bureaucratic system), writing and rewriting proposals for the various extra funds often offered last minute by the board, lobbying and pleading for additional positions (example: We qualified for an assistant principal, but tried, unsuccessfully, to get the line switched so it could release the lead teachers from some of their classroom duties), dealing with stalled paperwork for some of our already-chosen faculty, filing the constant flow of reports, responding to almost daily requests from the bureaucracy for new forms of control and reporting, guiding visiting friends and officials on tours of the building, attending meetings required by various board departments, dealing with relationships among the teachers and with outside partners.

The staff as a group faced countless decisions that would gradually give shape to the school. Take the daily schedule, for example. The teachers wanted to balance a fairly traditional approach that allowed them to teach each traditional subject to each student, with a block schedule that would focus on more integrated teaching and learning. They considered but rejected options such as having students work with only half the faculty for a given part of the year. This would have cut in half the number of students each teacher saw, but would have split the staff into two smaller teams. When the teachers tried the block schedule, they found at first that some of them, as well as many of the students, were-n't ready to use it effectively. And the first integrated study unit that the teachers designed using the block schedule did not work well. Students wasted much of the class time set aside for research, and even though they were given some choices of what to learn about, many seemed directionless. The teachers repeatedly extended the project deadline, which only prolonged the agony. When teachers have had no opportunity to practice new approaches, even a strong desire to make them work does not guarantee immediate success. How-ever, by the second year the faculty began to devise ways of combining structure and choice effectively, along with strategies to utilize the block periods more ef-fectively.

Ultimately, the teachers worked out a schedule that balanced their many needs. An "A" block schedule features 100-minute periods with students at-tending half their subjects Tuesday and the other half Thursday; and a "B" schedule uses 50-minute periods to rotate students to all their classes each day on Mondays and Fridays. From the start, a half hour of advisory was included at midday, paired with lunch so that half the school eat while the other half attend their advisories. On Wednesdays, the students go out to their internships on busses for half the day (supposedly leaving common planning time for the teachers, though new board rules about the number of adults on trip buses un-dermined that arrangement). And on the other half of the day, students attend "choice time" sessions that include chess, dance, drama, student government, poetry writing, and other special topics.

Gradually, however, the staff has experimented more and more with the sched-ule. They realized that if they wished to declare a special schedule, all they needed to do was decide the night before and put up signs, or announce it in classes first thing in the morning. Because all students (except seniors) study the same sub-jects, schedule conflicts simply don't exist. The students proved to be far more flexible than expected. Math teacher Mark Fertel became the time management expert, and modified schedules began to appear whenever a special project, school trip, or visiting speaker required it. Did the kids need extra time to finish their science projects, with editing help from the teachers or time for word pro-cessing in the computer lab? Change the schedule. We'd discovered one of the great advantages of a small school. No large traditional American high school could operate this way. Of course, many teacher-hours went into planning alter-nate schedules and discussing how and whether they might work.

The use of integrated learning activities, already mentioned, presented a similar challenge. The faculty at first attempted these in schoolwide units. The first unit, titled "Here We Are," was meant to help the students learn about the building, the neighborhood, and the city where our school was located. The teachers chose the main topic and offered a choice of subtopics to the kids. But it was difficult and time consuming to marshal study material for many of the subtopics, and the students lacked the study skills or the motivation to find information on their own. We worked intensely to add interest and reality to the project by bringing in visitors for the students to interview and organized an entire day when students rotated through group interviews with neighborhood leaders, architects, educators, and older adult grads who'd gone to school in our building. But without student buy-in or sufficient informational background, the interviews meant little to them.

As the unit stretched from November into December, it bumped up against the physics teacher's plans for science fair projects. Because the students felt the pressure of his grading, the science projects began to take precedence. And though the kids needed help with write-ups of their science experiments, the other teachers hadn't organized to provide it. Both projects suffered as a result; but the staff learned that better planning and shorter, more focused units could improve the situation.

In the spring, the teachers took a more circumspect approach to integrated learning. Three teachers, Kathy Daniels in English, Peter Thomas in social studies/geography, and Aiko Boyce in art, collaborated on a very focused plan. Thomas would instruct the students on the relationship of geographical features and the organization of societies. Students were to work in groups inventing their own "island civilizations" to illustrate these concepts. Daniels would help the students create written documents that would reflect their imagined societies. And Boyce would show them how to make topographical maps using flour and salt, and map hangings made by crochet. The choices were narrower, but there was meaningful content, a manageable structure, and plenty of creativity. Students had been acquiring computer graphics skills from Boyce and plugged these into their stories and documents. The kids grew engaged, the products delightful. This was a major step.

A grant from the JCPenney Corporation provided the teachers with summer and during-the-year planning time to design integrated units for the next year. Buoyed by this, the teachers surveyed the students to gather input for topics for Year 2, so that student choice could be deepened. With guidance from integrated curriculum experts James Beane and Barbara Brodhagen, surveys were designed to help students ask questions that mattered to them, first about themselves and then about the world. The strongest common concerns proved to be students' own futures, and social peace and understanding.

In Year 2, now with both freshmen and sophomores, the teachers worked in grade-level teams. The first freshman integrated unit attempted once again to tackle the "Here We Are" topic, whereas the sophomore teachers focused on

"Windows and Mirrors," a multicultural inquiry comparing some aspect of one's own culture to a different one. Although things went somewhat better, the teachers were still overwhelmed by the massive amount of information students needed but couldn't gather very effectively by themselves.

Then in early spring, the sophomore team designed a unit they called "Isms," on various forms of discrimination—sexism, heterosexism, racism, ageism, ableism. They tried still another variation in the structure, and this time it worked. For a week, teachers provided content for the students, each teacher focused on one "ism," using regular 50-minute periods. History teacher Kate Lang, for example, provided brief background readings on various key pieces of legislation and famous court cases relating to civil rights. The chemistry teacher, Doug Spalding, provided stories about young adults' struggles with gender roles and homosexuality. At the end of the week, students chose an "ism" to explore further, and a mode of expression for their own projects. The modes included photography, videography, posters, children's books, a collage "wall of respect" that featured heroes who'd struggled against the "isms," both famous people and members of the kids' own families. During the second week, using block schedule time, students gathered information, planned, and executed their projects.

We now had a structure that solved many of our challenges. Students whose research skills or motivation were still shaky had plenty of content to work with. Whatever the projects, students had engaged with important material in history, literature, art, and politics. There was also plenty of time for further inquiry on their own choice of topics within a decent range of possibilities. And the time schedule was designed according to teaching and learning needs, rather than the other way around.

Leadership for these scheduling and curriculum developments came from a variety of sources. At first, the lead teachers set the tone. The university partners pitched in suggestions. Math teacher Mark Fertel came in almost every Monday of the first year with a new schedule to consider. History teacher Kate Lang took the initiative to design the "Isms" project. Yet what a long process of planning, work, and frustration it had taken to get to this point. And this was just one set of tasks facing everyone. Others, such as establishing after-school activities, deciding on rules of student conduct, and preparing students for standardized testing, demanded attention. And some, like discipline policies, were simply left to wait, because there seemed to be little energy or time left to address them.

Students' Roles and Responses

We'd like to think that intense innovation and student-centered approaches would elicit delighted enthusiasm from our students and inspire them to take leadership initiatives themselves. And in the long run, this can indeed develop. However, during the initial months of a new program, particularly with teenagers who have become well accustomed to the traditional schooling that also bores them, the response can be extremely trying. Although our students asserted in their applications that they wanted to come to a different kind of school, most had little idea what that entailed. "This isn't real high school!" they whined. "Where are the textbooks?" And because they represented a wide range of achievement and motivation levels, many were glad to spend much of their time socializing or acting out. Students complained—about the lunches, about the closed-campus rules, about several of the teachers—but took no positive action to get their needs met. The relaxed atmosphere seemed like an invitation to test the rules. Many students accepted the street culture dictum that every conflict be settled with physical violence. And in even the best of settings, the hormones and energy levels of 13-year-olds can be nearly uncontrollable.

Even though there was no planned-out broader discipline policy, the faculty responded rather firmly, policing the halls between classes, requiring passes for students leaving classrooms during the periods, meting out punishments for the inevitable sexual escapades, banning T-shirt logos to squelch even the suggestion of wannabe gang gestures. This is when we understood that it had been best to start with a staff toughened by years of experience in city schools. Fortunately, firmness was not the only quality of the student–teacher relationship. Individual students received plenty of attention. When we found that many students were struggling with physics, the science teacher added extra help periods to the "choice-time" options. As the teachers began to better organize and coordinate efforts, students found that they'd get help from the English teacher in writing up reports for science, and help from the art teacher to add computer graphics to their essays. Students who acted immature in classes seemed to grow up instantly, if sometimes temporarily, when helping younger children during internships in neighboring schools. Students who were learning to use video cameras in their internships began taping school events.

Bit by bit, student by student, positive experiences added up. After Christmas break that 1st year, said Sonja Kosanovic, the students mellowed and grew more trusting:

> In the fall I'd say hello to kids in the hall and they'd ignore me. After Christmas they started opening up. When I sponsored a "Spring Extravaganza" talent show, half the school participated. It may have been chaotic but it was an important step. In May, half the entire class applied to be peer mediators, and that showed their commitment.

Sophomore Edgar Arrellano explained proudly, "It's such a small school, you get to know everyone, Black and Hispanic, kids all together. At the beginning of the year groups were fighting with each other, but gradually we got together." Fellow student Itanzia Wilcox added, "We call it 'stomping with the big dogs.'" Even though there's still more they want happening at their school, the students noted how integrated projects, choice-time activities, internships, and caring teachers all helped to mold the positive climate.

By the 2nd year, student leadership began to show itself and have an effect on the school. The peer mediation team was trained and took up regular duty to help settle conflicts—surprisingly the first such program operating in a Chicago high school. One of the seemingly most irresponsible students joined with a more successful boy to propose and lead a Wednesday choice-time activity. The student council requested (and the faculty agreed on) a student role interviewing candidates for the new teaching positions for the next year. Colead teacher Kathy Daniels reflected:

> I don't know if it's just maturing or also that they're coming to realize we value their opinions. But just last week some of the freshmen who like to complain a lot served as tour guides for open house and we listened as they told next year's new kids and their parents all the things they loved about the school.

Perhaps the most telling event was also a sad and frightening one. During our second year, a sophomore boy was shot and killed on a Saturday night in his own neighborhood (nowhere near the school) and Monday morning the school erupted in grief. Teachers who had worked in tough neighborhoods testified that killings there had brought only the faintest reactions at school. Here, the students refused to sit docile and listen to the school board's "crisis team" spout platitudes. In ones, twos, and threes they stood up, walked out of the library, and started searching for ways to express their feelings. It was frightening and difficult trying to keep some of the angry boys in the building, though we mostly succeeded. Then, down the hall, a cluster of kids gathered. We fearfully hurried to investigate, but found they'd pulled out the video cameras to record memories of their classmate, to be given to his family. Still other students headed to the computers to compose poems, letters, and banners, which they posted around his locker, not unlike the "offrendas" they'd learned about when studying the Mexican Day of the Dead traditions. By Wednesday, they and the teachers had organized a memorial service with choral music and readings of poetry, and even the boy's family attended. No one should ever, ever have to discover it this way—but we knew they'd become a community, with many active, responsible members.

Adult Relationships

In many respects, the teachers at the Best Practice High School have worked well together under tremendous pressure. Everyone pitches in, works long hours, and all tolerate well the fact that no one could possibly, in the beginning, do all the myriad tasks to make the school everything they want. Kathy Daniels observe:

> Teachers haven't been in positions before where they could take leadership roles. They're a strong faculty, so when a need or a project comes along, they just jump in and do it. I can't say exactly when this started. In the beginning, they tended to look more to Tom and me. They're also really good at negotiating with each other. For example, at the beginning of this year, one teacher started off very forcefully stating what was needed. At first, the others gave in, but gradually they began to express their own ideas and work things out together. A lot has to do with getting to know each other and to realize that their own ideas matter.

Yet at times there have been strains and difficulties, and it's important for several reasons to talk about them, particularly as they relate to the challenges of leadership. One reason for this glasnost is that if we are to create new and better schools, then people need to understand the complex difficulties of starting one, rather than just the glories and successes. The problems may not be identical in other efforts, but perhaps there are underlying issues and tensions we can tease out.

Another reason for examining the less harmonious side of the endeavor is simply to recognize that good new schools will be created not by ideal supermen and women, but by normal human beings. If improved institutions can come into existence only through the intervention of perfect leaders possessed of no flaws, quirks, conflicts, or stylistic incongruities, then there's really no hope for us. The question is whether a well-designed structure, guided by people whose intentions and abilities are good enough though not perfect, can create a powerful and constructive learning experience for children. We've seen that it can.

So we want to tell the story in brief of at least one of our struggles. It would no doubt be narrated differently by other of the participants. The content of the issue was the manner of disciplining students. But the underlying tension was really about the roles of the teacher-leaders and the university partners.

Because the school began with a small staff and no free administrator or released teacher (our principal serves as more of an overall manager for the three small schools housed together in our building), we very quickly faced the question of how to handle unruly students whom a teacher wished to remove from the room (or hallway) or recommend for in-school suspension. With the student body we'd chosen, this was not an uncommon matter. Teachers sent students to the office, where they usually faced an aide, a woman who, though she loves the students deeply, deals with them in a strong, authoritarian style. And because she had many other duties and demands on her time, and was not always present herself, responses were not always consistent. It didn't seem fair to blame her, for this was not the job she was hired to do. Nor had detailed policies and procedures been worked through by the faculty.

The situation troubled the university partners greatly. It unsettled some faculty as well, but so many other challenges presented themselves at the twice-weekly staff meetings that this one was simply put aside for the most part. Perhaps some hesitated to bring it up. When the university folks finally did raise the issue, their comments were perceived as critical, judgmental, too focused on negatives, and unappreciative of the achievements and strides the school was making. This in turn brought into play the unspoken, deeper question of what the external partners' role really was.

Before the school had started, almost all the work and much of the decision making fell to us, the university professors. It was we who had free time to visit prospective sites, sit on board committees, lobby politicians, and draft budgets, whereas the teachers were hard at work in the schools where they were teaching at the time. The day the students arrived, this instantly changed. Now the school belonged to the teachers, and we became visitors. We might carry furniture, help conduct classes, vote on policy, help select new faculty, but it was not our job to deal with the kids and teach every day, nor were we the school's supervisors. We weren't paid by the Board of Education, we had no formal authority, no clearly defined role, only the history of our partnership and the understanding that we could do a great deal to help.

Another way to think about it is that in an endeavor like this one, everyone brings to the table a fantasy of the outcome. Perhaps in America, the start of any new institution bears this utopian tinge. But inevitably, the individual fantasies don't match perfectly, and the reality is something else again. That's when the negotiations and adjustments begin. Even when people agree on the outlines, life proves far more complex than anyone expected.

For example, although we'd all said we believed in a teacher-run school, we hadn't really thought about what that meant if the university partners disagreed with something the teachers decided! Or if we disagreed with how they decided it. Without assigning ourselves a parental role, we began to feel we were in a situation similar to that parents face when they try to give advice to their grown children. It's liable to be seen as meddling, a lack of confidence, or overly critical. And because the teachers had inevitably come from highly authoritarian schools with limited opportunities for real self-governance and were just now trying out and treasuring their new powers, it's not surprising some would see our comments this way. Were the teachers too sensitive, too focused on issues of power and control? Were the university partners too impatient to solve all the school's challenges at once? Perhaps both groups played a role in the conflict.

With several issues following this pattern, the university partners pulled back a bit. Although we were not about to relinquish our involvement, we were unsure what to do, how much to say, and what actions would contribute, strengthen, and develop the school. We began to choose tasks and issues more carefully. We did a lot of observing and thinking, and some teachers perceived this as neglect. It was not an easy time for anyone. But by the middle of the second year, several interesting developments began very gradually to alter the relationships still further.

For one thing, there were more staff to address various tasks and concerns. Time and energy were becoming available, so that subgroups of teachers could move beyond the daily crush of demands and take on some of the unresolved problems. For instance, a faculty group convened one Sunday morning over brunch to devise a new procedure for disciplinary problems. They invited one of the university folks, but it was essential for the teachers to work on this by themselves so we respectfully declined the invitation. Although the discipline issue wasn't yet fully solved, the staff was beginning to acknowledge it.

Another development was that as the school grew—with a new freshman class in September 1997, the school had doubled in size—there were simply more activities, more avenues for expression and experiment, no longer created and guided by just one small team. Now the freshman teacher-team and the sophomore team each planned separate integrated study units, with different approaches, making any one decision seem less crucial. If one way didn't work, we'd learn from the other. While the peer mediation group met in one room, the Black Heritage contest team met in another, and the Gallery 37 artists in a third. As more students responded to the opportunities and supports being offered to them, the school began to find momentum of its own. If the basic tone of the place allowed students to bloom and feel empowered—and it did—then there was less need to debate any one issue. Control, power, even making the "right" decision about a problem, simply receded as key concerns. Utopia may not have been restored, but a new, more realistic, more mature set of relationships began to take shape.

As of this writing, each of the three university people has taken on a particular task at the school. Steve Zemelman helps guide the peer mediation program and serves on the Local School Council, the formal governing body that evaluates the principal and approves the discretionary budget. Marilyn Bizar is helping design a portfolio assessment process, and works with the professional development program that brings teachers from other schools to observe what we're doing. Harvey Daniels is helping our first seniors to set up digital portfolios to be used in college applications. All of us provide information on curricular concerns and do the grant writing that brings funding to the school for special needs and projects. And all of us participate in policy decisions and the hiring of new teachers. Our part in the leadership of the school has become more focused and more organic.

Deepening

As the first year spun itself out and the second proceeded, teachers took more and more initiative beyond their own classrooms. At first, sheer survival was the goal, and any leftover energy was reserved for the most pressing issues. But increasingly, teachers would simply propose and execute the special activities that add up to create a community. When this writer suggested a peer mediation program, one teacher, Sonja Kosanovic, plus the counselor, and later the assistant principal, eagerly joined in to review available programs, obtain training for ourselves, recruit and select mediator candidates, and train them. Kosanovic also organized the spring student talent review. Aiko Boyce, the art teacher, helped students publish a yearbook. Arthur Griffin, the physics teacher, organized a trip to Great America, the region's main theme park, to celebrate the students' accomplishments in science (and to study the laws of motion that described the workings of some of the rides). History teacher Kate Lang helped students plan a Day of the Dead celebration. Sports teams were coached by Peter Thomas, the geography teacher, and Pat Gregory in physical education.

Choice time offered special roles for teachers as well. Math teacher Mark Fertel became the chess guru. Librarian Jackie Chappell led a poetry-writing group. Because Arthur Griffin also led the choir at his church and had taught choral music as part of his previous position, it was natural for him to organize a school choir. In the second year, too, the faculty began to divide up governance tasks such as recruiting new teacher candidates—an important task, because we were growing by a full class level each year, and a new complement of teachers would be hired annually for two more years. In a long-established institution, all these tasks might seem more like simply "jobs" to be distributed among the faculty, but in a new school, each of these actions becomes an exercise of leadership, helping shape the school. People took on responsibilities because they wanted to move the school toward some vision they held, rather than because "duties" were being assigned.

Now a strong school culture has evolved. Teachers take turns leading staff meetings. Ad hoc committees form swiftly to address problems that come up. Teachers plan in the grade-level teams more than in departmental groups—which means they can focus together on the needs of individual students or the whole class. When they interview new teacher candidates (and everyone who can, attends these interviews), their questions show that they believe deeply in the approach and philosophy the school has adopted.

Perhaps this is one of the best advantages of a teacher-run school. Staff members take initiative not because someone tells them to, but because they want to—even when they're exhausted and overloaded. Is it that such a school attracts such educators? Or rather that the structure of shared responsibility inspires commitment? "These are all people who take initiative," Sonja Kosanovic asserted:

> You can't sit back, here. There's so much opportunity, why would you want to sit back? I have the same work ethic I had at my previous school, but it was frustrating there. All I got were "No's" to my ideas before. When you keep going back to the administration and the answers are always "No, no, no," you feel less and less hope. Here, ideas get a hearing, they're respected, and we trust each other. You can't be selfish or territorial and work at our school.

The School as a Model

Another way to view leadership in an innovative school is to ask whether it is able to influence the larger system it resides in, or simply becomes an isolated little island in the traditional sea. From the start, active modeling and dissemination were elements in our original proposal. And in the second year we obtained grant funds from the Prince Charitable Trust, the Lloyd A. Fry Foundation, and the Chicago Annenberg Challenge to start a visiting staff development program. The McDougal Family Foundation has also contributed to this effort. Teachers from other schools are invited to the high school for 2-day seminars that combine separate workshop sessions, observation in BPHS classrooms, and conversation with our teachers.

This effort is particularly important, for one of the greatest obstacles to change in city schools is teachers' unspoken belief that "these newfangled strategies can't possibly work with my unruly and unskilled kids. They're only possible in the suburbs." Because we've observed progressive strategies work wonderfully in the most difficult and discouraging neighborhoods in Chicago, real-life demonstrations of success in settings the skeptics can identify with just might prove convincing.

Like every other task in this work, nothing has come easily. Schools and teachers have almost no tradition of cross-visitation. Responsible teachers are understandably reluctant to leave their kids for a day. And because substitutes frequently fail to arrive when requested from the board—or if they do appear, display doubtful competence—principals are hesitant to let their teachers go. Often it's only possible if an assistant principal, counselor, or other freed staff member can cover the classroom. We wondered, as well, whether seeing more effective classrooms and school structures might only create frustration, because the visiting teachers don't have the freedom to reorganize their schools to follow our model.

Yolanda Simmons, our teacher-leader in charge of this project found that to ensure participation she had to radically redefine her job and spend extensive time visiting prospective schools to build relationships with principals and teachers. Then, once the teachers attended a session, enthusiasm mounted. We spaced out the 2 days of the workshop so it wouldn't be too disruptive to the visiting teachers' classrooms. And the teacher-leader added visits to the schools between and after the workshop sessions, to help participants try out the new strategies they'd learned about. Change in existing schools and classrooms is a labor-intensive process.

This still leaves us with the larger question, however, whether the Chicago Board of Education or any other large educational bureaucracy is likely to support a broader shift to small progressive schools. Will real leadership for an innovation like teacher-led, student-centered small schools ever come from the core of a large school district? We started with Deborah Meier and Linda Darling Hammond's doubts on this question. In our own experience, we've certainly known individual Chicago administrator, who've supported small schools. Those who encouraged and guided the original request for proposals that we responded to, and who helped launch Chicago's initial group of new small schools did all they could to make them work. Their power was clearly limited from the start, however, and seemed to diminish sharply as the effort moved along.

Yet our high school couldn't have won its struggles for a chemistry lab, or for the awarding of Chapter I funds based on growing enrollment rather than last year's numbers, without someone influential wanting us to succeed, or at least acquiescing in our continued success. After all, if powerful leaders wished to eliminate our school they could do it easily, through any one of several maneuvers. For example, they could simply declare our building was needed for other programs. In the past, innovative programs have withered when forced to move, for even if a new location is found—nearly impossible in itself—parents fear sending their kids to some new, unknown neighborhood and pull them out. The present administration in Chicago claims it's supportive of small schools, and praises the work of the activists in the city who have lobbied for them. And five new charter schools opened in September 1998, most of them structured as small and innovative schools.

On the other hand, as the Chicago administration prepares, with new state and federal construction funds, to build 22 new schools to relieve overcrowding, not a single one has been designed to house small-school clusters. And whether intentional or a product of bureaucratic habit, the endless flow of new directives, rules, curricular mandates, and assessments all inhibit or undermine small-school structures. What does it mean to have a teacher-led program if centrally mandated and designed end-of-semester tests control what's offered in the courses? How can innovation succeed if the board appoints a new principal who has no belief in or understanding of teacher autonomy, as happened in another of the small schools?

More broadly, we must consider what sorts of leadership are demonstrated by the top administrative figures in the Chicago system—by CEO Paul Vallas and board president Gery Chico. And the main phenomenon to notice is that the key initiatives lie elsewhere than in small schools. Two in particular have brought the Chicago school leadership great acclaim from news media and politicians nationwide, and these make clear the extent to which small, innovative schools are simply irrelevant in the larger flow of events here. The first was the establishment of a system in which schools with fewer than 15% of students scoring at or above national norms on the ITBS were placed on "probation." Probation schools' programs are reviewed, and a probation manager, a probation partner, and some fresh support dollars are brought in to help make changes. The principal and manager are given the power to fire teachers summarily, and if the school doesn't improve, the entire staff can be replaced.

Though we agree that schools with such low scores need help, this approach makes clear that progressive curriculum innovation is not what the administration seeks. First, the probation decision depends on a measuring stick with major flaws. The ITBS yields surprisingly inconsistent results between different forms and from year to year (see Bryk et al., 1998). Second, the calculations fail to take mobility into account, so that a school's program is held accountable even for students who have just moved into its attendance area and who haven't actually experienced its educational efforts. Third, any principal under pressure to improve will quickly realize that the quickest way to up the scores is to concentrate on just a few borderline students who, if they improved slightly, would raise the school's percentage at the national norm. The kids who need help the most can be conveniently neglected. At the other extreme, the approach in some schools is to coach kids for the tests intensively, all year round, a practice that deprives them of much learning and obtains only mild score increases.

The other high-visibility effort by the present administration was to begin retaining students who failed to score high enough on the ITBS at Grades 3, 6, and 8. After a second try during summer school, third- and sixth-graders who still don't measure up repeat their year, whereas eighth-graders go to "transition centers" instead of to high school. Though numerous research studies and extensive experience with such approaches in other districts have shown that the main effect of this strategy is only to increase the dropout rate (Pick, 1998; "Test Scores Jump." 1998), Chicago's school leaders have pressed ahead. The transition centers were commanded into existence with barely a few weeks' notice and no real planning.

We can't examine all the problems with these policies in depth here, but we can point out that these policies yield high publicity impact, while establishing innovative small schools offers a far less dramatic story to the newspapers. Even President Clinton has praised Chicago for its no-nonsense boldness. Meanwhile, more knowledgeable observers are already finding that recent test score increases in the high schools reflect only that the lowest scoring students are no longer present, whereas grade levels not yet affected by retention show no improvement. The real result of the policy is already starting to show up—a significant increase in the student dropout rate. It will be tragic if school policy unwittingly repeats the mistakes of the past and simply limits educational access for children of poor and minority families.

One direct effect of the more dramatic policies on progressive innovations such as small schools is that while the innovators continue their struggle, the new efforts begin to soak up all of the board's discretionary funds. For example, the Chicago board is expanding the eighth-grade transition centers into full 4-year alternative high schools, establishing a new, lower track for many students. The funds are indeed headed elsewhere than small schools. Ironically, however, in the long run the increased dropout rate should have the odd effect of reducing board expenditures, because there will be fewer students to teach.

Small schools with unique and autonomous programs, in other words, are unlikely to be eliminated from the scene, but also unlikely to be replicated very extensively at this time. In sum, then, central office leadership in Chicago is not presently taking action to support or expand progressive reforms in curriculum and instruction such as the Best Practice High School, and is, in fact, focusing its efforts elsewhere.

This chapter does not have a neat and comfortable ending. At the present time, leaders and supporters of progressive schools like the Best Practice High School have plenty of work to do and battles to fight. We've got new schools to aid and nurture, successes and problems to document. At the same time, it seems unwise to simply allow retrograde and draconian policies to go unchallenged. Leadership appears to require a delicate balance, on the one hand continuing to work with school administrators to create and maintain new, progressive programs, and on the other, maintaining pressure to change repressive policies. It may be that only when the public, the media, and the policy makers themselves are educated to recognize the social cost and the lack of real educational improvement left behind by this spate of get-tough rulings, will any broader change become possible.

And yet over the decades, with each wave of reforms in the approach to teaching and learning such as those we're trying at Best Practice High School, the efforts are stronger, clearer, and built on a firmer base of prior experience, better research, more well-designed applications. This is no time to stop.

Analysis of Leadership

This case exemplifies one way that school leadership has been redefined with the advent of school reform in Chicago. The reform law helped to focus the educational community on the importance of school leadership, while shifting the emphasis from administrative leadership to that of shared school-based leadership of parents, teachers, community members, and students. The legislation focuses attention on these key players in the school community and on their evolving leadership roles. The Best Practice High School brings together these forces to create a new school from the ground up. The reform legislation created the opportunity, and a group of dedicated people seeking something better seized upon it.

What is evident in this case is the importance of the collaboration of different groups in the design and creation of this new school. It is clear that leadership in the creation and running of a new school requires dedication and perseverance in the face of many obstacles. Of particular interest was the relationship between the "outside" university collaborators and the teacher-leaders of the school. The issue of student discipline surfaced tensions concerning the rights and responsibilities of each of these groups, which are still being resolved. More than any other school case examined, students have been permitted leadership roles within the school, particularly in the selection of new faculty and in the resolution of disputes between students. Because new patterns and roles are being developed, the journey has been fraught with missteps and potholes, and yet those who have participated agree that it has been worthwhile.

EXTENDING THINKING

Questions

1. Zemelman states that it is more effective to start a new school than to reform an existing one. Do you agree? What are the issues to be considered?
2. Best Practice High School is a teacher-led school that shares a building with two other small schools. Sylvia Gibson was chosen by

the teachers from all three schools to be the principal of the whole building, leaving the running of the schools up to the teachers. What special skills would be necessary for her to work successfully with three schools where most of the decisions were made by the teachers? Consider the implications of this type of administrative role in the areas of management and leadership.

3. From a teacher's perspective, reflect upon the pros and cons of working in a teacher-led school.

4. Best Practice High School is a small school by design. How can small size be beneficial for teachers, students, and parents? What are some of the problems that are created by small size?

Activity

1. In this case, one of the challenges faced was working with the large bureaucratic school district. Consider the ways in which your school is impacted by school district policy and procedures. In what ways does the district provide assistance and in what ways does it provide obstacles.

Reflection on Cases 7 and 8

High schools differ from elementary schools in internal structure. Departments organized around disciplinary areas encourage a form of teacher leadership that links with the administration of the school. This structure may tend to protect teachers against change in their teaching practice. In any case, those monitoring results from the reform effort note the failure of high schools to show increasing achievement among students.

The case of Amundsen is useful in representing some of the complexities inherent in reform. The newly Local School Council (LSC)-elected principal saw as his first priority the creation of a safe environment for the students attending Amundsen. Changes in neighborhood ethnic composition, and the changing school populations that resulted, had led to a decline in school achievement over the years as less well-prepared students entered the school. Many better prepared students from the neighborhood were electing to attend other schools. Thus, the principal with the support of the LSC attempted to modify the composition of the school by having Amundsen designated as a special school with a focus on environmental issues, with the goal of retaining better prepared students from the neighborhood. This attempt, however, did not lead to increased achievement in the short run.

With the increased attention on test scores that resulted during the second wave of reform, Amundsen was placed on the "watch list" in 1995 and on "probation" in 1996, with 1 year to raise scores or be "reconstituted." The principal viewed this new pressure as an opportunity for the school, and its departmental teachers, to take positive steps to make changes in curriculum and learning. The initiative during the first years of instructional change seemed to come through the leadership of the assistant principal and outside collaborators—the state, local universities, and other high schools. The case reveals the deep ambivalence of the high school teachers to change their content focus of teaching to include the development of student writing and reading strategies. The activities around writing improvement, including the collaborative model forged, laid the basis for subsequent changes in the area of reading. However, as the case shows, the effort focused on reading faced many obstacles and the results were hard won. Teacher leadership schoolwide began to gain some momentum as teachers witnessed the success that their students were having.

The ambivalence expressed at the end of the case reflects two dimensions of the reform process. The first is the realization that a preoccupation with test results diminishes available time, narrows instructional richness, and diminishes the learning opportunities for students. The second recognizes the tendency of many high school teachers to adhere to traditional practices, even when they are no longer appropriate for a new student body, and acknowledges the viable wedge toward changing practice that comes through the pressure of accountability.

With so many entrenched cultural traditions in high schools, one might conclude that an easier solution to reform would be the creation of new schools. Yet, the description of the development of the Best Practice High School details a myriad of unpredictable and foreseeable obstacles. The process experienced within the group of teacher, university, and community planners demonstrates many of the same problems faced by all schools dealing with the Chicago Public School bureaucracy. Gaining appropriate space, having sufficient planning time, and securing needed resources all posed major problems.

Many administrative matters—hiring faculty, recruiting students, planning special student activities—required the attention of the teachers and their university collaborators during the planning phase. Other issues surfaced once students had arrived and classes were in session. In addition to the collaborative planning of an instructional program, many tasks normally handled by administrators fell to teachers. It was clear from the case that only an extremely dedicated group of teachers would or could assume this range of responsibilities and make the time needed available.

The division of labor between the teachers and the university collaborators has become clarified through a number of events, including those concerned with student discipline. Teachers who interacted daily with students wanted to be responsible for establishing disciplinary policies and practices, as well as those concerned with instruction and learning. University participants assumed responsibility for such functions as guiding the peer mediation program, serving on the LSC, working with the professional development program for teachers from other schools, developing links with colleges, providing information on curricular concerns, and writing grants.

Although relatively little was written in the case about parent involvement, other than through participation on the LSC, students have begun assuming leadership responsibilities in the school. This, too, was an evolving process that involved replacing the resistive forms of response they had learned in their prior schools, with knowledge about how to contribute constructively. Through internships, such as working in neighboring schools with younger students or with video cameras, students learned new roles. Through school events, such as the spring talent show, they got to know students and faculty in different ways and grew more trusting. By the second year, student leadership began to show itself through participating in such activities as peer mediation, leading choice-time activities, and participating in the interviewing of candidates for new teaching positions. The small size of the school facilitated the development of student leadership, and within the small schools, it was the nature of the relations among faculty and students that nurtured the trust needed for responsible student action.

SECTION 6

Insights Into Leadership During Times of School Reform

Rebecca Barr
Marilyn Bizar
National-Louis University

In this book, we are interested in the forms of leadership that the reform made possible, and how they came about. The Chicago school reform, by devolving powers to the local level, created possibilities for new forms of leadership. These were taken up in some schools, but not in others. We believe that the patterns followed provide lessons about leadership in all schools undergoing some aspect of school reform. By reflecting across these eight school case studies, we can make visible the complex set of conditions that interact to give rise to new forms of leadership, as well as the factors that inhibit their occurrence.

We examine emerging forms of leadership in relation to the formulations of school leadership developed in Section 1. We argued earlier that it is useful to distinguish "leadership" from "management" forms of school leadership. There has been a tendency to view leadership positively as indicating progress and innovation, and management as a reactive, traditional style. Based on the work of Achilles and his colleagues (1999), we believe that it is more useful to consider school administration as composed of leadership as well a management functions, with leadership conceptualized as the risk-taking force leading to new forms of schooling and management as the conservative force maintaining what has proven effective in the existing school culture.

Indeed, it is only in the context of agreed-upon ways of doing business, that one can see what is in need of change. The principals described by Keedy's study (1991) worked in out-of-control schools without an agreed-upon culture. What was needed first was to establish roles, get students under control, and establish a new departmental structure and equitable teaching loads, before they could think of leadership to establish more innovative forms of practice. Moreover, establishing routines ways of doing business, as well as the incentives and beliefs that support compliance to them, can be a lengthy and complicated process. Once the fabric of the school culture is in place, principals are then in a position to effect changes, including distributed leadership activities to establish more shared forms of governance.

From a sociological perspective, leadership roles may be either institutionally sanctioned or based on personal authority. In some settings such as schools with an established culture, a person steps into a role for which social patterns have already been established. This person is expected by others in the situation to make decisions and to carry others along. The role is sanctioned by the institution and the person assuming the role is perceived through the set of expectations shared by that school community. That is, although the person may posses personal qualities that "fit" him or her for administration, these qualities are viewed through the lens of institutionally determined expectations.

In some situations, however, persons other than the principal may emerge into leadership roles. Because of personal characteristics—knowledge, wisdom, social sense—these people may be looked to for guidance. This form of more spontaneous leadership may be viewed as supporting institutional goals or as a threat to those of institutionally sanctioned leaders. As Waller (1961) insightfully noted, "Institutional leadership tends to break down under conditions of peculiar strain, and personal leadership, with its continual modification of measures, steps in to take its place" (p. 191). This formulation may apply in times of reform when other leaders, such as teachers or members of the Local School Council (LSC) emerge to offer competing forms of leadership.

The formulation may also apply to situations when principals pursue opportunities to encourage leadership in others. Principals with the personal characteristics of imagination, planning skills, a predisposition to situational opportunities, and an ability to cope with "turbulence" may experiment with new forms of governance. Similarly, those selected to participate in leadership roles, whether they be teachers or community members, usually share some of the same personal characteristics. They have a vision for the school and are willing to engage in new forms of planning and instructional practice.

Scholars studying "effective " schools conclude that the principal is key in determining the effectiveness of a school (Brookover, Gigliotti, Henderson, & Schneider, 1973; Dwyer, Barnett, & Lee, 1987; Edmonds, 1979; Venezky & Winfield, 1979; Weber, 1971). Blumberg and Greenfield (1980), for example, studied the characteristics of successful schools and the form of leadership involved. They noted that principals who are good leaders are highly goal oriented, hold a vision for their school, have a strong sense of clarity about their role, are alert to opportunities to influence what is going on in the school, and can communicate effectively with all constituencies in the school community.

These principals have long-term goals, have a high tolerance for ambiguity, and are able to work in loosely structured environments.

Reform creates the opportunity for various forms of shared leadership. The activities for which principals are responsible include curriculum development, instructional improvement, pupil services, community relations, and financial and facility management, as well as others. As discussed earlier, it is easy to see how teacher leadership might make significant contributions, particularly in the areas of curriculum development and instructional improvement. It is similarly clear that parents and community members should have contributions to make to issues of curriculum, pupil services, and community relations.

Yet, the empowerment of teachers and community members to assume leadership roles is a complicated process. An open climate encouraging the questioning of existing practice must be modeled by principals to provide the climate for others to become entitled and trusting. Principals who share leadership roles must not only support the initiatives of others, but also help in developing agreed-upon standards and procedures so that the organization will work well. In other words, the principal is still the manager of the school and responsible for the way the school works and supports the learning of children.

The cases presented earlier reflect the practice of leaders in schools. Although principals are central to most of these stories, in some settings other forms of leadership emerge and the school culture shows corresponding changes. In the following sections, we look carefully across the eight cases to identify these patterns. The remainder of the section is organized around the five questions that we posed in Section 1:

1. How has the leadership of school principals been shaped by the reform initiative?
2. How have leadership roles of teachers been shaped by the reform initiative?
3. How have community members contributed to school decision-making?
4. How has the culture of schools been influenced by reform?
5. How have teaching and learning been shaped by reform?

We pursue these questions in light of the descriptions presented in the eight case studies. The cross-case analyses enable us to see how the window of opportunity created by the reform legislation becomes manifest in local school settings. We close the final section with a summary and discussion of our tentative ideas about leadership in times of reform.

How Has the Leadership of Principals Been Shaped by the Reform Initiative?

As argued in Section 1, a window of opportunity was created in individual schools by the nature of the site-based restructuring. But the specific ways in which leadership was to be exercised were not clearly specified. School reform did, however, alter the definition of the principal's role in several ways. The principal gained additional power by having a budget with discretionary funds. Greater control was achieved over the hiring of teachers. Principals also were given more authority over the selection of curricular materials, professional development, and during the first years of reform, over assessment. The budget and the school improvement plan were to have been linked directly to the instructional programs of the school. These were areas of increased responsibility and power for principals. At the same time, the legislative changes could be seen as encouraging a principal to shift away from more traditional forms of leadership, to forms of shared leadership where goals and courses of action are established through collaborative decision making with community members and teachers.

The problem for a principal is how to maintain the institutional authority inherent in a management role, while at the same time engaging in shared forms of leadership. Traditional forms of institutional management tend to lack flexibility and to become nonfunctional under conditions of change and stress. In contrast, personal leadership has within it a flexibility to be responsive to new problems as they arise. The influence gained through a personal style of leadership arises from knowledge, social presence, and other personal characteristics. Authority that derives from roles and offices is enhanced by educative experiences and temperamental characteristics; it is this combination that enables principals to function effectively during periods of reform. The institutionally prescribed norms and behaviors were changed and the legislation encouraged subordinates with good personal leadership qualified to come forward.

The role of Chicago principals was redefined to demand skills and strategies that were not part of the repertoire of many principals. Key to the power of leadership is the ability to galvanize support of school participants and to build consensus and commitment to the school's goals and vision. In this, principals need to be effective communicators who can enlist others in reenvisioning the school culture and transmit this vision for others. Sergiovanni (1990, 1996) focused on the cultural aspects of leadership, which include articulating school purposes and mission, socializing new members to the school, and maintaining traditions and beliefs. The effect of this form of leadership is to bring together school participants and create a sense of community through their empowerment. He argued that principals, who are successful cultural leaders, lead in ways that enable shared leadership to develop. These flexible leaders share power, and thereby build a culture that is ripe for teacher growth and empowerment.

However, there are many obstacles to this form of leadership, not the least of them being principals' reluctance to relinquish power (Eubanks & Parish, 1990). Traditional administrators are likely to be concerned that empowerment will reduce the school and teacher accountability for carrying out a unified improvement plan and will place decision-making authority in the hands of untrained and unprepared persons (Conley, 1991). These types of administrative concerns are based in a lack of trust and respect for teachers and parents.

The cases provide a highly varied set of portraits of how principals faced with a changing set of conditions respond to the challenge. At the elementary school level, Ms. Morgan from Jackson Elementary provides an image of a traditional leader who is invested in the institutional definition of her role. She evidenced a rigid form of management that became dysfunctional under the stressful conditions of school reform. Her high need for control became evident in her curtailment of the activities and deliberations of the LSC and in her interactions with teachers. She seemed to be unable to share leadership activities with either the LSC or the teachers. Her inability to share power seemed to have deep roots in an underlying lack of trust and respect for her teachers and parents, justified because of what she saw as the collusion of teachers and community in the abuse of Jackson children. Although shared decision making could not become a reality at Jackson under her traditional administrative style, the postscript at the end of the case reveals that a cultural change was possible with a new principal.

In spite of her controlling management style, the LSC did vote to rehire Ms. Morgan for another 3 years. That unresponsive principals would be allowed to continue under reform is not, however, a forgone conclusion. Another of our cases involved the entrenched and traditional school administrator who was the first principal of Anzaldúa. Because of his unresponsiveness to teachers and instructional concerns, as well as his misuse of funds for purposes other than teaching children, the LSC voted not to rehire him. The rising up of a school community against the administration of an existing principal is unusual, but occurred in this case because teachers and some parents from the community became aware that the principal was not serving the needs of Hispanic children in the school.

In several other cases, we saw tensions develop as new principals became leaders in schools with well-established cultures. It is difficult to know how the energetic leadership of Nelda Hobbs at Field School should be characterized. When she came in, she saw that what was needed was establishing the safety of the school and the neighborhood for Field children. She undertook these activities single-handedly, but seemed to have the support of parents, community members, and the LSC. She then moved on to getting teachers involved in improving the instructional program. She based her approach on the advice of consultants and the research literature suggesting that small schools, especially those organized around teacher interests, create a sense of community.

It is clear that some teachers forming small schools were greatly energized by the opportunity to work and plan with a group of like-minded teachers. But it was also clear that not all teachers felt so empowered. For the latter teachers who failed to "take up" the invitation, the change seemed to be an imposed one, over which they had limited control and limited personal investment. So what can a leader do when only some teachers opt into collaborative teaching groups and more interactive forms of classroom instruction? We cannot know the answer to this question because Ms. Hobbs decided to retire rather than face the problematic process of being rehired by the LSC. Yet, we would like to think that if she had had the opportunity to continue as principal for several more years, other small schools might have followed the lead of those who thrived under this form of organization.

The case of "T," the newly hired principal at W school is a challenging one to think about because we can only see his actions secondhand through the eyes of the LSC chair. What seems to be the case is that the principal was an articulate person who had given some thought to his philosophy of education. He impressed the LSC members who had spent considerable time informing themselves about what are considered to be "best" instructional practices. Yet unexpectedly, at his selection celebration, when a parent suggested visiting classes, his negative reaction was completely at odds with the way the selection committee had perceived him. Though he was adept at the language of reform, it quickly became clear that he was more comfortable in operating in a more traditional way that employed control and management. Because of what happened, the LSC felt betrayed.

But perhaps there is another way to interpret what occurred. Among T's goals would have been to gain respect and authority in the eyes of the teachers, while at the same time assuring them that he had their best interest in mind. One of his first acts in relation to the LSC was to establish that parents could not visit classrooms. Perhaps T sensed that the LSC was encroaching into the territory of instructional matters, an area that he and the teachers considered to be their prerogative. By not permitting parents to visit classrooms, he would have accomplished two things at once: rejecting the direct instructional involvement of the LSC and winning the support of the teachers. The close lay involvement of parents and LSC members creates conflicts over the professional domain of teachers and principals and poses a threat to professionalism.

A second problem T faced was the extremely low level of involvement on the part of the teachers as indicated by their activities during professional development. We do not have evidence on how T confronted the problem in getting them to improve their instruction. As the postscript showed, although continuing to adhere to a fairly traditional management style, he was able to get teachers to incorporate more interactive forms of instruction into their classrooms. As a result, test scores improved, suggesting that learning had also improved. Hence, more traditional forms of management are not always inimical to the goal of reform to improve instruction and learning.

The activities of a new principal are revealed in a third case. At Irving School, Madeleine Maraldi worked hard to build the kind of culture that would support a dialogue about teaching and learning between herself and her teachers. The strategies she used are instructive. She shared test results with her teachers and then had them focus on causes. When there was a universal failure to identify classroom instruction as a possible cause, she had them identify only those causes that were under their control. As a next step, she had teachers select an area of instruction that was most in need of improvement. Writing was selected. She established a computer writing lab and hired a teacher. But when it became apparent that teachers were not engaged in learning how to teach writing, she increased accountability by saying that the following year they would be responsible for bringing their students into the lab and supporting their writing development. The change in responsibility resulted in an enormous increase in teacher involvement. Finally, to increase the focus on reading, she offered to have classes take field trips to bookstores so that children could select and purchase books. Teachers signing up first received the special monies that had been tagged for this purpose. In other words, inducements led teachers to do what was expected, and the culture of the school changed in response.

The change in teachers' involvement did not occur overnight. They needed to become convinced that she wanted their input about children and instructional matters and that she valued it. When she eliminated her role as a teacher evaluator, she communicated to her faculty that they were capable of self-evaluation and they were trusted to look at their teaching honestly. What evolved was, in a very real sense, a community of teachers and learners who were willing to become innovators and try the kinds of teaching strategies that would place them at the edge of their comfort zones. But as previously discussed, directives and inducements were part of the process.

At Saucedo, teachers were similarly involved in decision making. But this was a process that began long before the reform legislation was passed. As a result, the structures for working effectively with teachers, parents, community, and students were in place from the beginning. The image that emerges from the interview with Karen Morris was that of an extremely hard-working principal, actively engaged with others in the school, and familiar with the workings of the school from morning to night. Work on budget and school plans was left for the weekend at home. Long before reform, she had provided her teachers with a variety of professional development experiences in such areas as reading, writing, and the arts. She was also in communication with the school community long before reform began, and the community could see the influence of its hopes on the expansion of the school to include lower grades. Ms. Morris was trusted in the community to have the best interests of their children at heart, and she valued their ideas and their needs.

The story of reform for Karen Morris was the continuation of a dialogue that had already been established inside and outside of school. New tasks such as developing a school improvement plan and a school budget were easily accomplished because the school community was already talking about what the priorities and future directions of the school should be. As we commented earlier, to some extent the complex role of the principal is invisible in this case. The case description fails to detail her numerous daily interactions with students, teachers, and parents. It doesn't show the skill she needed to sense serious problems and to take decisive action. It shows instead a well-crafted pattern of intersecting activities that Karen, with the help of others, keeps in balance.

The two high school cases differ in their conceptions of the principal's role. At Amundsen, the principal seemed to see his role less as an instructional leader than as a guide generally responsible for setting the direction of the school. To further the work with teachers, particularly in areas of instruction, he appointed an assistant principal to interact with teachers to determine areas of instructional priority and with consultants to obtain the professional development support that would lead to test score improvement. Rather than seeing himself as an instructional leader, the principal's role seems to be more akin to that of a superintendent or a person in a top management position. He worked through his appointees, in this case the assistant principal, to realize his goals for the school.

In the Best Practice school, the nominal principal was not directly engaged in the activities of the school. She served a coordinating role among the three small schools sharing the building and between them and the central office of the Chicago Public Schools (CPS). Leadership roles for the school are assumed by teachers and outside partners. The effective leadership of the school, the teachers with their university supporters, had relegated some minor management functions to the nominal principal, but retained decision making for collaborative action among the teachers.

The complexities of the role of principal, particularly during the years of reform, become apparent through these case studies. They seem to point toward several evolving sets of ideas.

First, most principals who continue administering schools from a traditional management perspective and limit the access of teachers and parents to school decision making will not survive in a situation in which community members and teachers have control over the hiring and firing of teachers.

Yet, several cases serve to complicate this assertion. Ms. Morgan did survive in spite of a very restrictive form of management. Similarly, principal T in W school exemplified a traditional autocratic administrative style, but used his authority to bring in forms of instruction that were responsive to the needs of children. He thereby gained the respect of most LSC members. His approach failed to capitalize on the knowledge and insights of teachers and community members, but his vision for the school included the pursuit of good instruction and learning. Finally, Nelda Hobbs who exemplified a progressive form of leadership chose to leave the principalship of Field School rather than face an LSC that opposed her. Other principals, off the record, expressed similar views; they considered leaving their positions because of the political nature of actions of some LSC members. Perhaps what allows a principal and LSC to work effectively together is a shared set of goals and visions for how schools should operate. Such like-mindedness may allow for not only the retention of the principal, but also the accomplishment of instructional and learning goals.

Second, the principalship has become an increasingly complicated role entailing the ability to work with a variety of groups, skill with school-based management and trouble-shooting, as well as ability to recruit teachers and knowledge of long-term planning and budgeting resources. As described best by Karen Morris of Saucedo School, the newly defined position not only entails a never-ending set of challenges during each school day, but also long hours on weekends attending to budgetary matters and school plans. Myriad demands leave little time for principals most committed to the teaching and learning of children to spend time in classrooms. The case studies also reveal that Chicago children are extremely fortunate to have a set of committed leaders who are willing to dedicate their lives in this way to their education.

Finally, changing the complex set of expectations that define the roles of principals, teachers, and parents takes a substantial period of time. For change to occur at all, it must usually be supported and sustained by the leadership of the principal. For example, the exciting instructional innovations initiated by Pete Leki were not initially sustained because of the lack of support on the part of the principal and teachers. Over time and with the development of mutual respect, the teachers, LSC, and the principal have forged a culture that now works to support outstanding learning. To engage teachers and others in shared decision making, principals must become directly involved in instructional and community concerns. Perhaps the case of Madeleine Maraldi of Irving School best exemplifies the year-by-year developments that are needed by a leader to gain the trust and respect of teachers and to empower them to participate in the improvement of instruction.

How Have Leadership Roles of Teachers Been Shaped by the Reform Initiative?

Although teachers are leaders in their classrooms, they are usually followers in the school community. The institutional force of leadership is given to principals and the form of leadership developed has implications for the roles of teachers. When principals retain most decision making, teachers get carried along in a dependent form of relation. When more collaborative forms of decision making are operative, teachers contribute knowledge and gain deeper understanding about the reasons for decisions and their implied actions. Leadership is won, not given. What is given is authority that can be employed well or frittered away.

Clearly, the relationship between leaders and followers is not reciprocal (Waller, 1961). Leaders are hugely invested in courses of action, particularly those they have established. In contrast, teachers as a group have relatively little investment, particularly when they have not participated in the determining the activity or goal. In other words, leaders entering into relationships engage the whole of their personalities, whereas subordinates invest in only minor ways. To the extent that teachers become involved in democratic forms of leadership, their investment increases correspondingly.

The early years of reform posed special challenges for teachers. For years before the reform legislation, a variety of minireforms had swept the CPS and teachers had learned that the best response was no response. Professional development had been of a "one-size-fits-all" form imposed by the central office. Thus, except in a few schools, it was clear that many teachers lacked opportunities to learn new instructional strategies. Similar to past initiatives, the restructuring legislation itself was also externally imposed.

Moreover, teachers were not central participants in establishing the legislation to reform the Chicago school system. Their lack of initial involvement had implications for the minor roles they were given in the implementation of the law. In its first draft, the legislation was silent on the role of teachers except for its specification that two teachers would serve on the LSC. The final draft of the legislation provides for the creation of a Professional Personnel Advisory Committee (PPAC). The PPAC is to be composed of teachers whose role is advisory to the LSC and the principal, especially in the areas of curriculum and instruction.

Inherent in the legislation is a contradiction of sorts. Decentralized management presumes cultural change in the workplace to support the engagement and empowerment of teachers. But from the legislation, it is not clear how the leadership roles of teachers might evolve. Because of the advisory nature of their role, teachers might assume a role in decisions relating to curricular and instructional matters. Teachers might, for example, assume new roles and responsibilities related to the school improvement plan (SIP). All of this would depend to a great extent on whether the principal and LSC chose to heed the advice of teachers.

It would be hoped that teachers would define their roles so as to collaborate in the decisions that directly affect their lives and the lives of their students. Yet, such participation would mean greater investment of the part of teachers, and their becoming convinced that the extra time and effort would pay off in their classrooms. The eight case studies are useful in exploring how teachers became involved in school leadership and reform. Did the PPAC become viewed as an important influence on decision making, particularly in the realm of curriculum and instruction? Did the teachers serving on the LSC become influential leaders among teachers and members of the community? What influence did the principal have in encouraging teachers to assume leadership roles?

PPACs were formed in most of the case study schools, and in most, teachers were eager initially to participate. In Jackson, for example, all teachers became members of the PPAC. But in this school and in others, teachers experienced a difficult time carving out an advisory role. Teachers on the LSC did not solicit the views of the PPAC or teachers more generally. Again, this is most clearly show by the Jackson case in which the LSC teacher representatives became power brokers delivering a renewed contract to the principal. Yet, when the teachers attempted to initiate a new departmental scheme in the middle grades, the principal vetoed this plan without debate. No attempt was made to help teachers develop their knowledge by being involved in the refinement of a plan. The silencing of teachers and the LSC had the effect of eliminating teacher voice from any form of decision making. Only a chosen few participated in laborious tasks, such as the development of the school improvement plan, which was then edited by the principal.

At the opposite end of the spectrum were a subgroup of teachers at Anzaldúa, who in collaboration with parents on the LSC, engaged in action that led to the dismissal of the principal. This exemplifies the unusual situation in which teachers act without the encouragement and blessing of the institutional leader. Although members of the PPAC did participate in the development of the school improvement plan and the budget, it was the perception of many teachers that these were not the primary forums in which teacher leadership was exercised. Instead of through institutional roles, most teachers saw themselves as having an impact on curricular and instructional decision making. Leadership, then, seemed to depend more on the knowledge and other personal characteristics of teachers than on their institutional roles. The degree of personal leadership varied greatly among teachers with members of nontraditional small schools assuming the role of nudging others toward a form of schooling that was culturally responsive to the needs of children. But even in this, there were disagreements as to what this might be, with some teachers advocating traditional forms of instruction as best serving the future needs of students.

A unique form of leadership was also described in the postscript of the Anzaldúa case in which teachers from the BETA small school left Anzaldúa to form their own small school, building on earlier initiatives. This is similar to the innovative work undertaken by teachers at the Best Practice High School. They, in cooperation with university partners, created a new school for a diverse set of high school students. Similar to the new BETA school, for the Best Practice High School, there is a nominal administrator, but all decisions concerning the working of the school and the instructional program are decided collectively by teachers. These would seem to be examples of collective teacher governance models. The role of the institutional leader is minimal, and he or she exerts little influence on decision making and practice.

Quite different forms of leadership were shown in other school cases. In Saucedo Academy, Karen Morris has been promoting teacher empowerment over many years. Teachers have worked together on a variety of teaching and curriculum approaches including process writing, integration of subjects, hands-on science and math, and using computers. To realize her vision of a teaching/learning community involving teachers, children, and their parents, she constantly looks for ways to connect people together. In the case of Madeleine Maraldi at Washington Irving School, we see a strong principal who works relentlessly to get teachers to become actively engaged in new forms of instruction. Her refusal to evaluate her teachers was symbolically an important stance because it underlined her perception of them as professionals. In both of these cases, the principals value teacher leadership. But not all teachers respond eagerly to the opportunities proposed. Whereas some teachers eagerly assume leadership roles, many others are less trusting and have less investment in collaborative decision making. Both of these principals express, in somewhat different ways, the belief that for teachers to engage children interactively in challenging instruction, they must be similarly empowered to participate in the key decisions affecting their teaching lives.

Field Elementary and Amundsen High School both have much more diverse groups of teachers in terms of their willingness to become engaged in leadership roles than do some of the other school cases. Nelda Hobbs of Field School wished to pass instructional and curricular control over to the teachers through the establishment of small schools. Some teachers and their students thrived in this more creative environment; many others, however, were slow to assume responsibility. The administrators of Amundsen understood that it was crucial to have the teachers become an integral part in the change process. Yet, as the case reveals, teachers who worked in a setting that was resistant to change were not ready participants. Being on probation became the impetus for selected groups of teachers to work collaboratively, and through this experience, they became enthusiastic participants in improving their instructional practice.

The teachers of W school seemed to resist new ways of thinking about instruction, as indicated by their sabotage of professional development activities and their limited response to the opportunity to work with the LSC chair on an integrated science curriculum. Yet as the postscript reveals, the principal imposed on teachers more interactive forms of instruction, which they gradually incorporated into their classrooms. That undemocratic forms of administration led to increased levels of students participation in classrooms works against our assumption that teachers need to be respected and valued decision makers before they will engage their students in more actively in classroom decision making. T represents an anomaly, a principal who advocates constructivist forms of collaborative learning for students, but mandates that teachers should be similarly engaged. Or alternatively, perhaps he simply uses constructivism and ideological rhetoric, and thus no anomaly exists.

In sum, the ways in which teachers became engaged were almost as numerous as the cases. In all of the case study schools, teachers represent a diverse group, at quite different places in their willingness to assume new responsibilities and to try new approaches to instruction. The clearest case of teacher leadership was in the case of the Best Practice High School where teachers, in cooperation with university partners, created a new instructional program for a diverse set of high school students. In a similar way, the activist group of teachers from Anzaldúa started their own small school, building on the instructional thinking they had begun earlier.

In the other schools, teacher involvement was much more varied. At W and Jackson during the early years of reform, for example, most teachers did not seem to want to take on the new responsibilities. At Field, Anzaldúa, and Amundsen High, some groups of teachers became involved and exerted considerable energy and time rethinking instruction, but others adhered to their traditional approaches. At Irving and Saucedo, many more teachers became involved in meaningful ways because the principals of these schools encouraged and rewarded their involvement in rethinking instruction.

These cases make clear that a centrally important, ongoing challenge for principals is how to get more of their teachers involved in implementing engaging forms of instruction. The cases of Irving and Saucedo are perhaps most useful in showing the creative ways principals enhanced the development of their teachers by making opportunities available and by providing an attractive set of incentives for those teachers who might not choose to make changes on their own.

How Have Community Members Contributed to School Decision Making?

The legislation established a LSC composed of parents, community representatives, teachers, and the school principal. At the same time that the legislation expanded the power of the principal, it also required the principal to share power with the LSC in two areas: approval of the budget and approval of the SIP. In a third area, involving the hiring and firing of the principal, the LSC was given sole decision-making authority. What the Chicago reform did was to put in place a form of site-based management that gave authority to principals, while at the same time, establishing an alternative power base in the form of the LSC.

The role of principals in individual schools became similar to that of superintendent in districts in their accountability to a school board. As is well known from the literature on the school superintendency, relations between superintendent and school boards represent highly contested areas. Typically, in a district there are several schools involved, which has the effect of diffusing the focus of the board. In the case of the LSC, the focus of contestation is potentially more volatile because a high proportion of the board members are parents, there is a single school involved, and meetings are held on location.

There is little dispute that the LSC has the authority to act autonomously in the hiring and firing of the principal. Yet, as previously discussed, this power adds stress to the working relationship with the principal. Questions are being raised if laypersons have or will be willing to acquire the expertise to make judgments about the qualification of professional educators. Inherent in the legislation is potential conflict between the principal and the LSC, and in many schools, this was indeed an area for conflict.

The field of contestation between the LSC and school professionals expands when the LSC members believe that they also have been given the authority to participate in the running of the school. Such activity by laypersons may be viewed by school professionals as interference in their areas of expertise. In a time when many laypeople are as well educated as teachers, this challenge raises the issue of the unique knowledge that teachers can point to as warrants of their professionalism.

Nevertheless, because LSC members are outsiders in terms of their knowledge, because they have less opportunity to develop personal relations with teachers, and because they are not physically present in the school on a full-time basis, their power to control the work of the school is limited. More to the point, how might a constructive role for parents and community members be envisioned?

As discussed in the first section, the initial reform legislation gave new powers, but the way in which leadership would evolve in particular schools could not, however, be predicted. Several of the elementary school cases provide windows into the complications that can arise in this relationship. The case written by Pete Leki is particularly useful in showing the dynamics from the perspective of the LSC chair. At W, we see a council that took its role seriously, even to the point of securing consultants so that it could be informed about the characteristics of effective school leaders and best practices for classrooms. The LSC chair's heavy investment in reforming science instruction raises another set of issues. As we discussed earlier, highly informed parents may pose special threats to teachers, both in terms of challenging teacher competence and in providing a competing source of leadership. This may explain why the principal, through such actions as keeping parents from going into classrooms, attempted to establish and maintain his own control.

In a second instructive case, that of Field School, the relationship between the new principal and the LSC chair was contentious from the beginning, with the chair seeking a desk in the principal's office. These disputes seemed to be ongoing during the tenure of the principal, although it does seem that the LSC supported Hobbs' initiatives to make the school safer and to improve instruction. But the emotion and energy involved in doing business with a group who in Hobbs' mind were not qualified to make instructional decisions seemed to wear Hobbs down. In the end, she decided to retire early rather than to campaign for reappointment as principal and to face another contentious 3 years. That many of the LSC members were perceived to be unqualified to approve budgets and school improvement plans, as well as to select school leaders, was a recurring theme in this case.

A somewhat different perspective is represented in the case of Anzaldúa School. The LSC proved to be the vehicle through which a group of teachers, those in the minority, were able to rid the school of a leader who silenced the comments of many teachers and parents, who was partial to a traditional group of teachers, and who did not seem to have the interests of children at the center of his agenda. Without the support of the teachers, the Anzaldúa LSC would probably not have been able to have acted decisively to change the principal.

In the five other schools, we see almost no discussion of relations between school professionals and the LSC. At Jackson School, the principal tightly controlled the activities of the LSC, a strategy that was effective in suppressing contributions they might wish to make. In this school, both the principal and the teachers shared a lack of confidence in the qualifications of the parents and community members to make the sorts of decision that were to be made by the LSC.

The principals of Saucedo and Irving say relatively little about the LSCs, other than brief allusions showing that they were responsive to new proposals from the LSC that were in the interests of children. The parents in Saucedo Academy, for example, with the support of the principal, seemed to have developed open communication with school personnel that helped in solving problems and in enhancing the programs of the schools.

In the two high school cases, there is little discussion of LSC activities. It is hard to know from these cases whether a workable relation, with a division of labor, had been achieved between school professionals and the parents and community members of the LSC or if the extent to which they could have a voice had been limited.

The cases reveal the variety of ways in which relations between the principal and the LSC evolved in schools. The relationship can be contentious, but through contestation of issues, school professionals become aware of areas of concern to parents and the community. On the other hand, such conflict may lead certain good principals to "opt out." Relationships can be controlled, particularly by principals who are traditional managers. Whether such control is for the good of the school can only be judged over a period of time. One basis for making this judgment would be to see if and which of the LSC's high-priority goals the school leadership had taken up. Particularly the case of Saucedo suggests that the relationship can be most productive when it is formed on a basis of mutual respect and trust, but it also suggests that such developments take time.

The issue of the qualification of the LSC to make instructionally relevant decisions is a thorny one. It is easy for school professionals to dismiss the potential contributions of parents and community members on the basis of not speaking the language or of having limited education. The underlying reasons for wanting to discredit these perspectives may have to do with the intrusiveness of the LSC into areas that teachers feel they have special expertise. In the case of better-educated LSC members, it may be that teachers and principals feel threatened, particularly by well-educated parents. Being highly educated doesn't necessarily mean that parents have constructive ideas for improving schooling. The high level of parental education may generate conflict based on relative status, not over workable ideas.

The case of Saucedo is probably the most useful case in thinking about the potential contributions of parents and community members. Parents and community members are a valued resource because of their unique knowledge about their children and the community. When listened to, they can identify problems that need to be considered. When a history of discussion of issues has been established, parents and community members along with school professionals can consider the merits and limitations of alternative courses of action. It probably takes a principal and teachers, secure in their own professional knowledge, with a willingness to be flexible, to welcome the ideas of parents and community members and use them to help guide decisions, *and* parents prepared to acknowledge the expertise of teachers and the principal.

How Has the Culture of Schools Been Influenced by Reform?

As discussed in Section 1, change in the organization of schools cannot occur without fundamental change in the culture of schools. We define culture as composed of the values and activities of participants: the school lives of administrators, teachers, and students, what they strive for, and the way they conceptualize the nature of schooling. We argue, further, that the values and actions of school leaders are particularly important in establishing the culture of schools.

These cases detail the processes that were engaged in by participants of eight schools as they attempted to implement site-based management. These cases allow us to examine how values and expectations changed within the schools and how different patterns of activities were established. As stated succinctly by Deal (1987):

> Culture is a social invention created to give meaning to human endeavor. It provides stability, certainty, and predictability. People fear ambiguity and want assurance that they are in control of their surroundings. Change creates existential havoc because it introduces disequilibrium, uncertainty, and makes day to day life unpredictable. (p. 7)

Traditional forms of educational practice are both stable and durable (Cuban, 1984). Schools evoke predictable scripts for those who enter them, and these serve as the basis for educational rituals that are the foundations of educational practice. These shared scripts and expectations forge the culture of the schools and classrooms and give meaning to the process of education. Because of the stable nature of these scripts, schools are extremely resistant to improvement, reform, or restructuring (Deal, 1987).

In 1971, Sarason echoed a phrase that continues to haunt those committed to making changes in schools. He observed that the more things change, the more they remain the same. One explanation of the strong resistance to change pertains to the formal, hierarchical structure of schools and classrooms. The roles of school participants are narrowly defined and adequate levels of interdependence and coordination do not exist (Corwin, 1972). Deal (1987) argued that to change a school, it is necessary to change the roles and responsibilities as they are defined by the culture. The institutionally redefined roles of principals must become reenvisioned, both by the principal acting in the role as leader as well as those who share leadership and those who follow. The reform initiative presumes reenvisioned roles for teachers, both within their classrooms and in their decision-making structure of the school.

In the eight cases, we see different ways in which leadership roles became redefined. Least stress was experienced by Karen Morris and teachers of Saucedo who had been developing their culture over a long time period. The process is a complex and long one before Morris' vision of a community of learners could be a reality. She regretted the fact that the many new managerial responsibilities that came with reform left her little time to spend with teachers in their classrooms.

In both Irving and Field, strong and determined new principals came in with visions of teachers as professionals immersed in decision making and concerned with student learning. Madeleine Maraldi showed great respect for teachers, while at the same time providing incentives for them to assume new responsibilities. Nelda Hobbs, with the support of the LSC, invited teachers to participate in the formation of small schools. Some took up the invitation creatively, others saw it as an unwelcome imposition. But in any case, school roles and ways of interacting were evolving. The culture within classrooms changed for the enthusiastic supporters, but probably not for the others. Similarly, in Anzaldúa, the creation of three small schools resulted in very different ways of interacting, making decisions about children's learning, and teaching and learning.

Cultural change can also occur in more limited areas of an institution. For example, role redefinitions for certain teachers occurred in Amundsen High. That is, teachers who engaged in the reading and writing projects adopted ways of thinking that changed their classroom instruction. Very limited change seemed to occur in Jackson Elementary and W School during the period of the case studies, although the postscripts suggest that greater change had occurred in later years.

Finally, the case of the Best Practice High School shows that in beginning a new school one does not begin from the ground up. Instead, role expectations and familiar patterns of conduct come along with teachers and students from prior school experiences. Thus, in creating a new school culture, participants face many of the same problems that were experienced in the other school cases. It is a process that cannot occur in a limited time period, but rather requires situation after situation of working together to establish new expectations and ways of doing business.

The eight cases reveal in different way the complexities inherent in changing agreed-upon ways of doing business. Cultural change will occur when it becomes clear that principals are committed to new forms of practice. The cases also suggest that for the change to be stable, it must occur over long periods of time. Structural changes, such as the institution of small schools, by their nature may change the ways in which teachers interact as they assume new responsibilities. Whether such changes in roles and responsibilities penetrate into classrooms probably depends on the commitments of individual teachers.

How Have Teaching and Learning Been Shaped by Reform?

The school reform law, passed in 1988, alters patterns of leadership in schools to make them more responsive to the goals and values of the communities in which they are located. The reformers believed that these changes in governance would alter the culture of schools, their instructional environments, and ultimately the learning of students. Yet, no direct mechanisms linking governance to instruction and learning were specified. The implicit logic of this expectation seemed to be that as shared leadership became more common within schools, teachers would participate in various forms of decision making in which diverse perspectives would be considered. These experiences, in turn, would lead teachers to abandon transmission forms of teaching in favor of instruction that actively engages students in decision making and learning. This perspective assumes that the dismally low achievement characteristics of students in poor urban areas result from the limited involvement of students in learning. As a corollary, it also assumes that constructivist forms of learning that engage students will results in higher achievement.

In 1995, a more direct link between governance and student achievement was established. Under the leadership of Paul Vallas, the central administration of the CPS reframed the reform initiative in terms of accountability, and focused on direct instruction of students as the means for enhancing achievement. A different body of research was brought to bear showing that some students, particularly those from minority groups, often profit from explicit forms of direct instruction.

Thus, in understanding how teaching and learning have been shaped by the reform, there are two quite different periods to consider. During the first years of the reform from 1988 to 1995, local school governance was initiated based on the premise that it would result in constructivist forms of classroom instruction that would eventuate in improved learning. From 1995 to the present, a centralized accountability program ensued that might have affected achievement through an increase in more traditional forms of instruction.

The case studies provide some support for a link between the decision-making activities of teachers and more constructive forms of teaching. Activist teachers from Anzaldúa who formed the BETA small school developed forms of instruction that were responsive to the culture and knowledge of students; in contrast, the more traditional teachers strongly valued bringing Hispanic children into culturally mainstream forms of instruction. Teachers from the Best Practice High School were committed to constructivist forms of instruction. Even at Field, some teachers working with like-minded colleagues in small schools developed highly engaging forms of teaching and learning.

More incrementally, with principal-driven situations, multiple opportunities were provided for teachers to enhance their instructional strategies at Saucedo Academy and Irving School. Teachers were given a voice in determining what professional development activities would be of benefit to them. These initiatives included new approaches to reading and writing instruction, as well as other areas of instruction. As indicated by the postscripts to cases, such opportunities were also developed at a somewhat later time at W School and Jackson Elementary. Thus, although not a central focus of the reform, activities occurred in most Chicago schools to improve teachers' knowledge and their classroom instruction.

The question of interest is whether this focus on instruction led to improvement in student learning. When the reform legislation was passed, proponents and skeptics agreed that the criterion for judging success would be improved student learning. A recent analysis of reading achievement patterns on the Iowa Test of Basic Skills (ITBS) between 1990 and 1997 found that "49% of [elementary] schools either showed test progress or maintained test scores above the national norm, 48% of schools showed no significant pattern of gains or losses and remained well below the national norm, and 3% of schools showed significant losses" (Designs for Change, 1998, p. 34; Summary, p. 2). Results have been less positive for high schools.

What is particularly interesting is that some Chicago schools showed improvement in instruction and learning during the first wave of the reform effort (1988–1994), which tended to be maintained thereafter, whereas others showed improvement during the second phase after an emphasis was placed on accountability and probation for schools not showing gains. Among the six elementary cases included in this book, three—Saucedo, Irving, and Anzaldúa—showed steadily improving learning gains during the first phase of the reform that continued in the years thereafter. The three others—Jackson, Field, and W—have made gains in reading and other achievement areas but mainly during the second phase of reform.

The question these data raise is how to examine these scores. Was it the accountability focus that brought up test scores or was it time? In the three schools that showed gains within the second phase of reform, the first years of reform in these schools were years of extreme struggle. Perhaps these schools needed more time to institutionalize some of the practices that were just beginning in 1989, or alternatively, these schools may have needed some external inducements in the form of accountability to focus on student achievement. More basically, whatever the initiating set of events, learning increments may depend on school communities establishing common goals and putting their conceptions into practice.

Both high school cases were documented during the second phase of the reform. Because of being placed on probation, the administrators of Amundsen High School solicited the assistance of a special consultant to guide a small subgroup of teachers to focus on reading and writing development in content areas. These teachers were then responsible for engaging their colleagues in special writing and reading projects. As reported in the case study, scores at Amundsen improved in recent years, following a concerted effort to improve reading and writing instruction. Best Practice, which admits students who are diverse in terms of achievement, realized above-average achievement during its 3 years of operation.

What ideas emerge about the relation between reform and improvements in instruction and learning? First, based on the results of Saucedo and Irving, it appears that the principal's investment and direct involvement in improving instruction is an important ingredient in the serious pursuit of instructional change. Although many of the schools brought in external partners or empowered teachers to develop their own approaches, these by themselves did not seem to be as successful as when the principal was directly involved. The involvement of the principal conveys symbolically the importance of all children learning successfully. Second, the pressure of public test results and the possibility of probation seem to represent an alternative force that can capture the attention of principals and teachers in an effort to improve achievement test scores. A negative side effect from this form of pressure is that many activities involve drill on test materials that do not represent the interactive forms of instruction from which students show long-term learning benefits. The use of heavily scripted instruction designed by the central office for schools under probation drives out constructivist methods.

Summary and Tentative Ideas
About Leadership in Times of Reform

Leadership during times of urban reform is extremely challenging. The leadership and the management roles of principals have become considerably more complex because of the opportunities and tensions created by the Chicago school reform. Not only did principals have to become astute managers of human and budgetary resources, but they were also challenged by the dilemmas faced by many superintendents in working with community members (LSC). Beyond this, some principals took on responsibility for supporting leadership on the part of teachers and community members. In the following paragraphs of this concluding section, we summarize our emerging ideas about the various forms of leadership that evolved among principals, the LSC, and teachers, as well as some of the tensions and conflicts that became apparent. We also consider the implications of these new forms of leadership that reform made possible for the culture of schools and for the teaching and learning that occurred in classrooms.

Leadership of Principals. First, principals who continue administering schools in an authoritarian manner limit the access of teachers and parents to school decision making; consequently, their perspectives cannot influence the nature of instruction and its responsiveness to the needs of students. Nevertheless, even under a directive principal without parental involvement, instruction may improve. Second, changing the complex set of expectations that define the roles of principals, teachers, and parents takes a substantial period of time. For the change to occur, it must be supported and sustained through the leadership of the principal. Third, the principalship has become an increasingly complicated role entailing the ability to work with a variety of groups, skill in onsite management and troubleshooting, as well as knowledge of long-term planning and budgeting resources. Finally, principals must become directly involved in instructional concerns, developing the mutual trust and respect with teachers that are essential for shared decision making.

The Participation of Teachers.   These cases make clear that a centrally important, ongoing challenge for principals is how to get more of their teachers involved in implementing engaging forms of instruction. The cases of Irving and Saucedo are perhaps most useful in showing the repertoire of ways that principals enhance the development of their teachers by making opportunities available and by providing an attractive set of incentives for those teachers who might not choose to make changes on their own.

Parental and Community Involvement.   Parents and community members can be a valuable resource because of their unique knowledge about their children and the community. When listened to, they can identify problems that are in need of consideration. It probably takes a principal and teachers secure in their own professional knowledge to welcome the ideas of parents and community members.

School Culture.   In creating a new school culture, participants face many of the same problems whether they are working in established or newly created schools. Change in culture is a process that cannot occur in a limited time period, but rather requires situation after situation of working together to establish new expectations and ways of doing business.

Teaching and Learning.   First, teachers who are given the freedom and authority to make decisions collaboratively about instruction offer their students opportunities for challenging and engaging forms of learning if their ideas are challenging and engaging. Second, the investment and direct involvement of principals in improving instruction are important ingredients in the serious pursuit of instructional change. Third, the pressure of public test results and the possibility of probation seem to represent alternative forces that can capture the attention of teachers and lead to the improvement of achievement test scores if the remedies introduced are imaginative and productive. Coupled with the latter approach is the worry that multiple test drill activities will not lead to long-term learning benefits for students. Finally, institutional improvement takes time, and even when teachers begin to make instructional changes, these changes slowly become manifest in student achievement.

Final Reflections.   Above all, these cases have helped us to observe the real-life complexities in schools. The cases lay out the particulars in all of their richness, contradictions, conflicts, and struggles for power, as school participants attempt to find the best ways to help their students learn. We are struck by the many tasks that schools perform and the vast range of ways they can be accomplished. These cases underscore the importance of context and the limitations of attempting to draw generalizations that apply to all schools.

In addition, we find the cases confirming our respect for those good people who work to make schools into good places for students. Although our cases revealed many problems, they were also comforting in showing the large numbers of people, both lay and professional, who work to realize their dreams for what schools can be and what they can mean in the lives of our children.

References

Achilles, C. M., Keedy, J. L., & High, R. M. (1999). The political world of the principal: How principals get things done. In L. W. Hughes (Ed.), *The principal as leader* (pp. 25–57). New York: Macmillan.

Argyris, C. (1982). *Reasoning, learning and action.* San Francisco: Jossey–Bass.

Argyris, C., & Schon, D. (1974). *Theory in practice: Increasing professional effectiveness.* San Francisco: Jossey-Bass.

Banas, C. (1987, September 29). Enrollment's down, office workers up. *Chicago Tribune,* Sect. 2, p. 8.

Blumberg, A., & Greenfield, W. (1980). *The effective principal: Perspectives on school leadership.* Boston: Allyn & Bacon.

Brookover, W. B., Gigliotti, R. P., Henderson, R. P., & Schnieder, J. M. (1973). *School social environments and achievements.* East Lansing, MI: College of Urban Development.

Brooks, J. G., & Brooks, M. G. (1993). *In search of understanding: The case for constructivist classrooms.* Alexandria, VA: ASCD.

Bryk, A. S., Easton, J. Q., Kebow, D., Rollow, S. G., & Sebring, P. A. (1993). *A view from the elementary schools: The state of reform in Chicago.* Chicago: Consortium on Chicago School Research.

Bryk, A., Thum, Y. M., Easton, J. Q., & Luppescu, S. (1998). *"Policy brief: Examining productivity: Improving the assessment system of the Chicago Public Schools.* Chicago: Consortium on Chicago School Research.

Bryk, A. S., & Rollow, S. G. (1992). The Chicago experiment: Enhanced demostrative participation as a lever for school improvement. *Issues in Restructuring Schools, 3,* 3–7.

Cohen, D. K., & Spillane, J. P. (1992). *Policy and practice: The relations between governance and instruction.* (ERIC Document Reproduction Service No. ED 337 865). Washington, DC: Office of Educational Research and Improvement.

Conley, S. (1991). Review of research on teacher participation in school decision making. *Review of Research in Education, 17,* 225–226.

Cordeiro, P. A. (1999). The principal's role in curricular leadership and program development. In L. W. Hughes (Ed.), *The principal as leader* (pp. 131–153). New York: Macmillan.

Corwin, R. G. (1972). Strategies for organizational innovation: An empirical comparison. *American Sociological Review, 37,* 441–452.

Cuban, L. J. (1984). *How teachers taught: Constancy and change in American classrooms 1890–1980.* New York: Longman.

Cuban, L. (1990, February 28). Leading, managing defined. *Leadership News,* p. 7.

Darling–Hammond, L., Bullmaster, M. L. & Cobb, V. L. (1995). Rethinking teacher leadership through professional development schools. *Elementary School Journal,* 96(1), 87–106.

Deal, T. E. (1987). The culture of the schools. In L. T. Sheive & M. B. Schoenheit (Eds.), *Leadership: Examining the elusive* (pp. 3–15). Association for Supervision and Curriculum Development.

Deal, T. E., & Peterson, K. D. (1999). *Shaping school culture: The heart of leadership.* San Francisco: Jossey–Bass.

Designs for Change. (1998). *What makes these schools stand out. Chicago elementary schools with a seven–year trend of improved reading achievement.* Chicago: Author.

Duane, E. A., Bridgeland, W. M., & Stern, M. E. (1986). The leadership of principals: Coping with turbulence. *Education, 107*(2), 212–219.

Dwyer, D. C., Barnett, B. G., & Lee, G. V. (1987). The school principal: Scapegoat or the last great hope? In L. T. Sheive & M. B. Schoenheit (Eds.), *Leadership: Examining the elusive* (pp. 30–46). Association for Supervision and Curriculum Development.

Edmonds, R. (1979). Some schools work and more can. *Social Policy, 9,* 28–32.

Elmore, R., Peterson, P., & McCarthy, S. (1996). *Restructuring in the classroom: Teaching, learning and schoool organization.* San Francisco: Jossey–Bass.

Eubanks, E. E., & Parish, R. I. (1990). Why does the status quo persist? *Phi Delta Kappan, 72*(3), 196–197.

Fullan, M., & Hargreaves, A. (1991). *What's worth fighting for: Working together for your school.* Toronto: Ontario Public School Teachers' Federation.

Giroux, H. (1988). *Teachers as intellectuals: Toward a critical pedagogy of learning.* New York: Bergin & Garvey.

Giroux, H. (1994). Teachers, public life, and curriculum reform. *Peabody Journal of Education, 69*(3), 35–47.

Greer, J. T., & Short, P. M. (1999). Restructuring schools. In L. W. Hughes (Ed.), *The principal as leader* (pp. 89–104). New York: Macmillan.

Hawley, W. (1988). Missing pieces of the educational reform agenda: Why the first and second waves may miss the boat. *Educational Administrative Quarterly, 11,* 416–437.

Hess, G. A., Jr. (1991). *School restructuring, Chicago style.* Newbury Park, CA: Corwin.

Hess, G. A. (1994). The changing role of teachers: Moving from interested spectators to engaged planners. *Education and Urban Society, 26*(3), 248–263.

Hess, G. A., Jr. (1995). *Restructuring urban schools: A Chicago perspective.* New York: Teachers College Press.

Hughes, L. W. (1999). The leader: Artist? Architect? Commissar? In L. W. Hughes (Ed.), *The principal as leader* (pp. 3–24). New York: Macmillan.

Hughes, L. W., & Ubben, G. C. (1994). *The elementary principal's handbook: A guide to effective action* (4th ed.) Boston: Allyn & Bacon.

Jenkins, J. R., Ronk, J., Schrag, J. A., Rude, G. G., & Stowitschek, C. (1994). Effects of using school–based participatory decision–making to improve services for low performing students. *Elementary School Journal, 94*(3), 357–372.

Johnson, S. M. (1990). *Teachers at work.* New York: Basic Books.

Katz, M. B., Fine, M., & Simon, E. (1997). Poking around: Outsiders view Chicago school reform. *Teachers College Record, 99*(1), 117–157.

Katz, M. B., & Simon, E. (1994, June 14). Consensus is key to school reform. *Chicago Tribune,* p. 23.

Keedy, J. L. (1991). *School improvement practices of successful high school principals.* Unpublished manuscript. The West Georgia Regional Center for Teacher Education, West Carrollton.

Latham, A. S. (1998, April). Site–based management: Is it working? *Educational Leadershop,* pp. 85–86.

Little, J. W. (1984). Norms of collegiality and experimentation: Conditions for school success. *American Educational Research Journal, 19,* 325–340.

Malen, B., Ogawa, R., & Kranz, J. (1990). What do we know about school–based management? A case study of the literature. In H. Clune & J. F. Witte (Eds.), *Choice and control in Amercian education* (pp. 289–342). New York: Falmer Press.

Meier, D. (1998, January). Can the odds be changed? *Phi Delta Kappan,* 358–362.

Mirel, J. (1993). *The rise and fall of an urban school system. Detroit, 1907–81.* Ann Arbor: University of Michigan Press.

Moore, D. (1992). Voice and choice in Chicago. In J. F. Witte & H. Clune (Eds.), *Choice and control in American education: Vol. II. The practice of choice: Decentralization and school restructuring* (pp. 153–198). Bristol, PA: Falmer Press.

Norris, C. J. (1999). Cultivating creative cultures. In L. W. Hughes (Ed.), *The principal as leader* (pp. 59–88). New York: Macmillan.

O'Day, J., & Smith, M. S. (1993). Systemic reform and educational opportunity. In S. H. Fuhrman (Ed.), *Designing coherent educational policy: Improving the system* (pp. 250–312) San Francisco: Jossey–Bass.

Olson, L. (1997, June 25). "Annenberg challenge" proves to be just that. *Education Week.*

Olson, L., & Jerald, C. D. (1998, January 8). Barriers to success. *Education Week,* pp. 9–15.

Paris, S. G., Wasik, B. A., & Turner, J. C. (1991). The development of strategic readers. In R. Barr, M. Kamil, P. Mosenthal, & P. D. Pearson (Eds.), *Handbook of reading research* (Vol. 2, pp. 609–640). New York: Longman.

Pearson, P. D., & Fielding, L. (1991). Comprehension instruction. In R. Barr, M. Kamil, P. Mosenthal, & P. D. Pearson (Eds.), *Handbook of reading research.* (Vol. 2, pp. 815–860). New York: Longman.

Peterson, P. (1976). *School politics: Chicago style*. Chicago: Falmer Press.

Pick, G. (1998, April). Trying to succeed where others failed. *Catalyst*, 1, 4–9.

Ravitch, D. (1974). *The great school wars. New York City, 1805–1973. A history of the public school as battlefield of social change*. New York: Basic Books.

Rogers, D. (1968). *110 Livingston Street*. New York: Random House.

Ryan, S. R., Bryk, A. S., Lopez, G., & Williams, K. P. (1997). *Charting reform: LSCs–Local leadership at work*. Chicago: Consortium on Chicago School Research.

Sarason, S. (1971). *The culture of school and the problems of change*. Boston: Allyn & Bacon.

Sarason, S. (1990). *Predictable failure of eductional reform*. San Francisco: Jossey–Bass.

Schlechty, P. C. (1991). *Schools for the 21st century: Leadership imperatives for educational reform*. San Francisco: Jossey–Bass.

Sebring, P. A., & Bryk, A. S. (1993). Charting reform in Chicago schools: Pluralistic policy research. In *New directions for program evaluation* (No. 39). San Francisco: Jossey–Bass.

Sebring, P. G., Bryk, A. S., & Easton, J. Q. (1995). *Charting reform: Chicago teachers take stock*. Chicago: Consortium on Chicago School Research.

Sergiovanni, T. (1990). *Value–added leadership: How to get extraordinary performance in schools*. New York: Harcourt Brace.

Sergiovanni, T. (1996). *Leadership for the school house*. San Francisco: Jossey–Bass.

Shipps, D. (1997). The invisible hand: Big business and Chicago school reform. *Teachers College Record*, 99(1), 73–116.

Test Scores Jump, Retention a Factor. (1998, June). *Catalyst*, 26.

Venezky, R., & Winfield, L. (1979). *Schools that succeed beyond expectations in teaching reading* (Tech. Rep. No. 1). Newark: Department of Educational Studies.

Walberg, H. J., Bakalis, M., Bast, J., & Baer, S. (1988). *We can rescue our children: The cure for Chicago's public school crisis—with lessons for the rest of America*. Chicago: Heartland Institute.

Walberg, H. J., & Niemiec, R. P. (1996, May 22). Can the Chicago reforms work? *Education Week*, 39.

Waller, W. (1961). *The sociology of teaching* (Reissue). New York: Russell & Russell.

Weber, K. E. (1971). *Inner–city children can be taught to read: Four successful schools*. (Occasional Paper no. 18). Washington, DC: Council for Basic Education.

Weick, K. (1982). Administering education in loosely coupled schools. *Phi Delta Kappan*, 63(10), 673–676.

Wilson, C. (1971). Education in Harlem—I.S. 201 in perspective. In J. H. Clarke (Ed.), *Harlem USA* (pp. 222–242). New York: Collier.

Wilson, W. J. (1987). *The truly disadvantaged. The inner city, the underclass, and public policy*. Chicago: University of Chicago Press.

Wylie, C. (1995–1996). Finessing site–based management with balancing acts. *Educational Leadership*, 53(4), 54–57.

Zemelman, S., Daniels, H., & Hyde, A. (1998). *Best practice: New standards for teaching and learning in America's schools*. Portsmouth, NH: Heinemann.

Author Index

Subject Index

LSC, *see* Local School Council
LSIC, *see* Local school improvement
    council

M

Magnet schools, 56, 106
Management
  site-based
    concept of leadership in school re-
      form, 3, 5
    Jackson Elementary School, 39
    "W" Elementary School, 103
  style of principal and reform initiative,
    237
Maria Saucedo Scholastic academy
  analysis of leadership, 74–75
  background, 47–48
  building a neighborhood school,
    55–64
  creating a teaching/learning commu-
    nity, 69–72
  extending thinking, 75–76
  guiding philosophy, 64–69
  hopes for the future, 72–74
  reflection on reform, 48–55
  reform initiative
    decision-making contribution of
      community members,
      244, 245
    leadership role of principal,
      235–236
    leadership role of teachers, 240
    shaping of learning/teaching, 248,
      249
    school culture, 246
Minorities, 7
Mobility rates, 147
Modeling, 218–222
Monitoring, 187
Morgan Park plan, 182
Motivation, 73–74, 188
Multiculturalism, 108

N

National-Louis University (NLU), 184,
  185, 191

Needs assessment, 35
Neighborhood school, 55–64
New York City, 10
NLU, *see* National-Louis University

O

Options for knowledge, 180, 181

P

Parents
  Anzaldúa Elementary School, 149,
    165–167
  concept of leadership in school re-
    form, 6
  Jackson Elementary School, 29
  limited education and contributions,
    123
  Maria Saucedo Scholastic academy,
    49, 50, 54, 63, 65
  reform initiative, 243, 251
  Washington Irving School, 141
Parent–Teacher Association (PTA), 84,
  97
Parent–Teachers organization (PTO),
  54, 56
Peer mediation group, 198, 217
Peers, 161–165
Philosophy, guiding, 64–69
Political issues, 53
PPAC, *see* Professional Personnel Advi-
  sory Committee
Practicum program, 54
Prep periods, 70, 71
Principal
  Anzaldúa Elementary School,
    149–150, 158–161
  Best Practice High School, 206–207
  concepts of leadership and school re-
    form, 3, 4, 18
  Eugene Field School, 92–94, 101
  Jackson Elementary School
    contract negotiations, 31–34, 77
    leadership analysis, 44
    role and local school council,
      30–31, 78
    school improvement plan, 40–42